Nudge, nudge, think, think

Manchester University Press

Nudge, nudge, think, think

Experimenting with ways to change citizen behaviour

Second edition

Peter John, Sarah Cotterill, Alice Moseley,
Liz Richardson, Graham Smith, Gerry Stoker
and Corinne Wales

Manchester University Press

Published by Manchester University Press
Altrincham Street, Manchester M1 7JA

www.manchesteruniversitypress.co.uk

British Library Cataloguing-in-Publication Data
A catalogue record for this book is available from the British Library

ISBN 978 1 5261 4055 5 paperback

First published 2019

Typeset by Servis Filmsetting Ltd, Stockport, Cheshire
Printed in Great Britain
by TJ International Ltd, Padstow

Contents

Figures		*page* vii
Tables		viii
The authors		ix
Foreword by Greg Clark, MP		xi
Prologue by Cass R. Sunstein		xix
Acknowledgements		xxxii
Introduction		1
1	Nudging and thinking	13
2	Testing	38
3	Recycling	61
4	Volunteering	77
5	Voting	96
6	Petitioning	108
7	Giving	123
8	Donating	138
9	Debating	161
10	Including	176
11	Linking	189
12	Summary of key findings	207

Contents

13   Epilogue: the future of nudge and think   220

Note on results from the experiments   242
Glossary   245
References   247
Index   278

Figures

2.1 An experimental study design   *page* 45
3.1 Recycling participation rate by group   69
3.2 Proportion of households recycling food waste   72
5.1 Responses to door-to-door and telephone canvassing   103
5.2 Voter turnout rates in Wythenshawe after the
     intervention (%)   104
6.1 Subjects signing petitions in field experiment (by number
     of other signatories)   118
7.1 Percentage of households donating books from each
     treatment group   132
8.1 The information nudge for organ donation registration   153
9.1 Change in preferences by policy question   171
10.1 Satisfaction with the DVD (number of participants)   184

Tables

1.1	Nudge and think compared	*page* 28
2.1	Validity	41
2.2	The Hawthorne effect	43
4.1	The CLEAR model	84
5.1	The script for the telephone and door-to-door canvass	102
8.1	Organ donation registration survey choices	149
8.2	Pre- and post-organ donor registration by group	156
8.3	Attitudes to organ donation	157
10.1	Brief for community interviews	181
A1.1	Effects of the experiments	242

The authors

Sarah Cotterill is Senior Lecturer in Health Services Research and Statistics at the University of Manchester. She undertakes research on behaviour change interventions in health services and public policy, and has expertise in the design and analysis of randomized controlled trials.

Peter John is Professor of Public Policy at King's College London. His books include *How Far to Nudge: Assessing Behavioural Public Policy* (2018) and *Analyzing Public Policy* (2012). He is a member of the academic advisory panel of the Behavioural Insights Team.

Alice Moseley is Lecturer in the Department of Politics at the University of Exeter. She was previously at the University of Southampton, where she was part of the *Rediscovering the Civic* project team. She has published on a variety of public policy topics, including joined-up government, evidence-based and behavioural public policy.

Liz Richardson is Reader in Politics at the University of Manchester. Her research interests include decentralized urban governance and citizen participation in public policy. Her work includes a co-authored book *Designing Public Policy for Coproduction*, published by Policy Press in 2016. She is a Trustee of the National Association for Neighbourhood Management (NANM).

Graham Smith is Professor of Politics and Director of the Centre for the Study of Democracy at the University of Westminster. His research interests include democratic theory and practice, climate politics, and the social economy. He is author of *Democratic Innovations: Designing Institutions for Citizen Participation* (2009).

Gerry Stoker is Centenary Professor of Governance at the Institute for Governance and Policy Analysis at the University of Canberra, and Professor of Politics and Governance at the University of Southampton. He is author of *Why Politics Matters: Making Democracy Work* (2nd ed. 2016) and co-author of *The Good Politician: Folk Theories, Political Interaction, and the Rise of Anti-Politics* (2018).

Corinne Wales was Visiting Fellow at the Centre for Citizenship, Globalization and Governance (C2G2), University of Southampton, where she was part of the *Rediscovering the Civic* project team when this book was conceived. She is now Deputy Director of International College, University of Dundee and has a continuing interest in conducting design experiments in pedagogical contexts.

Foreword

The Rt Hon Greg Clark MP, Secretary of State for Business, Energy and Industrial Strategy

The arrival of a substantially upgraded second edition of any book involved in the here-and-now of how to make good policy is an important moment and something of an accolade: it shows that the impetus behind the first edition was right; and it shows that the philosophy presented is sufficiently rich, flexible, and important to require an update in the light of a changed environment. Perhaps a second edition – rather than a reprint of the original edition – has some parallels to the re-election of the same party to power but with a new leader or manifesto.

So this second edition is an occasion for me to reflect on what have been the big changes at the everyday interface of politics and policy between 2012 and now, and how they relate to a central question of politics and policy: how should we seek to improve social outcomes by changing citizen behaviour?

Thinking back to the time of the first edition of this book I can remember a time of excitement about 'nudge': Kahneman's *Thinking Fast and Slow* had just been published. Cass Sunstein was 'Regulation Czar' in Obama's White House. Our own Behavioural Insights Team, as the then 'Nudge Unit', was at the heart of government, in the Cabinet Office, where I would soon become a minister.

There was a sense at that time that the markets of textbook economics had not worked as many of us had hoped – we were just out
of the Global Financial Crisis, and the UK's productivity was still (as
it still is) obstinately slow to recover its growth path. And 'nudge'
offered a new way to think about these problems; it opened up a field
of possibilities for policy. The policy wonks of the world could emit
a sigh of relief. The solution flowed from Kahneman and Tversky's
two-mode model of human cognition. Our everyday behaviour
mostly came out of 'system one' – the low-processing, fast-thinking,
default-setting mind; the rational mind of calculative economics and
public policy, system two, could occupy itself with setting objectives
and discovering, rationally and scientifically, how to set the knobs of
system one so that each of us behaved in such a way as to produce an
overall social good. The toolkit offered in the first edition of this book
flowed naturally from this picture of humanity and society: properly
harnessed processes of 'think' (system two), including consultative
processes that could uncover information that the policy-maker did
not have, would deliver policy goals and ideas. These would seek to
change citizen behaviour with particular regard to resetting the dials
of system one. And policies would be empirically tested – especially
using methods derived from public health (randomized control
trials) and from cognitive psychology (lab experiments).

By the standards of most breakthroughs in the policy world,
this programme has been enormously successful. It has cut smoking, increased organ donation, made tax-payments more prompt,
increased the rate at which people return to work, and offered any
number of improvements in well-being that required difficult behaviour change. It is now a part of mainstream policy-making. And
yet I have to say that the dreams we had for it in 2012 have not all
been satisfied, and nor has the urgent need that fed those dreams
disappeared – if anything quite the opposite. So I am very heartened

to see that this second edition of *Nudge, nudge, think, think* avoids all complacency and shares some of my diagnosis of the problem. Let me illustrate with an example that occupied a good eighteen months of my time as Secretary of State for Business Energy and Industrial Strategy – the case of domestic retail energy markets.

The brief history is this. In the early noughties, Britain fully deregulated domestic energy supply. Customers, it was assumed, would shop around for good deals; suppliers would compete for their custom; innovation in energy services, conservation, multi-utility models, and more would follow. Except that for the most part it didn't. By 2012, six big consolidated incumbent suppliers presided over a market in which almost three quarters of households were not active, in which prices to them were often hundreds of pounds higher than prices to switchers, and in which there was a dizzying confusopoly of tariff offers – as if some hand, invisible or not, had efficiently discovered a nudge to turn the problem of cognitive load to profitable corporate advantage. This situation gained political salience, fuelled by campaigns in the tabloid press, especially the *Sun*, which was quick to condemn a 'rip-off economy'. David Cameron used the institutional mechanisms at hand and in June 2014 called for a reference of the whole market to be made to the Competitions and Markets Authority (CMA). The investigation soon confirmed the scale of the problem: it was on 'an upwards trend, reaching almost £2 billion in 2015'.[1] Moreover, it diagnosed an entirely novel market failure, one very much in the nudge spirit of the times: 'weak customer response'.

Pause for just a moment to consider that diagnosis: the market is

---

1   CMA Energy market investigation, 'Summary of the Final Report', www.gov.uk/cma-cases/energy-market-investigation#final-report   [accessed   12 March 2019].

not working, said the CMA, not because firms were doing anything wrong, not because there were significant barriers to competing firms entering the market, but because customers were not behaving as the (old) textbooks say customers ought to. The CMA decided on a set of solutions that are straight out of what has become the 'nudge' mainstream – call it Nudge 1.0 – the most striking of which was the 'database remedy': the regulator would collect from suppliers a database of all customers who had failed to switch and would experiment with messages – nudges – to make them more engaged. When a good method of changing consumer behaviour had been found, it would be scaled and the problem would be solved.

But unusually, the CMA panel failed to reach unanimity on its conclusions. There are two very thoughtful pages of dissenting opinion by Professor Martin Cave at the end of the almost 1500-page final report that speak volumes to the limits of Nudge 1.0. I quote from them briefly:

> [T]he remedies proposed for the large majority of households will take some time to come into effect, and are in any case untried and untested. This makes it risky to rely on them. That is why I believe they must be supplemented by a wider price control designed to give household customers adequate and timely protection from very high current levels of overcharging.

> The [...] report's information remedies [are] designed to combat disengagement. A significant source of evidence on the effectiveness of such remedies lies in our experience of them over the past three years or more. We have seen a variety of measures covering such things as bill formats and customer prompts, barrages of publicity adverse to energy companies, concerning the level of their charges, and very large amounts of column inches, TV advertising and other advice devoted to explaining how to switch supplier. Yet none of these developments has made a dent in the proportion of customers of the six large energy firms (about seven out of ten) which remains on the standard variable

tariff (SVT). This is despite the fact that the SVT is currently more than £300 per year more expensive than the competitive benchmark for a dual fuel customer.[2]

His point might be paraphrased like this: we have too little evidence that nudge alone will deliver in good time, and the harm is too great not to adopt a more direct solution. After the CMA report, the newspapers did not let up on their campaign – they dubbed the database remedy a 'spammer's charter' – and the government sided with Professor Cave's view. We passed legislation to impose a price cap on default tariffs, and I am very pleased to have been able to appoint Martin Cave as the new chair of our energy regulator, Ofgem.

So where does this particular example leave 'nudge', and what of the new thinking presented in this second edition around 'think'?

Since 2012, not only in my role as the person ultimately responsible for competition and consumer policy, but also in my role as the initiator of the country's Industrial Strategy, I am more than ever aware that markets are social constructs and that the patterns of behaviour that firms, consumers, investors, and workers develop within them form a complex equilibrium that may deviate a very great deal from the textbook case.

When it came to domestic energy, what we really needed was a way to nudge *company* behaviour: we needed a pattern of rivalry that would reward good companies with a focus on price and service. I started with a hope that I could nudge the behaviour of the large energy suppliers by asking them to do the right thing, pointing out that the government and Ofgem would act in any case. This, however, failed: these companies responded to legislation, not exhortation. And perhaps it is in the nature of most corporate entities to be

---

2 CMA Energy market investigation, 'Final Report', www.gov.uk/cma-cases/energy-market-investigation#final-report [accessed 12 March 2019].

like this: they have clearly defined fiduciary responsibilities and they interpret them in ways that they have become comfortable with as institutions. In a sense, up to this point, the energy price cap story was a double failure for 'Nudge 1.0': neither consumers nor firms turned out to be nudgeable, however much all could see that overall we were in a very poor outcome.

The solution was therefore to introduce legislation requiring Ofgem to set a price cap on the default tariff that firms could charge. In terms of nudging *firm* behaviour, the early signs are encouraging for this policy: it is designed to allow an efficient producer a good margin, and a dynamic new tier of mid-sized companies now exists that is growing with the intention of establishing trustworthy brands. These firms have been supportive of the cap because it allows them profits while making it harder for incumbents to cross-subsidize competitive customer acquisitions.

But the price cap would not have emerged out of 'Nudge 1.0'. That had developed a tendency to focus on the behaviour change it knew best – the behaviour change of the person or household. In extreme cases, this turned into policy prescriptions of 'blame the consumer', or at least 'change the consumer'.

The first edition of this book recognized the danger within nudge that it might be seen as being manipulative and illegitimate; hence the importance of integrating 'think' processes into policy-making. I enormously welcome the fact that the second edition goes even further in this direction, with its repeated attention to the problem of how to design solutions that achieve a real buy-in from all stakeholders. Without this, I do not think we will be successful in truly decentralising and democratising decisions. In the case of retail energy policy, I have been very concerned with shaking any notion that we are 'blaming consumers'.

We are far from the end of the road with this policy problem. A centrally administered cap is *not* a long term ideal. Decentralized mechanisms, when they work, will always be better for innovation and flexibility. So we need to aim for a future that satisfies three conditions simultaneously: we do not blame the consumer, we avoid exploitation by those with market power, and, ideally, we avoid centralized price regulation as a long-term solution. This book and this research programme calls for 'nudge plus': policy-making that has a psychologically rich view of citizens, and which includes the importance in our lives of institutions which we can trust to 'have our backs'. This will clearly be needed to solve the retail energy problem in the long term.

What the policy-maker and the politician need today, in my view, is a much better understanding of how we can nudge *organisations and institutions* – firms, NGOs, regulators, and governments themselves – to become the trusted intermediaries without whom a complex modern life is impossible. 'Nudge plus' is a recognition of this challenge. Even if the great successes of 'Nudge 1.0' have allowed its limitations to be revealed, the philosophy of policy-making at its core – rigorous empiricism, a realistic model of behaviours, and a recognition that collective decisions must be *both* efficient and legitimate – has been carried over into the 'nudge plus' proposal of this volume.

Indeed, it is needed today probably even more than it was on the occasion of the first edition in 2012. I have elaborated on the very specific example of the retail energy price cap, but this should be seen in the wider context of a general need to rethink the architecture of decentralization. In very broad-brush terms, we can think of the period of 1945 to 1973 as being one during which policy – be it macro stability, price controls, utility provision, labour law, any number of regulatory interventions, or land-use planning – saw few downsides with centralization and direct intervention. The period 1979 to

2008 can be broadly considered one of reaction against this model, a period in which a consensus developed that decentralized market mechanisms should be encouraged wherever possible.

I think that the original hopes pinned on 'nudge' arose from the inadequacy of that model. What we want is a policy framework that will deliver the benefits of decentralization – efficiency, democratic buy-in, creative solutions that stay close to the problem at hand, development of innovation and talent in all corners of the country and at all levels. But modern markets, with information asymmetries between consumers and suppliers, sometimes do not deliver this. We need to build new frameworks and explore new mechanisms, whether it is in labour markets, innovation policy, utility regulation, competition policy, and right across government. 'Nudge plus' and the case-studies described in this volume recognize this key policy challenge and provide important elements of an answer. This is an absolutely crucial research program.

Prologue

Cass R. Sunstein, Robert Walmsley University Professor, Harvard Law School

Understanding nudges and nudging

Nudges are private or public initiatives that steer people in particular directions but also allow them to go their own way (Thaler and Sunstein 2008, Thaler 2015). A reminder is a nudge; so is a warning. A GPS device nudges; a default rule, automatically enrolling people in some programme, is a nudge (Ebeling and Lotz 2015). To qualify as a nudge, an initiative must not impose significant material incentives (including disincentives).

A subsidy is not a nudge; a tax is not a nudge; a fine or a jail sentence is not a nudge. To count as such, a nudge must preserve freedom of choice. If an intervention imposes significant material costs on choosers, it might of course be justified, but it is not a nudge. Some nudges work because they inform people; other nudges work because they make certain choices easier and more salient; still other nudges work because of the power of inertia and procrastination.

In recent years, a great deal has happened, and interest is exploding (Whitehead et al 2017). Nudge Units, often known as behavioural insights teams, can be found all over the globe. Prominent examples include the UK (Halpern 2015), the US, the Netherlands, and Australia, and superb work is being done within the governments of Canada, Ireland, Qatar and many other nations as well. The World Bank and the United Nations have enthusiastically embraced nudging and behavioural economics, with a focus on poverty, economic opportunity, development, and corruption. In domains that include environmental protection, public health, traffic safety, poverty reduction, consumer protection, tax policy, discrimination, and retirement savings, the results have been extremely impressive (Sunstein 2014, Halpern 2015). I will have a bit to say about those results here, but the full story remains to be told (for some glimpses, see Halpern 2015, Benartzi et al 2017).

There has also been an extraordinary outpouring of new academic thinking and research on behaviourally informed approaches, with particular reference to public policy (for a large sampling, see Sunstein and Reisch 2016). But it is an understatement to say that much more remains to be done. The use of nudging, and of behavioural economics, remains in its early stages. This book identifies important ways forward.

My major goal here is not to celebrate what has been learned, or to engage the many productive objections, clarifications, and refinements (Rebonato 2012, Allcott and Kessler 2015, Goldin 2015, Goldin and Lawson 2016), but more modestly to understand the nature of nudges and nudging, above all by cataloguing some common mistakes and misconceptions. Unfortunately, they continue to divert attention both in the public domain and in academic circles, and hence to stall progress. Once we clear them away, we will be in a position to focus on what really matters, which is (to cut a long story short) what will most improve human welfare (for a longer version, see Sunstein 2019b).

Without further ado:[1]

1 *Nudges are an insult to human agency.* In free societies, people are treated with respect. They are allowed to go their own way. Some people object that nudges are troublesome because they treat people as mere objects for official control (see Waldron 2014).

The objection is off the mark. One of the main points of nudging is to preserve freedom of choice – and thus to maintain people's capacity for agency. Many nudges are self-consciously educative, and hence they strengthen that very capacity; consider calorie labels, or warnings about risks associated with certain products. With information, warnings, and reminders, people are in a better position to choose their own way. Non-educative nudges, such as uses of healthy choice architecture at cafeterias or in grocery stores, also allow people to choose as they wish.

Perhaps it could be argued that if the goal is to promote agency, default rules are problematic. But because such rules are omnipresent in human life, it is not easy to make that argument convincing. Would it make sense to excise default rules from the law of contract? To say that employers, hospitals, and banks are forbidden from using default rules? In practice, what would that even mean? Those who are inclined to reject default rules out of respect for individual agency would do well to ponder the countless contexts in which such rules make life simpler and easier to navigate. (On the immense importance of navigability – more in a moment.)

---

1   I am not going to fuss here over definitional questions, though in recent years a great deal of work has been devoted to those questions. My hope is that the opening sentence of this prologue is clear enough, at least if it is informed by what immediately follows it. In the same vein, see Thaler and Sunstein 2008: 8, 'a nudge, as we shall use the term, is any aspect of the choice architecture that alters people's behavior in a predictable way without forbidding any options or significantly changing their economic incentives.'

A narrower argument would be that in certain settings, those who prize agency should insist on active choosing in preference to default rules. In *Nudge*, Thaler and I make exactly that argument in the context of organ donation, urging that when people receive drivers' licences, they ought to be asked whether they want to be organ donors. In some settings, active choosing is indeed better (Thaler and Sunstein 2008).

Note, however, that sometimes people cannot easily choose (because they lack bandwidth or expertise) or simply do not want to choose (Sunstein 2016a); they consider default rules to be a blessing. One reason is that people have limited time and attention, and they exercise their own agency by relying on default rules. If we aim to respect individual agency, we will often be inclined to favour those rules for that very reason (Sunstein 2017b). It is a complex question as to when active choosing should be preferred to default rules, or vice-versa. A simple framework, on which much more would have to be said: enquire into the costs of decisions and the costs of errors.

2 *Nudges are based on excessive trust in government.* The most intuitive objection to nudging is rooted in fear of government. To put that objection in its sharpest form: suppose that public officials are incompetent, self-interested, reckless, or corrupt. Suppose that your least favourite leaders are or will be in charge. Would you want them to nudge? Or suppose that you are keenly alert to public choice problems, emphasized by James Buchanan and his followers, or 'the knowledge problem', emphasized by Friedrich Hayek and his followers. If interest groups are able to push government in their preferred directions, and if public officials lack crucial information, then you might insist: do not nudge! Reliance on private markets might seem far better (Glaeser 2006).

Indeed, behavioural science itself might be taken to put this conclusion in bold letters. There is no reason to think that public officials are immune to behavioural biases. In a democratic society, the electoral connection might mean that they will respond to the same biases that affect ordinary people (Kuran and Sunstein 1999). To be sure, structural safeguards might help, especially if they ensure a large place for technocrats, insistent on science and on careful attention to costs and benefits. But in any real-world polity, behavioural distortions are difficult to avoid.

These are fair and important points, but if they are taken as an objection to nudging, they run into a logical problem: a great deal of nudging is inevitable. So long as government has offices and websites, it will be nudging. If the law establishes contract, property, and tort law, it will be nudging, if only because it will set out default rules, which establish what happens if people do nothing. As Hayek himself wrote, the task of establishing a competitive system provides 'indeed a wide and unquestioned field for state activity', for 'in no system that could be rationally defended would the state just do nothing. An effective competitive system needs an intelligently designed and continuously adjusted legal framework as much as any other' (Hayek 1943: 40).

As Hayek understood, a state that protects private property and that enforces contracts has to establish a set of prohibitions and permissions, including a set of default entitlements, establishing who has what before bargaining begins. For that reason, it is pointless to exclaim, 'do not nudge!' – at least if one does not embrace anarchy.

The second answer to those who distrust government is that because nudges maintain freedom of choice, they offer a safety valve against official error. Those who favour nudges are keenly alert to the public choice problem and the knowledge problem, and to the possibility that public officials will show behavioural biases. Many of them are influenced by Buchanan and (especially) Hayek. If one distrusts government, the real focus should be on mandates, bans, subsidies and taxes. To be sure, nudges ought not to be free from scrutiny, but they should be a relatively low priority.

It is true, of course, that some nudging is optional. Government can warn people about smoking, opioid addiction, and distracted driving, or not. It can seek to protect consumers against deception and manipulation, or not. It can undertake public education campaigns, or not. If you think that government is entirely untrustworthy, you might want it to avoid nudging whenever it can. In the abstract, that position cannot be ruled out of bounds. Public choice problems, and the knowledge problem, are real and important. On highly pessimistic assumptions about the capacities and incentives of public officials, and highly optimistic assumptions about the capacities and incentives of those in the private sector, nudging should be minimized (Glaeser 2006). But private actors nudge, and sometimes it is very much in their interest to exploit cognitive biases, thus causing serious harm to countless people (Akerlof and Shiller 2016). Would it be a good idea to forbid public officials from taking steps to reduce smoking and distracted driving? In any case, the track record of real-world nudging includes impressive success stories, if success is measured by cost-effectiveness (Benartzi et al 2017).

To be sure, nudges, like other interventions from such officials, should be constrained by democratic requirements, including transparency, public debate and independent monitoring (including continuing evaluation of how they work in practice). Constraints of this kind can reduce the risks (without eliminating them). The fundamental point is that those risks are far larger with other tools, above all mandates and bans.

3 *Nudges are covert.* Some people have argued that mandates, bans, and taxes have one advantage: they are transparent. People know what they are. No one is fooled. By contrast, nudges are covert

and in that sense sneaky, a form of trickery (Glaeser 2006). They affect people without their knowledge.

For countless nudges, this objection is hard to understand. A GPS device nudges, and it is entirely transparent. Labels, warnings, and reminders are not exactly hidden; if they are, they will not work. When an employer automatically enrolls employees into a savings plan, subject to opt out, nothing is hidden. (If it is, there is a problem; the right to opt out should be clear.)

Why, then, have intelligent people objected that nudges are covert? Is there anything at all to that objection? One possibility is that when people participate in a randomized controlled trial, they may not be informed of that fact. (A randomized trial might not work if people are told about the various conditions.) But I suspect that the real answer is that *some nudges work even though those who are affected by them do not focus on them, or even think about them* (Rebonato 2012). While such nudges are hardly hidden, people may be unaware of them, or at least unaware of their purposes and effects.

For example, a cafeteria might be designed so that the healthy foods are most visible and placed first, and people might choose them for that very reason. Such a design is not hidden – on the contrary, it should be obvious – but people may not be aware that their cafeteria has been designed so as to promote healthy choices. To be sure, they know that the fruits are more visible than the brownies, but they might not know *why*, and their decision to select a fruit might be quick and automatic rather than reflective. Or people might not think much about the default rules that come with (say) an agreement with a rental car company. If people are automatically enrolled into some kind of insurance plan and allowed to opt out, they might say, 'yeah, whatever', and simply go along with the default. (By the way, *Nudge* identified only one new heuristic, and it's that: the 'yeah, whatever' heuristic.)

In that sense, it is correct to say that some nudges can work even if, or perhaps because, people are unaware that they are being nudged. Note, however, that emerging evidence finds that the effects of such nudges are not diminished even if people are told that nudging is at work. Though research continues, transparency about the existence and justification of default rules appears not to reduce their impact in general (Bruns et al 2018). For some people, such clarity may even increase that impact, by amplifying the informational signal that some default rules offer (McKenzie et al 2006). On plausible assumptions, drawing attention to the healthy design of a cafeteria will actually increase the effect of that design, because it will convey valuable information. (To be sure, it may produce 'reactance' in some consumers.)

4 *Nudges are manipulative.* In a variation on the claim that nudges are covert, some people have objected that nudges are a form of manipulation (Conly 2013). But return to the points I have just explored: if people are reminded that they have a doctor's appointment next Thursday, no one is manipulating them. The same is true if people are given information about the caloric content of food or if they are warned that certain foods contain shellfish or nuts, or that if they take more than the recommended dosage of Benadryl, something bad might happen.

To be sure, we could imagine a graphic warning about opioid addiction, or about the use of cell phones while driving, that would create immediate fear or revulsion, or intensely engage people's emotions; it might be objected that nudges of this kind count as a form of manipulation. To know whether they do, we need a definition of manipulation. To cut a (very) long and complex story short, philosophers and others have generally converged on the view that an action counts as manipulative if it bypasses people's capacity for rational deliberation (see Barnhill 2014; Barnhill's own account is more subtle). On any view, most nudges do not qualify. True, some imaginable nudges might cross the line, but that is very different from saying that nudges are manipulative as such.

5 *Nudges exploit behavioural biases.* Some people object that nudges 'exploit' or 'take advantage of' behavioural biases. Indeed, some people *define* nudges as exploitation of behavioural biases (Rebonato 2012). That does sound nefarious. But the objection is mostly wrong, and while people can define terms however they wish, this particular definition is a recipe for confusion.

Many nudges make sense, and help people, whether or not a behavioural bias is at work. A GPS is useful for people who do not suffer from any such bias. Disclosure of information is helpful even in the absence of any bias. A default rule simplifies life and can therefore be a blessing whether or not a behavioural bias is involved.

As the GPS example suggests, many nudges have the goal of *increasing navigability* – of making it easier for people to get to their preferred destination (Sunstein 2019a). Such nudges stem from an understanding that life can be either simple or hard to navigate, and a goal of helpful nudging is to promote simpler navigation. I wish that *Nudge* had made this point clearer and had connected nudging to the central idea of navigability.

At the same time, it is true that some nudges counteract behavioural biases and that some nudges work because of behavioural biases. For example, many human beings tend to suffer from present bias, which means that they give relatively little weight to the long term; many of us suffer from unrealistic optimism, which means that we tend to think that things will turn out better for us than statistical reality suggests. Some nudges try to counteract present bias and optimistic bias – as, for example, by emphasizing the long-term risks associated with smoking and drinking, or by suggesting the importance of retirement planning. Similarly, default rules work in part because of inertia, which undoubtedly counts as a behavioural bias. But it is misleading – a form of rhetoric, in the not-good sense – to suggest that nudges 'exploit' such biases.

6 *Nudges wrongly assume that people are irrational.* Some critics object that nudges are based on a belief that human beings are 'irrational', which is both insulting and false.[2] This objection takes different forms.

In one form, the objection is that while people rely on simple heuristics and rules of thumb, there is nothing wrong with that; those heuristics and rules work well, and so nudging is not needed and can only make things worse. In another form, the objection urges that the whole idea of nudging is based on weak psychological research and on an assortment of supposed laboratory findings that do not hold in the real world. In yet another form, the objection is that people can and should be educated rather than nudged. In what seems to me its best form, the objection urges that people's utility functions are complex and that outsiders may not understand them; what seems to be 'irrationality' may be the effort to trade off an assortment of goals (Rebonato 2012). A mundane example: people might eat fattening foods not because they suffer from present bias, but because they greatly enjoy those foods. A less mundane example:

---

2   The least lovely, and the most peculiar, version of this claim comes from a German psychologist: 'The interest in nudging as opposed to education should be understood against the specific political background in which it emerged. In the US, the public education system is largely considered a failure, and the government tries hard to find ways to steer large sections of the public who can barely read and write. Yet this situation does not apply everywhere' (Gigerenzer 2015: 362).

Where to begin? I will restrict myself to noting that it is rarely a good idea to insult nations.

people might fail to save for retirement not because they suffer from optimistic bias, but because they need the money now.

No one should doubt that heuristics generally work well (that is why they exist), but they can also misfire. When they do, a nudge can be exceedingly helpful. Many nudges are developed with reference to well-established behavioural findings, demonstrating that people depart from perfect rationality. For example, default rules work in part because of the power of inertia (Johnson and Goldstein 2003); reminders are necessary and effective in part because people have limited attention; information will be more likely to influence behaviour if it is presented in a way that is attentive to people's imperfect information-processing capacities. These and other claims are based on evidence, both in the laboratory and real world. (It is always possible that they will be found to be imprecisely stated or wrong in important settings.) But those who embrace nudges do not use the term 'irrationality'. In fact they abhor it; 'bounded rationality' is much better. Nor does anyone doubt that education can work. As I have emphasized, many nudges are educative. More ambitious educative efforts, such as efforts to help people to assess risks and to teach statistical literacy, are usually complements to nudges, and rarely substitutes or alternatives.

It is also true (and exceedingly important) that people's utility functions are complex and that outsiders might not understand them; that is one reason that nudgers insist on preserving freedom of choice. To the extent that nudging is inevitable, it is pointless to contend that because of the complexity of people's utility functions, nudging should be avoided. To the extent that nudging is optional, it should be undertaken with an appreciation of the risk of error and with careful efforts to ensure that it promotes, and does not undermine, people's welfare. A GPS device does not decrease welfare. In general, information about health risks and potential financial burdens should increase welfare (Agarwal et al 2013).

Of course nudges must be tested to ensure that they are doing what they are supposed to do (Halpern 2015, Thaler 2015). Some nudges fail. When they do, the right conclusion may be that freedom worked – or that we should nudge better (Sunstein 2017a).

7 Nudges work only at the margins; they cannot achieve a whole lot. If experts were asked to catalogue the world's major problems, many of them would single out poverty, malnutrition and hunger, unemployment, corruption, diseases, terrorism, and climate change. On one view, nudges are an unfortunate distraction from what might actually help. With an understanding of nudging, we might have some fresh ideas about how to tweak letters from government to citizens, producing statistically significant increases in desirable behaviour. But that is pretty small stuff. If behavioural economists want to make a contribution, shouldn't they focus on much more important matters?

It is true that behaviourally informed approaches are hardly limited to nudges; mandates, bans, and incentives may well have behavioural justifications (Conly 2013, Loewenstein and Chater 2017, Thaler 2017). The policy programme of behavioural science is not exhausted by nudges (Thaler 2017). It is also true that some nudges produce only modest changes. But in multiple domains, nudges have proven far more cost-effective than other kinds of interventions, which means that per dollar spent, they have had a significantly larger impact (Benartzi et al 2017).

By any measure, the consequences of some nudges are not properly described as modest. As a result of automatic enrolment in free school meals programmes, more than 11 million poor American children are now receiving free breakfast and lunch during the school year. Credit card legislation, enacted in 2010, is saving American consumers more than $10 billion annually; significant portions of those savings come from nudges and nudge-like interventions (Agarwal et al 2013). With respect to savings, automatic enrolment in pension programmes has produced massive increases in participation rates (Chetty et al 2012, Thaler 2016).

New nudges, now in early stages or under discussion, could also have a major impact. In the US alone, automatic voter registration could turn millions of people into voters. If the goal is to reduce greenhouse gas emissions, automatic enrolment in green energy can have a large impact (Pichert and Katsikopoulos 2008, Ebeling and Lotz 2015). The Earned Income Tax Credit is probably the most effective anti-poverty programme in the US, but many eligible people do not take advantage of it. Automatic enrolment would have large consequences for the lives of millions of people. With respect to the world's most serious problems, the use of nudges remains in its preliminary stages. We will see far more in the future, and the impact will not be small.

It is true, of course, that for countless problems, nudges are hardly enough. They cannot eliminate poverty, unemployment, and corruption. By itself, any individual initiative – whether it is a tax, a subsidy, a mandate, or a ban – is unlikely to solve large problems, but denting them counts as an achievement. This book helps point the way.

Acknowledgements

The first edition of this book resulted from a research project that took place between September 2007 and June 2010 called 'Rediscovering the Civic: Achieving Better Outcomes in Public Policy', which was supported by the UK Economic and Social Research Council (ESRC), the Department of Communities and Local Government (CLG), and the North West Improvement and Efficiency Partnership (NWIEP) (RES-177-25-0002). With the publication of the second edition, we again have the opportunity to thank the funders for giving us the opportunity to engage in such an interesting and relevant piece of work, applying experimental methods to study public participation in the UK for the first time. It was a big act of faith by our government co-sponsors to fund a relatively slow-moving project. In spite of the time it took us to complete our work, we believe they found the research and findings relevant, as governments are always keen to know how to engage citizens in public policy. Our particular gratitude goes to Paul McCafferty, then head of Local Governance Research Unit at CLG, who helped organize the finance for the project. We are also very grateful to the team at CLG for their assistance throughout, in particular Arianna Haberis and Wendy Russell Barter.

Acknowledgements

We would like to thank the members of the advisory group to the project, who gave of their time so freely: Arianna Haberis, Jane Martin, Lawrence Pratchett, Joyce Redfern, Barry Quirk, Shamitt Saggar, Mike Saward, Henry Tam, Matthew Taylor, and Chris Wyatt. We also thank those who spoke at our final event on 23 June 2010, in particular Philip Blond, Toby Blume, Sue Goss, and the then Minister for Planning and Decentralization, Greg Clark MP, as well as members of the advisory group.

We owe a great debt to our administrator, the late Margaret Holmes, who coped so well in organizing such a complex and multifaceted project, especially its finances and sub-contracts, and who helped make the final event such a success. We are especially thankful to the researchers who worked alongside us, in particular Tessa Brannan, Hanhua Liu, and Hisako Nomura. Hanhua contributed to the first recycling randomized controlled trial and on our separately reported survey work. Tessa worked with Peter John on the original Wythenshawe Get Out the Vote experiment reported in Chapter 4. Hisako worked on the analysis of the deliberation project and came up with the food waste feedback experiment idea and led this part of our work, which we report in Chapter 3. We are very pleased that Helen Margetts collaborated with us on the research that forms the basis for Chapter 6, and we thank both Tobias Escher and Stéphane Reissfelder for their energy and ingenuity in planning and organizing the experiments at the Oxford Internet Institute. Patrick Sturgis also contributed his impressive skills to the statistical work on our deliberation project. We are grateful to Ben Smith and David Torgerson, who carried out many of the randomizations, in this way being the neutral third parties for this essential task. Don Green has been an inspiration, and we thank him in particular for spending a whole afternoon with us brainstorming our putative experiments and for commenting on the manuscript.

Acknowledgements

We thank again the original publisher, Bloomsbury Academic, keen on us right from the start. We benefitted from their online publishing experiment, which allowed so many people to download the text for free on Creative Commons, as well as encouraging them to purchase print copies of the book. We thank Frances Pinter for her support for the project. In particular, we benefitted from Caroline Wintersgill's enthusiasm and input throughout, especially her very helpful suggestions after reading the draft manuscript. We also appreciate the thoughtful comments of the publisher's anonymous reviewer. We are grateful to Kay Caldwell of Clere Story, who edited the manuscript, and to the copyeditors at Bloomsbury, in particular Howard Watson. We benefitted from the feedback of students on City University's Publishing MA, who were assigned the book as a project in the digitization and publishing module, and who asked Peter John a number of probing and useful questions about the enterprise.

We would like to thank the many people who helped deliver our projects in local government, the National Health Service, and the voluntary sector. We thank all those at EMERGE – in particular Lucy Danger, Mark Hill, Denise Lambert, Sebastian Serayet, and Jo-Anne Witcombe – who provided invaluable ideas and practical support with the recycling and food waste experiments, and Mark Husdan from Oldham Council's waste team, who worked closely with us on the food waste experiment, plus all the monitors and canvassers who worked on the projects. We gratefully acknowledge the work of Isobel McVicar at Community HEART, staff at Manchester City Council, all the people who staffed the drop-off points, and the colleagues and volunteers (Tessa Brannan, Bethan Harries, and Liz Pool) who helped sort the large number of books that arrived at the Institute for Political and Economic Governance's office as part of the pledging project. We are deeply appreciative to the staff at Ipsos MORI, in particular Lisa Valade-DeMelo, who helped us deliver the online deliberation, which was a leap into the unknown in designing a new kind of intervention. The company calmly complied with what may have seemed like endless requests to redesign the project. We would also like to thank Greg Naughton, who filmed the videos that were used for the online forums; Julie Martin and Niki Lewis, who worked so well with our design experiment in Wiltshire; and Share D'All, formerly of Hampshire County Council. Mike Amos-Smith of stories4change was a partner in the Building Links project, and his help included making YouTube videos and providing insightful comments. We also thank the eight courageous community groups who lobbied councillors with us.

For the volunteering experiment, we have huge admiration for our risk-taking local authority colleagues in Blackburn with Darwen Borough Council: Geoff Cole, Lesley Fox, Tanya Gallagher, Peter Little, Billy Maxwell, and Ross McQueen. Special thanks go to Sarah Henry for being one of our supporters throughout. Our thanks also go to NHS Blood and Transplant for advice and assistance with our two organ donation experiments, particularly Angie Burton, Christine Cole, Rachel Dance, and Professor James Neuberger, as well as again to Ipsos MORI who also helped conduct our online organ donation experiment. We appreciate the contributions of the postgraduate research assistants and the students involved in the university-based experiment.

For the second edition, we thank again Caroline Wintersgill, who championed the book as Senior Consulting Editor for Manchester University Press, and who helped persuade the press to publish the second edition. Frances Pinter was again in our ambit as chief executive of Manchester University Press. We thank the press for the help in getting the second edition off the ground, to Greg Clark for redrafting his foreword while a Cabinet minister at a very busy time in British politics, and to Cass Sunstein for writing us a new prologue.

Acknowledgements

Finally, we owe a debt of gratitude to the citizens themselves who participated in our project, and who showed they were willing to donate organs, recycle waste, vote, and volunteer in response to our prompts and interventions. As with the first edition, we are donating the royalties from book sales to local charities.

Introduction

We start with an example. In 2008 the environment department of an English local council located near to Manchester faced a problem: how to get a group of citizens to recycle more of their household waste. This well-run authority, with considerable green credentials, wanted to do more for the environment. It had already been very successful in persuading many residents to separate their waste. But very little recycling was happening on some of its publicly owned housing estates, where many tenants made little attempt to sort out their rubbish into cans, glass, and paper. Instead, they put all their waste into refuse sacks and deposited them in the general waste collection bins. There was even one small estate where no recycling was happening at all.

To try to get the message across to the residents on this estate, the council's officers sent leaflets to households, and then put up large, colourful posters at the entrances to the buildings and on the walkways. But these acts of encouragement had no effect. In the end the officers became so frustrated they instructed the waste collection service not to pick up the rubbish for a few weeks. The idea was that if the people living on the estate saw the growing pile of refuse sacks they would be shamed into recycling. Instead of picking up the rubbish in the normal way, the refuse collectors placed the sacks in the central grassed areas of the estate in full view of everyone. Over the weeks that followed, these courtyards became filled up with black refuse bags (the council regularly checked there was no public health problem).

Well, what happened? Did the citizens of the estate start placing glass, cans, and paper into their respective collection boxes? The simple answer is no. They ignored the message from the council. In the end the environment department gave up and the garbage trucks returned to their normal cycle of visits, collecting the black plastic bags with their unsorted waste. We do not know what the residents in the neighbourhood made of the mounting mountain of refuse. Was it clear to them that this was a form of punishment? Perhaps they thought the local council had failed them again? Maybe the collective action problem felt insurmountable? Regardless, the plain fact is that modern government, with its complex laws, access to finance, public relations/marketing skills, professionally trained employees, and information technology capacity – as well as the leverage it gets from democratic legitimacy – cannot get a group of citizens to behave differently if they do not wish to do so.

The story shows there are limits to what government can achieve with conventional means of bringing about change. It cannot command people to be more neighbourly or to save for their retirement, or to volunteer to help out in their community or – in this case – contribute to the environment by recycling more of what they dispose of. The kinds of problems that many societies now need to solve require changing the behaviour of citizens, whose private actions are hard to regulate by laws and commands alone. Even when these top-down tools of government work, there are some moral qualms about using them too much. Citizens in Western industrial democracies have come to value their individual freedoms, lifestyle choices, and right to have a say. They are less deferential, less automatically inclined to accept the claimed wisdom of experts, and more willing to challenge those in authority. Modern citizens want to be active choosers, or at least as much as they can be, and as a result top-down commands or crass incentives to change their behaviour are less likely to be effective and acceptable. The use of laws and commands, which was the normal reflex action of policy-makers in previous years, is no longer such an attractive option, at least when done without other complementary means of encouraging civic action. It is also possible for governments to provide financial incentives to support new behaviours, but even copious amounts of public funding need some citizen help to get the best value from public policies.

The important complements to finance and laws are what may be called the softer tools of government. These involve working more closely with citizens, understanding how they are thinking, and encouraging them to take – and to own – better decisions. It would involve a 'nudge' rather than a push or a shout, and would incorporate a 'think', that is, government and other public bodies allowing citizens to debate and to deliberate so they can decide what is best. We aim in this book to find out whether these alternatives can work.

Nudges are about framing choices. Citizens now live in a complex world, with many signals about what is the best thing to do. Given that people have only a limited amount of time to process all the information they get, it may be more practicable to use social cues to help decide what to do. In so doing, it may not take much effort to change individual behaviour, especially as citizens can take account of what others are doing. The nudge idea is about governments, working in cooperation with citizens, shaping the multiple daily choices people make in ways that could be better for society. It relies on citizens believing these social cues are right.

Think refers to another broad set of tools – stretching from con-sultation to handing over decisions to citizens – which have become prominently and widely established in the world of governance since the 1990s. Broadly, these multiple forms of public engagement rest on the assumption that citizens – given the right evidence, enough time, and an appropriate context – can come to the best judgement about what is good for them and their fellow citizens and then act. Solutions can be found to challenging issues, and the pathways to behaviour change can be illuminated and smoothed because citizens have been involved in the construction of the answer and perhaps even in the framing of the issue. Both the legitimacy and likely effec-tiveness of any solution are thus increased, and its chances of being adopted are maximized.

This book is about these softer tools of intervention and asks two questions. What are the underlying mechanisms that these tools depend on? And will policies that use them work – that is, will their use lead to changes in behaviour that bring public benefit or value? In answering these questions, the book breaks new ground. It is one of the first accounts of these new tools of governance that at the same time seeks to find out whether they work or not. There are plenty of books that advocate the use of new kinds of public management by government, starting from Osborne and Gaebler's *Rethinking Government* (Osborne and Gaebler 1993), with its famous dictum that government should do more steering and less rowing (more commissioning and less direct provision), and reviews of new tools of governance (Salamon 1989, John 2011).

Central and local governments have been quick to adopt this kind of thinking, as they have the newer doctrines of behavioural eco-nomics and nudge, inspired by the book *Nudge* (Thaler and Sunstein 2008). The prime mover in this important public policy develop-ment is the UK's Behavioural Insights Team, which was formed by the 2010–15 Liberal Democrat and Conservative coalition government in the UK as a unit in the Cabinet Office, which applies behavioural insights to public policy (Halpern 2015). It was then spun out of government as a social purpose company. Its success shows the rapid rise and development of nudge, which has become a familiar policy tool delivering concrete benefits to policy-makers. Similar developments occurred across the world in countries as diverse as Germany, Singapore, Australia, Finland, Japan, and Peru to name a few examples (see John 2019). We return to these innovations, which have occurred since the publication of the first edition, in the final newly written epilogue to this book as well as in the empirical chapters that follow.

We are able to offer something different from standard defences of behavioural public policies: an analysis of the underlying thinking behind the most prominent new forms of intervention. While supporting many of the nudge initiatives, we argue that think complements them and deepens and broadens out the behaviour change programme. Think helps deal with the potential lack of legitimacy of nudge and its appearance of being manipulative. In general terms, nudgers should consider incorporating some elements of think into their interventions.

Most of all, and uniquely, we provide a systematic and rigorous approach to the study of the effectiveness of both nudge and think. This book reports the first attempt in the UK to show how randomized controlled trials can reveal what works when it comes to changing citizen behaviour. Experiments allow a reliable inference to be made between a cause and its effect. When it comes to introducing new medicines in Western industrial democracies it is expected that they will be the focus of rigorous randomized controlled trials before they are introduced. That is, the research measures the difference between a sample of the population who receive the treatment and those in a control group who do not receive the intervention. The same logic of testing should be applied to interventions in the non-medical field and specifically when governments are trying to change citizen behaviour. Policy-makers can construct simple randomized controlled trials or experiments to test what forms of nudge might work or what forms of think-based interventions are efficacious. This book not only offers particular examples of interventions that have made a difference, but makes a case for a general approach to testing what works, which is rigorous and achievable. In cooperation with thousands of citizens and dozens of local governments, community groups, and non-profits, we have been trialling practices and ideas about how to stimulate different kinds of citizen behaviour, and this book reports the findings. One brief word of definition before we proceed: when we refer to citizen or civic behaviour in this book, we mean behaviour that is primarily oriented towards the collective public good, rather than towards individual wellbeing per se, although of course many citizen or civic behaviours do bring individual benefits, including physical, social, or psychological benefits. We elaborate on this further below on the section 'Defining the good citizen'. However, broadly speaking, citizen or civic behaviour refers to prosocial acts that are primarily for the benefit of other people, society more widely, or the environment, but which may also bring additional benefits for the individual.

Plan of the book

The first part of the book examines nudge and think, before setting out our preferred methods of investigating them: randomized controlled trials and design experiments. Chapter 1, 'Nudging and thinking', discusses nudge and think in some depth. It explores the assumptions of nudge and think strategies and what they can offer to the challenge of stimulating citizen behaviour. It also engages with normative questions about whether the state or other public agencies should nudge citizens or encourage them to think. Chapter 2, 'Testing', is about how to find out what works. It argues that policy-makers and others should adopt an experimental approach when they do not know the answer about how to achieve their goals. The randomized controlled trial and its qualitative cousin, the design experiment, provide robust methods that can ascertain whether interventions designed to change citizen behaviour work or not. Chapter 1 and Chapter 2 set out the main message of the book: policy-makers should experiment to find out the most effective way of encouraging better citizen behaviour.

The second and more substantial part of the book is about the key outcomes that policy-makers are interested in; this part reports and discusses experiments aimed at shaping citizen behaviour. It starts out looking at mostly nudge-based strategies and then examines some think interventions. These empirical chapters examine some of the existing evidence (both observational and experimental), provide tests of our original and innovative interventions in different areas of citizen behaviour, and come to judgements about the state of the current understanding of how best to stimulate citizen behaviour.

Each of the empirical chapters takes a similar structure: first explaining why we should study this topic, whether it is recycling, donating, or another activity; we review what is already known about it; we describe the interventions and convey what we have found out. Finally, we set out the lessons for nudge or think and recommend additional literature so the reader may explore the topic further.

Chapter 3, 'Recycling', is about how to encourage household recycling of waste. A detailed case is presented of a nudge strategy that involved canvassing people on their doorsteps, encouraging them to recycle their waste and comparing the results with a randomized controlled trial. The findings show the strength of nudge in that the canvassing increases recycling, but it also shows the potential weakness of nudge as the effect reduces three months later. The chapter contains a second experiment that examines the role of feedback in encouraging recycling. The chapter concludes with a discussion of the implications of these findings for the advocates of the nudge strategy.

Chapter 4, 'Volunteering', reviews the evidence on promoting volunteering and ask what a nudge strategy could offer. The chapter contains details on a design experiment that asks citizens complaining to a local authority telephone call centre to undertake some civic-minded acts. What do these findings indicate about the challenge of promoting volunteering? By changing the choice architecture, is it possible to turn complainers to volunteers?

Chapter 5, 'Voting', shows how experiments can test a variety of strategies for mobilizing the vote in a Get Out the Vote campaign (GOTV). There is a vast literature on getting citizens to engage politically, but could nudge offer some additional insights? We report on an experimental intervention about how to get citizens to vote and reflect on its implications for stimulating citizen behaviour more generally.

Chapter 6, 'Petitioning', is about another individual political behaviour: signing a petition, a simple and powerful way for the voice of the citizen to be heard by those in power, made much easier by online tools. We report on an experiment which alters the information that people receive when making an e-petition. We seek to find out whether allowing people to view the number of other e-petitioners affects their willingness to sign.

Chapter 7, 'Giving', asks if a nudge, through creating social pressure to do something, can encourage people to follow through their good intention to give to charity. The experimenters asked people to pledge to donate a book from their home to help children in Africa.

Chapter 8, 'Donating', discusses an experiment about donating organs. We ask whether the nudge strategy of changing the choice architecture can encourage people to agree to donate their organs after their death. We then outline a second experiment testing whether a booklet alone or a booklet combined with a discussion (think) would cause people to be more willing to donate their organs. In this experiment, we are able to test elements of think and nudge together.

Chapter 9 is called 'Debating'. The idea of deliberation is well established as a think strategy. But can it deal with controversial issues of public policy in an online environment? This chapter reviews the literature on this subject and reports a unique experiment in large-scale online deliberation involving 6,000 citizens. Drawing on evidence from these online debates on community cohesion and youth anti-social behaviour, we show how online engagement can influence knowledge and opinions about public policy options.

Chapter 10, 'Including', finds out how public authorities use media technology (in this case a DVD) to raise the profile of excluded voices as part of a decentralization initiative. The design experiment highlights the crucial, but difficult, role of facilitation, in particular the impact it can have in creating more inclusive dialogue.

Chapter 11, 'Linking', is about the wider institutional context of public decision-making, which may need to be reformed if think is going to work. Thinking requires linking, and only makes sense if the ideas that citizens come up with are reviewed and judged openly by the policy-makers. Why participate if no one is listening? This chapter presents findings about how citizens link to government and reveals the extent of the gap between citizens and local representatives. It may be the case that the difficulty of linking elites to citizens is the central limitation of the think strategy. We report the results of an experiment that tests how responsive policy-makers are to requests from a citizen's interest group.

Chapter 12, 'Summary of key findings', brings the insights from the various empirical sections together, and draw out the implications for policy-makers. It is here we make the case for more experiments that can help us understand what drives citizen behaviour and then assess the best way governments can intervene to promote it. With robust evidence to hand, governments can thereby achieve better policy outcomes. We advocate a local and decentralized approach to citizen involvement and behaviour change that reflects how we applied the experimental method and the way we used partnerships with local interest groups and public bodies to develop a genuinely creative and evidence-based form of local policy-making. In this way, we argue that the leverage of nudge and creative potential of think can be brought together.

The final chapter, 'Epilogue: the future of nudge and think', is newly written for this second edition. It reviews the field since the book first came out and assess the future for the two ideas in light of the book's findings and subsequent developments in public policy. It has been a fast-moving agenda, especially for nudge, which has transformed from being the newcomer to an established policy tool; but it has also been important for think too, which has matured as a form of governance. This chapter asks whether policy-makers have followed our earlier recommendation for nudge and think to work closer together. We make a proposal for a modified version of nudge, called nudge plus, which incorporates elements of think, and takes forward our vision of a decentralized citizen-active form of nudging, which we argued for in the first edition.

Defining the good citizen

Before getting to the core argument about think and nudge, and our tests of what tools drive changes in citizen behaviour, we need to address a prior question: what kind of behaviour should governments and public agencies be encouraging? This is not a straightforward question to answer, for what makes for good citizen behaviour is temporal, unfixed, and dynamic. The good citizen of Athenian democracy was one skilled in the art of soldiering; the twenty-first-century good citizen might visit their elderly neighbour, engage in making decisions about local public spending, or help support their local park friends group. Civic behaviour can manifest itself in several ways (John et al 2011). We can think of examples of individual political action where individuals seek to influence decision-making through signing a petition or voting in elections. Also familiar is the practice of collective political action, where people work together to influence decision-making, perhaps in a community meeting to think through a tricky issue that seeks to define priorities and actions for an area. We can also recognize many examples of citizens adopting a do-it-yourself attitude and practice, when individuals act in the wider public interest, for example by driving an elderly person to the doctor, recycling household waste, or volunteering to do hospital visits. There are also collective forms of this kind of citizen behaviour, which could include being a member of a community group to clean up a local park, forming a social enterprise to run a community facility, or pledging to exchange favours formally via a time-bank (Richardson 2008). For this reason, governments and public agencies need to recognize a wider set of behaviours than they have done hitherto.

Having established what kinds of behaviour are important to encourage, what are the main motivators of civic action that we need to establish before intervening with experiments? Each individual will have potentially multiple motivations for engaging in citizen behaviour, some more self-oriented and some more regarding of others. For example, people who volunteer may be interested in helping their neighbours; or they do it out of loyalty to the area; or because their friends are involved and asked them; or they turn up to community events because they want to meet people and make new friends. Others may enjoy the challenge of getting a project off the ground and winning against the odds; or some may see it as a route to employment in the third sector. Individuals may have one reason or many, which may vary according to the task involved. Engaging in civic action can be about protecting a person's interests, or those of others, or can be about both.

Citizen behaviour requires effort. Exercising self-restraint and personal responsibility, becoming informed about issues that affect communities, and participating in consultations, or changing entrenched habits for collective ends all demand considerable exertion by individuals. The basic idea is that to have the society that people want, they need to agree to give more back, which has been echoed in statements from people as diverse as Bill Gates and Barack Obama. But voluntary acts might not happen without some external support and intervention. Of course, there are some self-organizing activities, such as neighbourhood support, families whose members care for each other, and various forms of local organizing, such as petitioning and campaigning; but in many cases, actions will not take place effectively and on a large enough scale without some intervention by an external agency. Most people engage civically in many ways in their lives. Citizens do things individually and collectively. The scale of citizen behaviour is already substantial but people could do more if were approached in the right way. At least that is the proposition we aim to test in this book.

1

Nudging and thinking

What is a nudge strategy and what is a think strategy? In this chapter we compare and contrast these approaches to changing citizen behaviour. We argue that even though the two strategies draw on different traditions of research, they are both a response to a shared understanding of the human predicament, which is that people are boundedly rational. Individuals seek to economize on the use of information, even when reflecting on big problems of the day, as well as when deciding to carry out a routine civic action. This does not mean that they are necessarily making wrong choices for themselves and others, but that policies based on assuming rational action will be limited in their desired impacts.

We then ask whether policy-makers should be trying to stimulate citizen behaviour. Are efforts to involve citizens more in public life too paternalistic and limiting of individual freedom? What people do in civil society, it could be argued, is up to them and is not for the state to dictate. We try to address this issue head on by arguing that shifting the architecture for citizens' individual and collective choices is as appropriate and legitimate an act for government as passing laws and regulations or creating systems of taxes and charges. Government is about citizens agreeing to tie their collective hands for collective benefit. Laws exist to protect our property and freedom, and taxes are there to pay for services societies think should be collectively provided. If supporting civic behaviour brings similar collective benefits then there appears no reason to rule it out. Most forms of policy intervention are desirable, provided there are checks and balances on what can be done.

How to change citizen behaviour: nudge and think strategies

Understanding what motivates people and what drives their behaviour is self-evidently central to policy-making. If policy-makers are trying to change human society for the better then they are likely to have some theory of what it is that makes human beings tick. Social scientists have not yet produced a fully evidenced understanding of human behaviour, but research to date has produced at least two schools of thought that can be identified. The key issue from the point of view of policy-makers is which school to side with. In this chapter we make the argument for looking at citizen behaviour through the summary ideas of nudge and think. Nudge is about giving information and social cues so as to help people do positive things for themselves and society. Think argues it is possible to get citizens to think through challenging issues in innovative ways that allow for evidence, and the opinions of all to count.

These ideas draw on different traditions of research and theory, which are explored in this chapter. The two approaches of nudge and think are different. For the decision-makers, they represent different models of how to intervene in society at large. As discussed in the previous chapter, the book by Thaler and Sunstein (Thaler and Sunstein 2008) called *Nudge: Improving Decisions about Health, Wealth and Happiness* deserves particular credit because, along with associated publications by its authors (e.g. Sunstein 2016a, 2017b), it has done much to set out so clearly the possibilities of tackling issues of behaviour change in new ways. Nudge offers a valuable framework for changing the choice architecture of citizens in order to achieve alterations in their behaviour and attitudes, which would constitute improvements for them and for society as a whole. Nudge summarizes ideas from the work of behavioural economics (Thaler 2015), a line of work going back mainly to the 1960s but with earlier roots (Oliver 2017), and which draws extensively on assumptions from psychology about heuristics, and is not necessarily about nudge (see Hargreaves-Heap 2013). But in practice, behavioural economics has been applied to a range of current problems, such as under-standing contributions to pension schemes. Researchers using this approach argue that citizens can be offered a choice architecture that encourages them to act in a way that achieves benefits for them-selves and for their fellow citizens. This is often about the provision of information, and how it may be structured or framed to achieve effects on individual behaviour. This relatively new social-science thinking has influenced policy-makers to redesign these policies and implementation procedures with these insights in mind.

A valuable account of how nudge ideas have been taken up in practice, and how they could be taken further, is provided in a 2010 report by the Institute of Government for the UK Cabinet Office called MINDSPACE (Dolan et al 2010, 2012), which seeks to encour-age policy-makers to think beyond the tools of regulation, law, and financial incentives. The report contends:

> For policy-makers facing policy challenges such as crime, obesity, or environmental sustainability, behavioural approaches offer a poten-tially powerful new set of tools. Applying these tools can lead to low cost, low pain ways of nudging citizens – or ourselves – into new ways of acting by going with the grain of how we think and act. This is an

important idea at any time, but is especially relevant in a period of fiscal constraint. (Dolan et al 2010: 7)

The MINDSPACE report, and our thinking in designing our nudge experiments, also draws on disciplines beyond behavioural economics, including health psychology, social psychology, and politics, all of which have made a big contribution to understanding how behavioural insights can enable more effective public policy aimed at changing citizen behaviour (see Spotswood 2016). As a result of this broad engagement across the social sciences, nudging has emerged as an important strategy for public authorities to adopt for changing citizen behaviour (John 2018). The good news, according to Thaler and Sunstein, is that policy-makers may be successful in nudging citizens into civic behaviour if they take account of the cognitive architecture of choice that citizens face, and if they work with, rather than against, the grain of biases, hunches, and heuristics. While not denying the power of sticks and carrots in changing behaviour, they argue for the relevance of insights from cognitive psychology privileging the design of those interventions which recognize that citizens are boundedly rational decision-makers. The recommendation is that governments consider default options when they offer citizens choices.

An alternative strategy for transforming citizen behaviour – labelled as think – emerges from the deliberative turn that has dominated democratic theory over the last three decades. While there are a number of different conceptions of deliberative democracy, they share a common insight: the legitimacy of politics rests on public deliberation between free and equal citizens. Deliberative theorists recognize that preferences are not independent of institutional settings. In fact, institutional settings play a role in shaping preferences. As such, decision-making procedures should not just be concerned with simply aggregating pre-existing preferences (for example, voting), but also with the nature of the processes through which they are formed. Legitimacy rests on the free flow of discussion and exchange of views in an environment of mutual respect and understanding.

Underpinning this conception of politics is a particular theory of citizen behaviour that has an epistemic and moral dimension. Free and equal public deliberation has an educational effect as citizens increase their knowledge and understanding of the consequences of their actions. But the value of deliberation does not simply rest on the exchange of information. The public nature of deliberation is crucial. Because citizens are expected to justify their perspectives and preferences in public, there is a strong motivation to constrain self-interest and to consider the public good. Miller refers to the 'moralising effect of public deliberation' (Miller 1992: 61), which tends to eliminate irrational preferences based on false empirical beliefs, morally repugnant preferences which no one is willing to advance in the public arena, and narrowly self-interested preferences. Citizens are given the opportunity to think differently and in so doing, deliberative theorists argue, they will witness a transformation of (often ill-informed) preferences. Deliberative democrats provide a clear account of civic behaviour: under deliberative conditions citizens' behaviour is shaped in a more civic orientation as they consider the views and perspectives of others. For many deliberative theorists, this makes deliberation (or a think strategy) particularly pertinent for including those whose voices are not often heard, and for dealing with particularly contentious public policy issues (Gutmann and Thompson 1996).

Theories of deliberative democracy are often charged with being far too utopian in their ambition: their aim appears unrealistic if it is to imbue all of politics with the virtues of mutual respect and understanding (Shapiro 2005). But recent work has been more practical in its objectives, with democratic theorists and political scientists turning their attention to the empirical question of the conditions under which the norms and procedures of deliberation (or something close to deliberation) can be realized. There has been particular interest in forms of empowered participatory governance (Fung and Wright 2003) and democratic innovations (Smith 2009) that aim to increase and deepen citizen participation in political decision-making processes. In recent years, such innovations have been increasingly institutionalized in public decision-making (Smith 2018).

A shared starting assumption: bounded rationality

Nudge and think are distinctive strategies but crucially the starting point for both is the recognition that people are boundedly rational. Citizens – those in government and those in civil society – are decision-makers constrained by the fundamental human problem of processing information, understanding a situation, and deter-mining consequences. There are limits to their cognitive capacity and the world is a complex place to understand: 'Humans are goal directed, understand their environment in realistic terms, and adjust to changing circumstances facing them. But they are not completely successful in doing so because of the inner limitations. Moreover, these cognitive limitations make a major difference in human affairs – in the affairs of individuals and in the affairs of state and nation' (Jones 2001: 21). Decision-making is conditioned by the cognitive limitations of the human mind.

Individuals reason, but not as heroic choice-makers. When faced with a decision they do not think about every available option or always make a great choice that is optimal to their utility, as assumed by many economists. Their cognitive inner world helps them to focus on some things and ignore others and it is driven by habits of thought, rules of thumb, and emotions. Rationality is bounded by this framing role of the human mind. People will search selectively, basing that search on incomplete information and partial ignorance, but terminate it before an optimal option emerges, and will choose instead something that is good enough. This is not to say that the behaviour of agents needs to be judged as irrational. On the contrary, people are rational in the sense that behaviour is generally goal-oriented and, usually, they have reasons for what they do. It is just that rationality rests on the interaction of the cognitive structure and the context in which individuals are operating, and as a result sometimes they make poor quality decisions.

The starting point for our understanding in this area is the pioneering work of the Nobel Prize winner Herbert Simon, who produced his powerful insights over sixty years ago (Simon 1945/1997). Decision-making is conditioned by the structure of the human mind and the context in which people operate. Decision-makers rarely comprehensively perceive the environment and weigh up all options against their preferences in the context of incentives and constraints, and then efficiently choose the options that maximize these preferences. Decision-makers have to deal with the external environment and their inner world, their cognitive architecture.

A second point, strongly emphasized by Simon, is that actors gain their purpose in this complex world of information processing through sub-goal identification (Simon 1945/1997). Individuals identify with institutions or, more broadly, cultures of which they become part and internalize the aims of these social groups (Goodin 2004). More broadly, people are social animals, who often look to know what the rules are in different situations and ask how it is that people are supposed to behave. Individuals search for the rules of appropriate behaviour rather than just maximizing their utility (March and Olsen 1989).

Nudge and think constitute different responses to the challenge of bounded rationality. A standard assumption of much government policy-making in the past has been that 'if we provide the carrots and sticks, alongside accurate information, people will weigh up the revised costs and benefits of their actions and respond accordingly' (Dolan et al 2010: 8). An awareness of bounded rationality indicates that there are obvious limits to the chances of such strategies succeeding. Operating with an awareness of the implications of bounded rationality would appear to be advantageous.

Nudge tries to go with the grain of human behaviour: understand the shortcuts and heuristics that people use to make decisions and then seek to bend or influence their environment – choice architecture – to get behaviour that is more beneficial for society and the individual. Since individuals make decisions in the present – the here and now – nudge strategies are about creating the conditions to make better choices in the moment. A nudge strategy advocates working by understanding the way that rationality is bounded and then nudging citizens in the right direction.

In contrast, a think strategy suggests that a public agency can seek to create the right institutional framework so that an individual can overcome some aspects of their bounded rationality. If bounded rationality is heightened by lack of information and lack of attention to the viewpoints of others, then public agencies might create the conditions in which these are taken on board, in this way nudging citizens to think. This could be a fusion of our two strategies. Overall, a think strategy aims to promote free and fair deliberation between citizens. As Fearon comments, 'democratic deliberation has the capacity to lessen the problem of bounded rationality: the fact that our imaginations and calculating abilities are limited and fallible' (Fearon 1998: 49). Deliberation offers the conditions under which actors can widen their own limited and fallible perspectives by drawing on each other's knowledge, experience, and capabilities. The odds of good judgements increase for two reasons: deliberation can be additively valuable in the sense that one actor is able to offer an analysis or solutions that had not occurred to others; or it can be multiplicatively valuable in that deliberation could lead to solutions that would not have occurred to the participants individually (Fearon 1998: 50).

Nudge and think have a shared starting point but present a different dynamic for change. They appeal to different views citizens have about what is politically possible and acknowledge the extent of social change that different kinds of people think can be achieved. This chapter explores those differences before returning to the issue of whether, and how, to go about changing citizen behaviour.

Nudge: from psychological insight into intervention

Nudge strategies build on cognitive shortcuts or social influences to develop an intervention that will shape citizen behaviour. We briefly outline some examples of the approach below (see Oliver 2017 for an in-depth review).

Cognitive-driven interventions

Prospect theory (Kahneman and Tversky 1979, Thaler 1980) concerns the endowment effect, which suggests that when individuals are already in possession of something, they are very reluctant to lose it. Cognitively, it is more important for people to hold on to what they have (that is, to prevent loss) than to gain something extra. Experimental research backs up this theory and demonstrates that ownership matters in people's valuation of a good, with owners placing higher value on the traded good than buyers do (Kahneman et al 1990). In public policy this translates into designing behavioural change strategies to emphasize losses rather than gains. Where people feel that they have something to lose, they may be more inclined to do something to prevent the loss occurring. For instance, smoking cessation policies that highlight years of life lost through smoking are more effective than those highlighting years gained by quitting. In a similar way, fines are likely to be a more powerful motivator for changing behaviour than rewards (Dawney and Shah 2005).

Another facet of cognitive architecture that displays less than fully rational behaviour is the use of psychological discounting (Frederick et al 2002). This theory suggests that immediacy is a major factor in our responsiveness to offers. We place more weight on the short-term than on the long-term effects of our decisions. If people are about to gain something, they would rather do so now than later. If they have to feel pain, they would rather experience it sometime in the distant future. Behavioural economists use this principle to explain why people often make imperfect economic decisions. Hyperbolic discounting occurs when we place a 'high discount rate over short horizons and a relatively low discount rate over long horizons' (Laibson 1997: 445). In other words, people overweigh short-term consumption while discounting the greater long-term gains that could be made by delaying consumption, creating outcomes that are suboptimal both from an individual and a collective perspective. It is this trait that makes many people reluctant to save for their retirement or inclined to ignore the long-term effects of a poor diet or exercise regime. Since we are all living longer, this psychological predisposition is one that public policies should address. Commitment mechanisms can be built into public policies to redress our propensity for short-term gratification and procrastination

(O'Donoghue and Rabin 1999). One example of this, which displays promising results, is a pension savings programme built on a buy-now-pay-later principle, in which employees have to commit to incremental savings with a two-year payment holiday to begin with (Thaler and Bernartzi 2004). Another is commitments to engage in exercise programmes for weight loss (Savani 2018). Discounting is a feature of analysis by economists as well, but the psychological literature suggests that people discount in a less consistent and rational way than some economists, working with formally derived micro-foundations, recognize. Moreover, it is possible to derive different micro-foundations using the findings of behavioural economics as foundations (Sugden 2018).

A closely related phenomenon is our propensity for maintaining the status quo (Samuelson and Zeckhauser 1988, Geng 2016). Limited by time, intellectual energy, and resources, the majority of people, most of the time, prefer not to change their habits unless they really have to. Research verifies that when confronted with a complex or difficult decision, and in the absence of full information about all the alternatives, individuals will often stick with their current position (Choi et al 2003). A powerful mechanism that can be used by policy-makers is to alter the choice architecture by shifting the default position to maximize social welfare (Thaler and Sunstein 2008). Automatically enrolling citizens for pension savings programmes (Cronqvist and Thaler 2004, Cronqvist et al 2018) or on to organ donor registers (Johnson and Goldstein 2003, Abadie and Gay 2006) are instances where changing defaults appears to work well.

A further aspect of behaviour recognized by social psychologists and relevant to the design of public services is the issue of cognitive consistency. Following Festinger (Festinger 1957), psychologists suggest that people seek consistency between their beliefs and their behaviour. However, when beliefs and behaviour clash (the phenomenon of cognitive dissonance), we frequently alter beliefs instead of adjusting behaviour. One way out of this difficulty from a behaviour change perspective is to extract commitments from people (Dawney and Shah 2005). Research indicates that when people make such a commitment they feel more motivated to adjust their behaviour to back up their expressed beliefs, particularly where commitments are made in public. Making a commitment to do something can change self-image and encourage people in future decisions to seek consistency with their previous commitments. Evidence in the field of environmental behaviour suggests that extracting public promises can help to improve composting rates and water efficiency as compared to simple information provision and advertising (McKenzie-Mohr 2000). Similar findings are reported in the area of voting behaviour, with those asked beforehand to predict their likelihood of voting more likely to vote than those not asked (Greenwald et al 1987, see also Smith et al 2003); and in blood donation decisions, where exposing people to what is called an active decision choice (that is actively putting the choice before them) increases blood donation rates in people who are uncertain on the subject (Stutzer et al 2006).

Interventions driven by social influences

Individuals do not live in isolation, and recognition of the interpersonal, community, and social influences shaping behaviour will strengthen public service designs. Social psychologists and sociologists suggest a number of important influences (for a review see Cabinet Office 2004). For instance, perception of how people see each other, particularly peers, matters. In the context of promoting energy efficiency within offices, there is evidence that the technique of information disclosure between firms creates a race to the top amongst firms keen to display their green credentials (Thaler and Sunstein 2008). Similarly, the concept of social proof suggests that when confronted with an ambiguous situation, we look to other people for cues on how to behave (Cialdini 2007).

Theories of inter-group bias stress the importance of group loyalties and identifications, and experimental work indicates that strangers divided into groups can quickly form such loyalties (Tajfel et al 1971). Group identities often develop and, generally speaking, we are predisposed to emulate the behaviour of those with whom we identify (Tajfel and Turner 1986). Techniques that exploit these intergroup biases and loyalties have been used in policy interventions to encourage neighbourhood commitment to recycling. Such insights applied to public policy can help create policy designs that provide the opportunity for people to emulate and learn from those with whom they identify. Existing peer support and community mentoring schemes already exploit these principles. Inter-group biases can also be channelled to encourage communities to protect and steward their local environments.

A further strand of work suggests that immediate social networks, based on social norms, including reciprocity and mutuality, influence individual behaviour (House 1981). Social norms are the rules that a group uses to determine what behaviours are acceptable. Public policy instruments can make use of social norms, by exposing people to the attitudes, beliefs, or behaviour of others in the peer group (see John et al 2014). This can be done by comparing individual behaviour to that of others; providing information on the (dis)approval of the behaviour by others; providing praise from a respected peer, or offering to expose behaviour to the peer group. Examples include community contracts and other forms of voluntary agreements, as well as campaigns to encourage organ donation or volunteering, which emphasize reciprocity or a sense of community.

Think in practice: from democratic theory to institutional intervention

Deliberative democracy initially emerged as a highly abstract the-oretical endeavour: the province of academic theorists. Since the late 1990s, however, an increasing number of political scientists and democratic theorists have begun to pay attention to the insti-tutional conditions that can foster deliberation. It is this literature – particularly work on democratic innovations that aims to increase and deepen citizen participation in political decision-making (Fung 2003a, Smith 2009) – that can inform think strategies. Radically different designs have the potential to promote deliberation. One of the most commonly celebrated is participatory budgeting, which emerged in Porto Alegre (Brazil) in the late 1980s, but the influence of which has been felt across Latin America, into Europe and beyond (Cabannes 2004, Nelson Dias 2018). Similarly, a great deal of atten-tion has been focused on mini-publics such as citizens' juries and deliberative polling, which ensure inclusiveness by aiming to engage a random sample of citizens. Recently the Irish Citizens' Assembly that recommended changes to the constitutional status of abortion, which were then ratified by a national referendum, has expanded the imagination as to how mini-publics might be employed. With developments in ICT (information and communications technol-ogy), there is now growing academic and practitioner interest in the potential of online discussion and argumentation platforms, as well as other forms of digital consultation, which in principle overcome barriers to participation associated with time and scale.

While the methods of engagement differ, these innovations in citizen participation often share similar institutional characteristics that motivate a civic orientation. First, they carefully construct safe havens in which deliberation is enabled: in other words, there is a recognition that the norms and procedures of deliberation need to be nurtured and do not necessarily emerge naturally. Second, part of the motivation to participate is that citizens have a meaningful influence on significant political decisions. The unwillingness of governments to create these conditions – in particular access to influence – means that the rhetoric of deliberation and citizen engagement is undermined in practice.

The evidence from studies of democratic innovations indicates that ordinary citizens are willing and able to deliberate on controversial public issues when such interventions are carefully constructed. Institutional design is crucial in altering behaviour: bringing citizens together from diverse backgrounds (often mobilizing participants from politically marginalized social groups) and constructing an environment in which contentious issues can be debated (Smith 2009, Setälä and Smith 2018).

Nudging and thinking compared

The starting assumption for nudge and think strategies may be the same but their responses to this challenge are dissimilar. To help clarify these differences, we set them out in Table 1.1, with the elements of each approach summarized in the two columns. This is designed to be a helpful simplification of the complexity of the two approaches (see John et al 2009 for our first attempt at this comparison).

The first difference is in the underlying view of human behaviour. Nudgers tend to assume that individuals are happy to fall back on past lines of thought and behaviour unless they are encouraged to do something different. The options for change centre on reminders and cues that accept where the individual is and then put in place a choice environment whereby society might gain from the realization of these preferences. The nudge strategy plays to the role

Table 1.1   Nudge and think compared

	Nudge	*Think*
View of subjects	Cognitive misers, users of shortcuts, prone to flawed, sometimes befuddled, thinking	Reasonable, knowledge hungry and capable of collective reflection
Costs to the individual	Low but repeated	High but only intermittent
Primary unit of analysis	The individual	The group
Change process	Cost-benefit led shift in choice environment	Value led outline of new shared policy platform
Civic conception	Increasing the attractiveness of positive-sum action	Addressing the general interest
Role of the state	Customise messages, expert and teacher	Create new institutional spaces to support citizen-led investigation, respond to citizens

of the state as educator and the role of the policy-maker as paternalistic expert, steering citizens down paths that are more beneficial to them and society at large. Once these are known, the designer of public policy can use these to good effect so that the result is hardly noticed by the individual. The nudge strategy accepts citizens as they are, and tries to divert them down new paths to make better decisions.

The think strategy has a different account of what makes humans tick. It assumes that individuals can step away from their day-to-day experience, throw off their blinkers and reflect on the wide range of policy choices and dilemmas. People can be knowledge hungry, learn to process new information and demands, and reach new heights of reflection and judgement. The institutional setting and organization of the think has to be right, but if it is then citizens can extend their knowledge and understanding of issues and work together to find solutions.

The think strategy would appear, then, to be more demanding than the nudge strategy in the effort required by the individual to engage. Nudge relies on the impact of any intervention being low cost. In fact, it can only work through being low cost, or else the individual would not cooperate. In contrast, in order to get going, the deliberative experience requires the incurring of some considerable costs. There needs to be some investment in acquiring information and then in debating with others, often in a particular context, away from the individual's normal environment. These costs have policy implications, so they need to be seen alongside the benefits. The costs are partly a function of the unit of analysis. While both can be individually and collectively achieved, nudge is about affecting individual choices, just as in classical economics, though of course if the nudge is done in concert with others it stands more chance of success. Deliberation, by definition, cannot happen alone in spite of the powerful role that individuals play in the process.

How does change come about? For both strategies, change is achieved by altering how the individual sees the attractiveness of a different course of action. The nudge strategy seeks to improve the messages that citizens receive and the opportunities they have to participate so they see the costs in different, more congenial, ways. For the deliberative democrat, the change is about tapping into and giving life to values that are discovered and brought out through debate and reflection. Once these values are uppermost, the costs and benefits to the individual will look different and the motivation to make sacrifices to achieve them will alter. This links to the civic conception implied by each approach. The nudger does not think that the individual is entirely selfish – there is a civic conception in the nudge scheme. But the civic is limited to small acts, which might amount to a bigger societal change. The deliberative democrat would not be happy unless the general interest has been considered. Citizen behaviour in deliberative forums is understood in these terms.

Finally, these two approaches differ as to the expected state action. For the nudger the role of state is about getting the messages right and giving low-level incentives and costs to get to the desired kind of behaviour, although it may require frequent and repeated application to be effective. The role of the policy-maker is as an expert, someone who is able to say what is the best course of action and who is smart enough to design interventions that achieve these goals. These actions may be quite modest, even though they require a lot of thought, and they usually involve the modification of a routine or procedure. In contrast, for the think strategy to be successful, the policy-maker needs to be open-minded and willing to act as an organizer of citizen-driven investigation. Crucially, the state needs to do more than provide institutions that can help citizens deliberate: if the strategy is to be sustainable, it has to follow up on the recommendations that emerge, otherwise participants are likely to be disempowered and further disengaged from the political process.

Should public authorities change citizen behaviour?

So far we have assumed that the involvement of citizens in tackling social and economic problems is desirable. But why assume that and why consider it appropriate to design policy to stimulate citizen behaviour? Our starting point is that government on its own will find it hard to address some of the common challenges of society because no matter how much money it throws at an issue or how many regulations it passes, many problems will not go away. In a period of fiscal austerity, the spending option may no longer be easily available, so governments have to rely even more than before on citizens helping themselves and others. It is also the case that governments in many modern industrial societies can no longer rely on deference and obedience to messages from a benevolent centre as they probably did before. Citizens will question the authority of government or simply ignore it.

One response is to involve citizens directly in public policy, so as to get their consent in such a way that they own the policies and, as a result, change their behaviour in an intended direction. Another is to argue that policy-makers need to go with the grain of the way individuals make decisions. They should design solutions that encourage citizen behaviour rather than act against it or crowd it out. Moreover, government policy could be improved by involving citizens in such a way that they help public authorities adjust the implementation of public policies to reflect the particular circumstances and problems of a policy sector and locale or neighbourhood. In this way, as Braybrooke and Lindblom argue, government can become more intelligent if it is guided by responding to information, in this case from citizens (Braybrooke and Lindblom 1963). The logic of this argument is that if governments are going to be successful in a more challenging age, they need to use different kinds of instrument, ones that are smart and nimble, which are guided by the way that citizens are supported, and are driven by the active contribution of citizens (John 2011). The blunt instruments of financial allocation and regulation may only be partly successful as they need more human-centred complements. The ways that governments communicate with citizens and involve them have to become smarter and more effective.

But even if there are gains to be yielded from the kinds of policies we describe here, should government still back off because it should not interfere with individual freedom and choice? After all, it is often argued that the whole idea of representative democracy is that citizens elect governments to get on with the job of government;

the media and public opinion keep them in check between elections, and the threat of being up for re-election keeps them on their toes to manage policies effectively. In subsequent elections, citizens can re-elect a government to carry on managing affairs in the same way or elect another government to do things differently. With governments in charge, the job of the bureaucracy, local government, and other agencies is to do the best job of administering public services on behalf of the citizen in as efficient and cost-effective a way as possible. Does it not appear inappropriate for government to expect citizens to contribute their time to shaping services and even to produce some of the outcomes themselves, either directly through co-producing services, or indirectly by altering their behaviour so that they, and other citizens, get a public benefit? Moreover, the public might expect a right to keep their private lives private from the state, to be free from interfering public agencies that wish to change their behaviour. If somebody wants to have an unhealthy lifestyle, they should be allowed to lead it. They are entitled to elect a government and to pay taxes for a health service to pick up the pieces.

When is it right for the state to intervene in issues of behaviour? Assessing the morality of seeking to steer people's choices in certain directions is, of course, not a new dilemma for policy-makers, and issues of whether it is right to intervene apply equally well to the use of standard tools such as law-making, regulation, or taxation. What makes the issue more challenging in the case of nudging is that standard forms of intervention are more open and explicit about their intentions. (Although we can ask how much people really understand about the details of regulations and taxation. And we know also that policy tools of all types can be made less visible to reduce public resistance.) The tenor of nudging can be 'we the government know better what is good for you than you do and we have found a sneaky way of getting you to make the right choice'.

This problem becomes more acute when considering some of the techniques that governments can use to change behaviour. With the insights of behavioural economics as a guide, it can appear that public agencies are using the dark arts of manipulation to alter citizen behaviour to get to good ends for society. In this sense a think strategy trumps nudge on the grounds of transparency. But even think can invite the same attack. If society accepts that governments should involve citizens in decisions about the delivery of services, is not this a form of compulsion or an invitation to a self-selected minority to make decisions for the rest of society? Democratic governments, which are supposed to be responsive and to respect individual freedoms, may feel uncomfortable at taking such a direct control over the private lives of many citizens without their active consent. In the rest of the book, naturally, we answer this question in the negative, largely because citizens expect governments to get on with the job of making effective policies and only want to blame them when things go seriously wrong. But it is clear that behaviour change is a sensitive area, where extra attention to the democratic principles of transparency and responsiveness should guide policy-makers in the design of these interventions, even more so than other policies. If not, these interventions risk being seen as illegitimate and they will become ineffective as a result. Interventions designed to foster behavioural change need to be as public as possible, with as much support from the public as is feasible. One line of defence for nudge strategies promoted by Thaler and Sunstein (Thaler and Sunstein 2008), and appearing under the label of libertarian paternalism, is that at least the choice does remain with the citizen – it is just the architecture of choice that is altered to support what are judged by democratic governments to be beneficial outcomes.

Another important point is that our current choice architecture is neither natural nor morally neutral – in fact, in many ways it is pernicious and undermines citizen behaviour. Individuals make decisions in the light of social mores and norms influenced by the market, commercial advertising, peer pressure, and ignorance, and habit. Choice architectures are constantly evolving through strategic action on the part of different actors and the unintentional impact of everyday activities. Policy-makers, by seeking to steer the choice architecture, are just one more framer of choice for the citizen. Unlike other influencers they are at least authorized through the democratic process to promote the common good. And one way to do this is to encourage civic behaviour.

If the qualms about intervention can be met, there remains, of course, the issue of competence. Can we trust governments to make the right choices for us? Prabhakar argues:

> Behavioural economics assumes that government knows best. But often this may not be the case. For good reason, government might find it difficult to unpick the different parts of a policy problem … government might lack proper evidence to guide its decisions. Government might only know the right nudges in a limited number of areas where there is plenty of evidence. (Prabhakar 2010)

Policy-makers, after all, face the same challenge of bounded rationality as citizens in civil society. In a different way, think strategists have been challenged because of their tendency to assume they know what is best for people (Stoker 2006). People are supposed to choose between options, not on the basis of self-interest but rather on the basis of a judgement about which of the options will advance the group's agenda. And whether they make the right choice or not depends in large part on whether the participants follow the procedures and norms of deliberation (Fung and Wright 2003). There is a danger that in trying to design out difficulties, think strategists are fostering forms of governance that in practice can become rigid and deeply constrained and not all that participatory, because only what are considered acceptable behaviours and reasonable demands are allowed to find their place in its processes and outputs. In their different ways, both think and nudge may be perceived as having authoritarian tendencies if they are not introduced to the reference points of citizens with a great deal of sensitivity, so that the individuals are ultimately in control of their fate, even if governments play a role in structuring the information to the citizen and affecting the institutional context in which action and debate takes place.

These arguments are a useful qualification to overenthusiasm about changing citizen behaviour but are not convincing enough to suggest governments should abandon the project. When government regulates and taxes citizens how does government know it is doing the best thing? The answer in all cases is surely that the key issue is a judgement for which, in a democratic society, citizens can hold government to account at some point. Moreover, our existing choice architecture is a construction of the decisions (or non-decisions) of actors, institutions, and practices that (explicitly or implicitly) promote non-civic behaviour. Looked at in this way it would be remiss of policy-makers to neglect the options for changing citizen behaviour.

Of course, nudge versus think is not the only take on what governments can do to encourage civic-minded behaviour. The traditional tools in the armoury of governments – regulatory and economic instruments – can and are used to shape civic actions. Tax incentives can provide a fiscal incentive to reduce carbon usage, or rewards can be offered for good behaviour on housing estates. The law can be used to compel people to be civic, such as those laws aimed at stopping dog-fouling on footpaths and in parks. But the attraction of nudge and think is that they are not about government commands, but about creating the conditions for better citizen choice.

Conclusion

In this chapter, we have reviewed the intellectual origins and implications of our two theoretical positions, summarized as nudge and think. These terms are, of course, simplifications of complex literatures and research programmes that have many manifestations, and range across different kinds of motivations and causes of human behaviour. We hope we have conveyed an important distinction between ways of thinking about behaviour change, with nudge being more concerned to provide cues for individuals to do better for society; and with think strategies being more interested in presenting individuals with opportunities to debate the key issues so they gain the resources and motivation to act. In many ways, think may be seen as a more positive alternative to nudge, and one that is more open and respectful of the individual. It is more transparent, too. In practice, these approaches are closer together than they might at first seem. Both acknowledge the limits to individual change and the lack of capacity individuals have in their everyday lives and decision-making for weighing up all the options that are open to them – the constraints of bounded rationality. Both these perspectives offer alternatives to policy-makers that are different from the top-down and commanding tools of the state that have been used so much in recent years; moreover, they are both capable of looking at public policy in a more citizen-centred way, a form of policy-making that is increasingly fashionable across the world. At the same time, because these interventions are new, they have attracted the suspicion of critics who see them as paternalistic and undemocratic – even think because of its reliance on selected groups of citizens. We hope to counter such concerns while recognizing that authoritarian regimes can also use these tools for their own ends.

As we shall show later in the book, most of these softer

interventions, in practice, are often some combination of nudge and think – for example, democratic innovations can be understood as the active design of structures that nudge citizens towards thinking. In this way, we offer a reconstruction of nudge that uses elements of think to make it more transparent, effective, and legitimate.

Most of all, these new tools of government need more testing and evaluation. And this is just what we do in the remaining chapters of this book. But before that – in the next chapter – we consider the best way to acquire robust knowledge about what works.

2

Testing

This book aims to identify the best strategies that policy-makers could adopt to encourage citizens to carry out collectively beneficial acts. Policy-makers need to know whether the nudge and think measures they introduce can achieve their desired effects or not. They require warrantable knowledge that tells them that if they do X then Y happens. They need to calculate how much of an impact a unit of a policy (X) has on a unit of an outcome (Y). They want to know how much an intervention costs in relation to the costs and benefits of other policy choices. In other words, they need a way of acquiring knowledge that apprises them of the causal relationships in the world, and informs them about just how much government and public agencies can influence those relationships in comparison with other ways of using their capacity and resources.

The argument that policy should be based on sound research seems obvious, but governments and public agencies often intervene without good evidence of whether the measures they introduce do in fact work: 'both decision makers and social scientists are content to rely on seat-of-the-pants intuitions rather than conduct the sorts of tests that could contribute to knowledge' (Green and Gerber 2003: 105). Getting it right might be the result of luck rather than foresight.

Policy-makers can get lucky, of course; but it is likely also that they are not serendipitous and there will not be a positive outcome resulting from an intervention – there might even be a negative one. To illustrate this point, Torgerson and Torgerson give examples of practices that were widely used in healthcare and believed to be effective until randomized controlled trials showed many years later that they did not work (Torgerson and Torgerson 2008: 4–7). In the 1940s and 1950s, oxygen was routinely given to premature babies after birth, and it was only after a randomized controlled trial found that oxygen led to significant increases in blindness that the practice was stopped. In crime policy, the programme called 'Scared Straight', which got young people to meet convicted criminals so as to shock them into not offending, was shown by a series of trials to have had the opposite effect to what was intended, actually increasing the risk of offending by juveniles (Petrosino et al 2003, 2013).

As a result of making policy based on poor evaluations, public resources have been wasted. Money could be spent on other items of benefit rather than on useless interventions, or taxes could be lowered. Null or negative results can even discredit the whole approach of involving citizens in public policy and can be used as evidence to say that governments should not interfere with civil society.

So what can be done about poorly evidenced public policies? One answer is to look for existing evidence. There are many sources that governments and other agencies can use when they select strategies to try to affect citizen behaviour – or any other outcome. They could trust the views they get from practitioners; make use of expert testimonies; commission reviews of the international experience; and rely on the personal experience of civil servants and ministers. Each of these sources has some value, but they should not be relied upon alone and can lead to the poor policies described above. Better are the many techniques in social science, such as case studies, analyses of the statistical evidence, and multi-method evaluations of existing policies. This is because the approach to collecting evidence is systematic, where great care is taken to try to relate an intervention to an outcome, and to rule out other factors that might have also caused it.

While not wishing governments to cast aside these existing sources of evidence (both informal and social scientific), the argument we present in this chapter is that experiments – especially randomized controlled trials – offer a much more valid and robust standard of evidence than any other method policy-makers have available. In fact, policy-makers should seek to use, as far as possible, the evidence from randomized controlled trials for their decisions on matters of public policy. At the moment, the commissioning and use of trials are all too rare.

To support this view, we offer an outline of the method of the randomized controlled trial and its qualitative equivalent, the design experiment. We argue that these different kinds of experiments have the capacity to provide robust evaluations of interventions designed to change citizen behaviour. The chapter contains an explanation of why experimental methods have tended to be neglected, and highlights some of the pitfalls of the approach and how they may be overcome (for more details, see Cotterill and Richardson 2010, John 2017). We conclude that there is still considerable untapped potential from the greater use of randomized controlled trials, both for social scientists and policy-makers.

Standards of proof

It is often frustrating for policy-makers to hear advice from social scientists. Quite often social scientists will say they do not know what works, or perhaps that the evidence is strong, but they do not know what the impact will be across the whole country. Or sometimes the opposite happens. A study is carried out which indicates that the government's policy works, but afterwards social scientists find the early evaluation was over-optimistic and produced some invalid inferences that did not apply later or elsewhere. These problems emerge from the challenge of making predictions and claims about the social world. The complexity of society creates a large number of interactions that vary from place to place. This makes it difficult to produce generalizations that hold over space, and over time, too (Pawson and Tilly 1997). Then there is the problem of knowing whether the evidence actually shows what it purports to show, which is about the limits of the instruments that researchers have at their disposal to observe the world.

The problem of making a generalization in social sciences comes down to the problem of validity, which is about the extent to which the research allows an inference to be made that there is the hypothesized causal effect (see Table 2.1).

The first issue with validity is external – whether it is possible to generalize from the intervention to other places and times. The

Table 2.1   Validity

External validity:
The extent to which the inference from a piece of research can be generalized to other contexts from where or when the research took place

Internal validity:
Whether the research explains what has happened – the extent to which it is possible to conclude that there is a hypothesized relationship between cause and effect

General validity:
The extent to which it is possible to make inferences from a piece of research

problem occurs because of the difficulty in reproducing the same conditions under which the original intervention or pilot was monitored – the complexity problem again. The second issue with validity concerns whether the instruments we have to hand validly observe the causal relations that are hypothesized to be happening in the real world – internal validity. One reason for weak internal validity is that the instruments do not always measure what actually happens. For example, views about the success of a policy might be drawn from survey responses of those who were involved with or who had participated in the intervention. But because those responding to the survey have a stake in the success of the policy, they may over-report the good aspects of the intervention and under-report the negative side. This happens not from any willingness to deceive but because the person responding has a perception of the policy from being involved in it, and that comes out in the survey response.

There is a further problem. It may be the case that the method does not offer a counterfactual as to what would have happened had the policy not been introduced. This is because the act of introducing the policy and measuring it may select favourable locations or create special conditions that affect its success but which would not apply when it is rolled out more generally across the country. This is similar to the survey response problem. Moreover, people who are more likely to achieve a desirable set of outcomes select into, i.e. choose to be become involved in, the programme to be evaluated, so, for example, pilots of employment schemes may end up training people who find it easy to get a job anyway so the result is more successful than it would be if the scheme were rolled out nationally. Or the areas that become selected into the research are those most ahead of the others in the first place or have more potential to improve. Even survey respondents may select into responding, with those more favourably disposed more likely to fill out a

Table 2.2   The Hawthorne effect

> The effect of the research on the outcome itself because research subjects respond to the interest being shown in them and change their behaviour accordingly. This may lead to the inference that an intervention has worked when it has not.

questionnaire, just as the students who fill out course evaluations are likely to be those who stayed until the end of the course, while those who were discontented dropped out long before. Moreover, the act of researching and evaluating may create what is called a Hawthorne effect (see Table 2.2), whereby those people affected by an intervention improve their outcomes because they are in the pilot. Participants do better because they feel more committed and enthusiastic when someone is observing them, as well as worrying about being watched and monitored.

These are examples of false positives, where the research shows something works but in fact it does not, and it is common to find evaluations of policy saying that an intervention has succeeded when it is based on observational evidence. Bias can work the opposite way, too. An intervention might show no impact, but that could be because factors independent of the intervention had caused every area or all people to reduce their performance. Simply observing the change in outcomes of those who had the intervention might lead the researcher to infer a false negative. What is needed is a counterfactual, which tells the researcher what would have happened in the absence of the intervention.

The advantages of comparison

In order to produce a counterfactual, most methods of evaluation build in comparison as a key part of their methodology. Drawing on the work of J. S. Mill, many scholars regard comparison as the key feature of social science, assisting in their understanding of the impact of institutions, cultures, and policy choices, by attempting to compare what happens with, or without, the occurrence of some hypothesized factor (Przeworski and Teune 1970). In evaluation research, it is possible to compare people, groups, or areas that were the subject of a policy intervention with others that were not, or perhaps with those who experienced the intervention later, or in a different or more systematic way. This evaluation can be achieved by using statistics to measure the impact over all cases, or over a sample, so that the average effect is observed, connecting variations in the factors that affect an outcome with variations in the outcome itself. Or else case studies can compare carefully selected areas and seek to understand why contrasting and similar areas produce particular outcomes. It is possible to be ingenious with the research design to improve the leverage, such as by looking at small variations within a case (King et al 1994, Gerring 2006). It can be instructive to observe change over time, particularly if it is possible to rule out other explanations for the change. For example, some evaluation research makes inferences from what are called interrupted time series, where the impact of an intervention over time is compared to a comparison group that did not receive the intervention (see Shadish et al 2002). Even though these observational studies have merit, they cannot rule out the possibility that the outcomes they compare may have been caused by things other than the intervention. This may be because the comparison group was different in some way, perhaps as a result of not being selected to have the intervention, or being selected to have it in different ways, or simply because something unexpected happened to one or both groups.

The advantages of randomization

It should be clear where the argument in this chapter is headed. The best way to compare individuals, groups, or areas that have had or have not had the intervention is to make a random allocation. Because the differences between the groups have been removed by randomization and, when the sample size is large enough, the only other factors that might cause a difference in outcomes – outside chance – is the intervention itself.

A diagram best represents how a randomized controlled trial works (see Figure 2.1). There are three stages, which in many respects resemble what researchers do in a standard research design, but there are important modifications in the randomized controlled trial. The first is the selection of a population of interest that should relate to the research question and be the units the policy-maker or researcher is interested in. The second is unique to the randomized controlled trial and involves randomization of the population into treatment (intervention) and control groups. The random allocation ensures that the membership of the treatment and control groups is

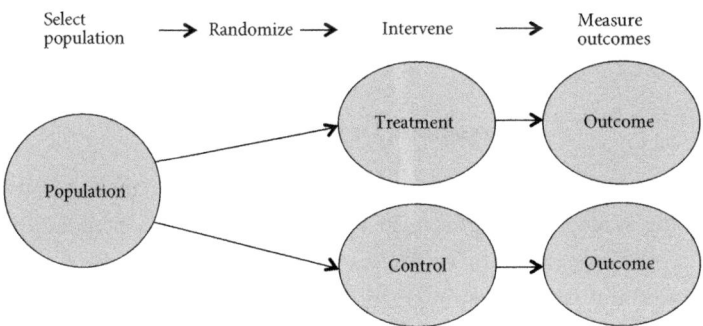

Figure 2.1 An experimental study design

very similar in all respects. Then – third – the outcome is measured after the intervention. The researchers can compare and contrast the measured outcomes across the groups and be safe in the knowledge that any differences in observed outcomes between the groups can reasonably be attributed to the intervention rather than to any other cause. As with other comparisons, it is possible to use inferential statistics to find out whether the differences between the groups have occurred simply by chance. A well-designed randomized controlled trial can provide a convincing estimate of the effect of an intervention, revealing how much effort or amount of resources it takes to produce a certain level of outcome.

There are variations on the basic design, such as having more than one treatment group. There are different kinds of randomizations, such as stratifying by some factor known to affect the outcome, or randomly allocating areas over time as a gradual implementation of a policy (the stepped wedged design). It is preferable, where possible, to measure outcomes both before and after the intervention. There are other desirable features of experiments, for example that they should measure real behavioural outcomes, such as votes, recycling, or charitable donations, rather than observations or survey responses. But the basic features of the trial remain the same with randomization at its core.

An example: Get Out the Vote

An example helps think through the power of the method. Voting is the subject of Chapter 5, so this example is also a preparation for what we report there. The experiment we describe here aims to find out whether an intervention in the form of a Get Out the Vote campaign, such as a door-knocking campaign, can increase the propensity of voters to turn out at an election (see Green and

Gerber 2015). It is impossible to know this simply from surveys that ask people whether they have been canvassed and whether they have voted, because of the inaccuracy of people's memories of voting and of receiving campaign information. In addition, it is possible that the people who are known to be more willing to vote are more likely be canvassed, as well as more likely to respond to the survey. This combination might just produce a correlation between canvass and vote rather than showing that the canvass had an effect. By contrast, an experiment with a simulated Get Out the Vote campaign can find out whether canvassing works by randomly allocating voters into two groups and then canvassing only one group. In this way there is a randomized population and a measurement of the outcome in the form of actual votes, checked from electoral registers after the election. Comparing the number of people voting in the treatment group and the number voting in the control group allows us to estimate the effect of the treatment. If the number voting in the treatment groups exceeds the control group by more than might be expected by chance, then canvassing has had an effect, and this can be calculated by the percentage point difference in voting.

Randomized controlled trials as the gold standard

Social scientists, health professionals, and government researchers refer to randomized controlled trials as the gold standard for evaluating the impact of interventions (Cabinet Office 2011). Trials are better than other kinds of evaluation because they are able to offer a genuine counterfactual of what would have happened without the intervention. For this reason, the trial has become the main source of knowledge acquisition about the impact of treatments, services, and tests in health research, and is regarded as a superior form of evaluation for interventions in education and crime (see Torgerson and Torgerson 2008), as well as in development (Glennerster and Takavarasha 2013).

If an experiment is well-designed and conducted effectively, researchers and policy-makers are able to infer whether there is a causal impact from the intervention or not. If the result is replicated again in several trials, they are in an even stronger position to make causal inferences (Torgerson and Torgerson 2008). Researchers are at pains to stress that they do not want to advocate randomized controlled trials as the only form of policy evaluation. There are some drawbacks, as with all methods, and we will discuss these later in the chapter. Other methods can be very useful for different things, such as determining stakeholder perceptions of a policy, which can be ascertained from a survey, or establishing whether the income of a particular group went up or not during the period of an intervention. Qualitative research can be helpful alongside a trial to understand how and why the intervention worked in the particular context. Our message in this chapter is that these methods are not ideal for determining the impact of a particular intervention as distinct from other influential factors affecting the outcome. Experimental research provides a more secure foundation for causal inference in these contexts.

We make an argument for field experiments, which take place in the real world. Druckman and colleagues argue that field experiments 'take advantage of *naturally occurring* political contexts while simultaneously leveraging the inferential benefits of random assignment. Because of their "realistic" foundations, field experiments can be especially relevant to policymakers' (Druckman et al 2006: 627; italics in the original). As Green and Gerber point out, there are more opportunities created to make the case for experiments in real policy settings than many social scientists have recognized (Green and Gerber 2003). Advocates of field experiments argue that the weight given to a body of research should be in proportion to the uncertainty associated with its bias (see also Gerber et al 2004). In other words, researchers need to observe the maxim: 'The more dubious the leap from research findings to a proposed application, the less weight should be accorded to the findings' (Green and Gerber 2003: 100). On this basis, political scientists should attach far less value to observational research. Moreover, laboratory work may be vulnerable to challenge because of the contrived settings in which it is conducted.

The implementation of new programmes, the diversity created through decentralized structures, and even financial constraints that encourage piloting rather than full-throttle roll-out provide a context in which experimentation can come to the fore. Experimenters need to work closely with policy-makers and social actors in order to both create the opportunities for field experiments and also achieve the mantle of relevance by helping in the search for solutions to tractable research and policy questions. Green and Gerber provide a rallying cry for experimenters to step forward and engage with policy-makers, arguing that:

> through systematic intrusion into the world, experimentation may encourage political scientists to rethink the relationship between political science and society. By continual interaction with those who are sceptical of social science, these intrusions force political scientists to ask whether decades of investigation have produced anything of demonstrable practical value. This question looms large over the future development of the discipline. If scholars can demonstrate the practical benefits of science, those who have the discretion and resources to effect change will learn to seize opportunities to acquire knowledge. (Green and Gerber 2003: 110)

The relationship between field experiments and public policy could be symbiotic. Experiments can offer significant advances in knowledge creation and can make social science relevant. According to

Roth, one key use of experiments is to enable academics to engage with the policy process (Roth 1995: 22). This is partly because policy-makers can identify the robust evidence produced by experiments and can relate to the headline results, whereas other kinds of research are often inconclusive (for example, case studies) or are hard to penetrate (such as the technical language of panel regression analysis).

Using the experimental method

Experiments are not a panacea for evaluating public policy interventions. They are much better than any competitor so they should be adopted when an appropriate opportunity arises. As with any method, they need to be adopted carefully and with due consideration to ethical values. Researchers should not claim more than can be inferred from the results. Because of this, as Shadish, Cook, and Campbell argue, experimenters have largely abandoned earlier claims to produce unvarnished, superior knowledge in favour of a more nuanced claim about producing better knowledge (Shadish et al 2002: 29–31). The experiment is a profoundly human endeavour, affected by all the same human foibles as any other human enterprise, though with well-developed procedures for partial control of some of the limitations that have been identified to date (Shadish et al 2002: 30). Experiments are not to be put on a pedestal but they are a cornerstone scientific method and are rightly becoming a tool that is increasingly adopted by political scientists because of their unrivalled capacity to establish causal inferences (Gerber and Green 2012). Their limits should not be seen as undermining this research method, but as the product of mature reflection, which encourages a more sensitive application of randomized controlled trials. After all, if too much is claimed from trials, policy-makers are bound to become disappointed. Moreover, there are ways to overcome these problems without great difficulty.

The first limitation is that experiments tend to be carried out in particular localities rather than as a nationwide trial, usually because of the complexity of arranging interventions (see below). These local results mean it is sometimes hard to generalize from localized experiments to other parts of the country, or from country to country. In the language of methodology, experiments are strong in internal validity but weak in external validity (see Table 2.1 above). The response of the experimenter is to argue that the knowledge base is improved by the accumulation of evidence. In this way, when trials are repeated in several contexts, and at different times, with different populations and different delivery partners, knowledge is accumulated. When the same basic results keep appearing, we know for certain that there is a robust relationship. Meta-analysis – the analysis of many trials in one data analysis – can help to get a sense of what the general relationship is.

A related issue is that experiments tend to isolate those aspects of an intervention that are capable of being randomized, but are less good at evaluating the intervention as a whole. Some aspects of an intervention can be randomized more easily than others and are selected for the evaluation, which means the experiment does not fully evaluate what government is doing in its policy intervention, for example, or it encourages government to select policies in easily randomized units rather than in other more useful ways, which are not susceptible to trials. A new policy may take time to work, whereas the experimenter might be tempted to pull out the short-term effects (though this problem is not unique to randomized controlled trials). The challenge, once again, is to accumulate knowledge about different aspects of an intervention and to match them with other kinds of evidence.

Experimenters need to be careful to address a number of technical issues when implementing experiments. In particular, randomization may be hard to achieve in practice. It is possible to have an unbalanced randomization purely from random error so that the two groups do not start from the same point. One solution is to control this in a regression model, where covariates isolate the effects on the outcomes as well as the intervention. The other solution is to do checks on the randomization and to repeat the randomization in the rare case that the groups end up unequal (experimenters differ on the merits of this). In general, this is a minor problem.

Another problem is that there may also be differential selection into the treatment and control groups, particularly if participants are invited into these groups or have a chance to drop out. The treatment itself may either encourage participants to drop out if they do not want to take part in it, or being in the control group might lead to disappointment followed by attrition. Differential selection also occurs if it is not possible to treat all the treatment group, as in a classic Get Out the Vote campaign described above, where not everyone will be in to answer their door to the campaign team. As in the case of breaches to randomization, this means that the groups are not the same, because the treatment group divides up into people who were contacted and people who were not contacted. But, as with randomization, it is possible to allow for how people select into the treatment and still produce a valid estimate of the treatment. Again, this is not usually a major problem, but these statistical procedures tend to detract from the purity of the experimental method.

One key issue – and this relates to some of the experiments described in this book – is that the experiment may be compromised by the practitioners, even those with the best of intentions. It is possible that the treatment may not be administered properly or that the agency involved may begin another intervention at the same time (Cotterill and Richardson 2010). More generally, as we discuss below, it is difficult to carry out experiments in the field as they are often 'bedevilled by practical problems of implementation' (Jowell 2003: 17). Lack of training for the staff involved in delivering the intervention may create problems. Decisions made in the heat of the moment may prove problematic to the experiment. For example, researchers in a study of deliberation which sought to contrast a decision mode driven by consensus with a decision mode based on voting found that pressures of time moved the consensus group towards the voting style of decision-making, with the result that the comparison was less easy to sustain (Setälä et al 2007). Greenberg, Linkz, and Mandell review the long history in the US of experimental trials in the social policy field, and provide examples of where experiments have had to be abandoned or modified because of administrative and other problems (Greenberg et al 2003, see also John 2017).

Because of this it is tempting to try to experiment without government agencies randomizing what they do, but to mimic these kinds of contact by having the researcher carry out the intervention instead, for example by creating a canvass group, or by carrying out feedback. The problem here is that the experiment lacks the force of a government intervention, so the effects may be less than if the government agency was involved (though it may have the advantage that citizens might trust a non-governmental body more than tarnished central or local government). Where researchers have to recreate the environment of policy-makers, the results may not read across from the experiment to the real world of policy implementation.

Finally, experimental research can face a number of ethical challenges (see Teele 2014). A common but misplaced criticism is that if we think an intervention might work, how can experimenters justify only the treatment group receiving that benefit? The answer, of course, is that we do not know that a benefit will accrue to the treatment group and hence the need for the experiment. As in other forms of research, a version of the harm principle could be used to judge the conduct of the experimenters in their work so that experiments could be considered ethical unless they knowingly cause harm to others. Some experiments may involve misleading participants and here if such deception cannot be avoided the best approach is to get the informed consent of those involved in the trial and debrief them afterwards. Overall, fundamental ethical objections to experiments do not stand up to scrutiny, especially in the citizen behaviour field, where there are few negative effects of an intervention; but researchers should build in ethical principles into the design of their experiments as well as seek approval from subject review or ethics committees.

Overall, randomized controlled trials are the best way to find out whether an intervention worked or not, and to draw lessons about how – in our case – government may best stimulate citizen behaviour. They are not without limitations, but many of the problems they face are well known and there exist some well-understood and recognized ways to overcome them.

Design experiments

Sometimes it is not possible to carry out a trial because it is hard to randomize a population or there is not enough known about an intervention to design an effective trial. This suggests the need for an intermediate method, which can pilot the intervention and pave the way for a randomized controlled trial. What is sometimes called for is some sort of compromise to be struck between knowing everything and knowing something. Torgerson and Torgerson refer to the value of pragmatic trials (Torgerson and Torgerson 2008) and Stoker and John argue for the development of design experiments as a precursor to full-blown field experiments (Stoker and John 2009). They argue that design experiments also seek to manipulate the external world, but in a way that is different from the generalized causal inference of mainstream experimental evaluations, such as randomized controlled trials. The design experiment may be thought of as a qualitative experiment, which focuses on the design of an intervention as the thing to get right. The experimental aspect of the method is the manipulation of an intervention and its observation over an extended time period, usually in one location, until acceptable results emerge. This is a bit like the interrupted time series discussed earlier, where the researcher observes changes as a result of an intervention. In the design version, the experiment progresses through a series of design-redesign cycles. There is feedback to the core decision-makers and to front-line bureaucrats as a policy unfolds, so that the design of the policy is adjusted to work in a particular context (Stoker and John 2009: 356). Once an acceptable version of the intervention is established it may provide the starting point for a broader randomized controlled trial test of a policy.

Design experiments offer social scientists and public managers a new way of researching public policy innovations, providing insights about what works and supplying timely information to decision-makers as an intervention develops. The method draws on the experimental tradition in social science and public policy, which conceives of a policy or an intervention as a treatment, whose impact can be compared with that of a randomly allocated control group. In an analogous fashion, design experiments manipulate the external world, but in a way that is different from large-scale experimental evaluations, such as randomized controlled trials, which aim to make generalized causal inferences. The design experiment focuses on the design of an intervention as the core research problem. The methodology claims to provide an evidence base that shows how an intervention can work in its early stages, when the intervention is being developed; in this way, it may provide a staging post for a broader and more generalizable test of a policy. Trialists find it hard to conclude whether a repetition of the experiment in an alternative setting would replicate the results. The design experiment sidesteps these issues by avoiding generalized claims about causal validity. The method aims to provide detailed information about the case and its context, so that the observer gradually establishes the causal processes at work.

Design experiments need to be carried out at the outset of an intervention. The focus is on understanding and applying innovative techniques in teaching and learning. They aim for the engineering of the learning experience (Cobb et al 2003). The use of this tag is deliberate because proponents of design experiments see their origins in applied science, relying on a precise method that involves tinkering with the design of the intervention and learning from mistakes so the final product is finished to the highest standard. Just as with product design, the practitioners and researchers make minute adjustments to the specification, which they track in detail and perhaps adjust further over time. As Collins and colleagues write, 'the design is constantly revised based on experience, until all the bugs are worked out' (Collins et al 2004: 8).

Design experiments explore and test hypotheses as in classic experimental research. But instead of the once-and-for-all hypothesis test (in the form of a statistical verification common in randomized controlled trials, which may confirm or reject the hypothesis) there is a quick turnover of research questions linked to the main hypothesis, followed by rapid redesigns of the intervention – what Cobb et al call 'conjecture driven tests' (Cobb et al 2003: 10). The idea is not to test general theories but to understand the practical limits and possibilities of what the innovation is trying to do. Design writers (Collins

1992, Collins et al 2004) start with Simon's distinction in his book, *The Sciences of the Artificial*, between the type of theory building in the sciences of physics and biology, and that of the design sciences, or what he calls artificial sciences, such as engineering and computer science, which are more recent and where theory links to the tasks at hand. As Simon writes, 'We speak of engineering as concerned with "synthesis" whereas science is concerned with "analysis" … The engineer, and more generally the designer, is concerned with how things *ought* to be – how they ought to be in order to *attain goals*' (Simon 1996: 4; italics in the original). Simon believes design scientists grapple with the complexity of the real world in a different way from their pure science colleagues. The theory in design experiments is intermediate, standing somewhere in between the grand statements of educational theory and accounts of practical relationships on the ground (diSessa 1991).

The researcher's role is like that of a participant. In fact, there is no reason why practitioners cannot be researchers; many design experiments are practitioner-run projects and, where there are researchers, there is a very close collaboration. Sometimes design experiments are known as design partnerships. In general, the person doing the design experiment participates in the innovation and in its evaluation. Brown writes, 'As a design scientist in my field, I attempt to engineer innovative educational environments and simultaneously conduct experimental studies of those innovations' (Brown 1992: 141). Of course, researchers, like all participants, need to be alert to the potential conflict of interest between researchers and practitioners and the dangers of researchers going native and losing their claim to a scientific version of objectivity.

Design experiments have mainly taken place in schools, and their findings appear in specialist learning science journals and education handbooks (Schwartz et al 2008). What scope is there for a more general application? Our starting point is that there is a case for transplanting the design experiment method to other contexts on the grounds that if it works in education, then it should work elsewhere. Indeed, we have carried out a design experiment on drugs policy (Askew et al 2010). Some of these ideas appear in the use of policy innovation labs to redesign public policy from the ground up (McGann et al 2018). Design experimenters who operate outside the classroom experience cannot have the same level of involvement in, and direction over, their environment as teachers and education researchers. It is more difficult to imagine researchers taking on the role of a social worker or police officer than a teacher. However, if the same amount of involvement is not possible in non-education environments, it is still possible to have close collaboration and involvement with the delivery of the project. Design experiments favour small-scale innovation, in a relatively controlled environment, where the dialogue can take place with a limited range of policy-makers and workers, all of whom have signed up to the new way of doing business and to intense researcher-practitioner interactions. It is particularly suited to policy being introduced in neighbourhoods or small areas without the fanfare and public scrutiny, which would be given to a pilot area where it is assumed there is a wider programme ready to be rolled out.

Many of these limitations of the design experiment method are, in fact, its advantages. Only policy-makers and practitioners who are committed both to a long-term evaluation and to creating innovation can work on design experiments, avoiding the problem of overload and expectations that are too high. By being more specialized, and targeted to the innovators, the design experiment encourages a high degree of focus and commitment in those who participate. It also biases the role of the policy-maker towards trying out more imaginative ways of intervening. The payoff is that the causal mechanisms can be understood much more clearly in relationship to the instruments the policy-makers have to hand. Other organizations and delivery bodies wishing to implement the policy innovation will not need to start from scratch.

Conclusion

Experiments offer a powerful and robust way to evaluate interventions by public agencies and other people or bodies seeking to improve public welfare. The claim applies to both the randomized controlled trial and the design experiment. In either case, they provide warrantable knowledge for the academic, researcher, and policy-maker. They offer a high standard of validity through the systematic collection of evidence and the generation of the genuine counterfactual from which to compare the effect of an intervention. The randomized controlled trial allows the policy-maker and researcher to make an inference whether an intervention has worked or not, and by how much. This is the power of randomization: the only difference between the group that gets the intervention and the groups that does not is the intervention itself. Other methods testing interventions do not come close in evaluating the policies of government because they permit factors other than the intervention to influence the outcomes a researcher or policy-maker observes, and it is almost impossible to control for these factors. Experiments are not a nirvana for reforming policy-makers and social scientists, and we have discussed their limitations earlier in this chapter. Some of the problems of randomized controlled trials can be overcome by effective piloting. Hence our advocacy of the design experiment as a qualitative complement to randomized controlled trials. Other limitations can be anticipated and corrected for in the design of the research, whereas the problems of other research methods cannot be successfully addressed. Doubt will always remain that something has not been allowed for, even in the most complex of statistical models.

What we have not communicated so far is that experiments can be great fun, being near to the real world with its challenges and thrills (for example, see Cotterill 2014). Experimenters face the day-to-day ups and downs far more than other researchers (and we should stress that getting experiments implemented is messy and unpredictable, as many of the following chapters show). Delivering an experiment requires considerable ingenuity and resourcefulness as well as sheer determination. There is the thrill of pulling off the research in the form of an effectively implemented intervention and control. Then there is the excitement of getting the results back. The clean nature of randomized controlled trials means that they do not rely on complex statistical procedures for reporting, such as multiple regression models, but on a simple comparison of outcomes that cannot be manipulated (though, of course, regression plays an important role in analysing experiments). The excitement of getting a positive result cannot be understated, but the disappointment of a null or negative result also has the compensation that it is a secure addition to knowledge. The design experiment has this real-world excitement, too, as there is close contact with policy-makers while they design and refine their interventions. Armed with these two methods, we are in a position to say whether think or nudge is the best route to civic behaviour and collective action, and which aspects of these two ideas work best and by how much.

3

Recycling

Why study this topic?

The widespread provision of doorstep recycling collections and a growing public awareness of the challenges of dealing with climate change have, over the past two decades, led to extensive change in citizen behaviour. Many households now routinely sort their waste into a variety of containers provided by their local authority, ready for kerbside collection. But while most households have changed their behaviour, a significant minority do not participate, choosing to dispose of their recyclable waste in the household waste bin. While kerbside collections of green waste, paper, cardboard, bottles, and cans are now widely established in many parts of the developed world, public authorities have only recently started to introduce food waste collection schemes and are looking for ways to promote participation in this new service. Perhaps a gentle nudge can persuade households to sort their waste?

In this chapter we start by looking briefly at the current state of the evidence on what can nudge households to recycle. We then describe two randomized controlled trials, which test the impact of two different nudges on recycling behaviour. Both these experiments adopted a similar design: within a selected neighbourhood, half of the streets in the area were randomly assigned to receive an intervention to encourage recycling, while the remaining streets were placed in a control group and received no special attention. Recycling participation rates for all households were measured before and after the intervention to see if the intervention had been effective. The first experiment tested the impact of door-to-door canvassing on recycling; the second tested the impact of 'smiley face' and 'frown face' feedback postcards on participation in a food waste collection scheme. In this chapter, we reflect on the findings from these two experiments and finish with a review of the lessons they offer for nudge strategies.

What do we know about how to encourage recycling?

Research, using mainly observational data, shows that the design of a recycling service has an impact on participation in recycling; in particular, the inclusion of a wide range of materials encourages participation (Woodward et al 2005, Harder et al 2006). Offering appropriate containers also promotes recycling (Woodward et al 2005). A box is probably easier for terraced houses, which have storage and access issues, but wheeled bins will be more convenient for houses with driveways. Frequency of collection and day of collection have an impact, helping to encourage a routine or habit of recycling behaviour. Some recycling organizations alternate collections of recyclable and residual waste, with each being collected fortnightly on the same day in alternate weeks. This can work successfully (Wilson and Williams 2007) and challenges the public's perception that recycling is an add-on rather than a core feature of the waste system, but it can be controversial to cease weekly residual collections (Woodward et al 2005). Vehicles collecting recycling waste should be visibly different from residual waste collection vehicles, so the public can trust that their recyclables will not end up in landfill sites (Woodward et al 2005).

Promotional and educational campaigns can raise participation rates by ensuring that people understand the scheme and by motivating people to get involved. High visibility events and road shows can be successful in building awareness (Read 1999). Incentives can work in areas with low recycling participation rates (Harder et al 2006), but they may crowd out intrinsic motivation (Bryce et al 1997); a survey of householders found that financial incentives are likely to be less effective in encouraging recycling than service improvements and active promotion (Shaw and Maynard 2008). Feedback cards left by collection crews to highlight boxes that contain contaminated material can be effective in reducing the amount of contamination and is a cheap approach to adopt (Timlett and Williams 2008). A systematic review of field experiments on seventy interventions designed to influence recycling found that 'social modeling and environmental alterations' were the most effective (Varotto and Spagnolli 2017).

A study of five newspaper recycling schemes found that households are more likely to set out a recycling box if others in their street recycle regularly, but there is a danger that living on a street with high participation rates may encourage non- or infrequent recyclers to regularly recycle small amounts of material, rather than increasing the absolute amount of material recycled (Tucker 1999). One study found that households in shorter contiguous blocks (fewer than 15 houses) were influenced by the recycling actions of their nearest next-door neighbours, particularly in cul-de-sacs, but the influence of neighbours diminished as the length of the blocks increased (Shaw 2008). Harder and colleagues found that households on small roads tend to have a higher recycling participation rate (Harder et al 2006). Suggested factors include increased attachment to the neighbourhood, community spirit, and peer pressure.

Two randomized controlled trials to look at nudges and recycling

We tested two different types of nudge that might promote recycling behaviour: door-to-door canvassing and the provision of feedback of social norms. Previous studies of door-to-door canvassing suggest that it is more effective in encouraging recycling than simply providing literature (Reams and Ray 1993, Bryce et al 1997), but it is less effective in raising participation in areas where recycling is already high (over 60 per cent of households) (Timlett and Williams 2008). Doorstep canvassing has been found to increase voter turnout in elections by about 7 per cent in the UK (John and Brannan 2008; also see Chapter 5 of the current volume), replicating the treatment effects in US studies (Green and Gerber 2015).

The rationale behind the social norms approach is that most people underestimate the extent of pro-social behaviour among their peers and then use those low estimates as a standard against which to judge themselves (Schultz et al 2007). This assumes that people identify with groups and tend to emulate the behaviour of those they identify with (Tajfel and Turner 1986). Providing feedback is expected to lead to a general rise in pro-social behaviour by letting people know that the prevalence amongst their peers is higher than they thought. However, previous studies have shown mixed results. The provision of feedback on borough-wide recycling participation rates had no effect in changing householder behaviour in a London borough (Lyas et al 2004), but giving more specific feedback on the recycling activity of the individual household or the surrounding streets was successful in promoting recycling in the US (Schultz 1998). The provision of written feedback on the election turnout of near neighbours had a substantial impact on encouraging voters to go to the polls, but the high effect of 8.1 per cent is linked to a shaming element to the intervention: households were told that their voting behaviour was being monitored and would be made public to their neighbours after the election (Gerber et al 2008). Feedback may have an unintended effect of discouraging those who already recycle, by alerting them that some of their neighbours are not participating. One solution to this is to include a smiley face or a frown face in the feedback, to let households know what is commonly approved or disapproved of within society (Reno et al 1993). Such an approach was tested in a field experiment on household energy use: adding a smiley face (J) or a frown face (L) encouraged both above-average consumers to reduce their energy use and below-average consumers to continue their low consumption rates (Schultz et al 2007: 430).

The impact of canvassing on household recycling

The randomized controlled trial set out to test whether door-to-door canvassing is effective in bringing about behaviour change on recycling (see Cotterill et al 2009 for full details of the design and results). The research was conducted in two adjoining neighbourhoods, Old Trafford and Gorse Hill, which are within the area of Trafford Metropolitan Borough Council, close to inner-city Manchester. The housing is a mixture of terraced and semi-detached houses. The area is relatively deprived and ethnically diverse compared to other areas nationally. A kerbside recycling service was provided by EMERGE, a social enterprise, which was commissioned by Trafford Metropolitan Borough Council to provide a weekly recycling service to all households. All the streets in Old Trafford and Gorse Hill that received a recycling service from EMERGE were included in the research study: a total of 194 streets, with 6,580 households. Streets varied in size from 2 households to 190, with an average of 33.9 households per street. Flats and commercial properties were not included because they were not eligible for the recycling service.

The list of streets was randomly divided into two groups of equal size, one to be canvassed and the other to act as a control. The data was stratified by district (Old Trafford or Gorse Hill) and street length, prior to randomization. The treatment group contained 3,468 households in 97 streets, and the control group 3,112 households in 97 streets. Random assignment was done at the street level rather than at the individual household level: we anticipated that canvassing one household might have an effect on the behaviour of its neighbours in the control group, which would contaminate the experiment. A street-based design reduced the possibility of such contamination.

One of four canvassers visited all households in the streets in the intervention group. The canvassing focused on three factors that are expected to influence recycling behaviour: awareness, attitudes, and structural barriers (Shaw et al 2007). Canvassers made sure householders were aware of the day and time of collection and the materials that could be recycled; they promoted positive attitudes to recycling, and addressed barriers to recycling by providing any plastic bags required and ordering new boxes if they were lost or missing. They dealt with any problems or queries about the service or passed any difficult queries on to an EMERGE manager. The canvassers were encouraged to be enthusiastic and conversational on the doorstep. They were provided with scripts to use as prompts but were encouraged to adapt them to their own conversational style. Canvassers were asked to take a different approach dependent on whether the householders were currently recyclers or non-recyclers. Canvassers thanked existing recyclers for using the recycling box, reminded them of the variety of recyclable materials and asked any enthusiastic householders if they would like to become recycling champions. Canvassers took a slightly different approach with non-recyclers, encouraging them to recycle, promoting the day and date of collection and providing information on the materials collected, before asking if they could be counted on to recycle regularly. An information leaflet was delivered to every household canvassed including those where no one was at home. The leaflet described what materials could be recycled, outlined the service provided, gave details of the time and day of collection, and provided contact details for more information.

The canvassing took place over a period of six weeks in May and June 2008 between 3 p.m. and 7 p.m. Monday to Friday, and 11 a.m. to 3 p.m. on Saturday. These times were chosen to maximize the number of contacts, based on previous best practice (Waste and Resources Action Programme 2006). Our monitoring confirms that these times are suitable for a campaign of this type. Each street was canvassed twice. The second visits were arranged at a different time of day from the first visit to maximize contact. During the first canvass 40 per cent of households were spoken to. By the end of the second canvass, 61 per cent of households had been contacted: 2,129 of the 3,468 households in the intervention group. The contact rate compares favourably with other canvassing projects.

We measured recycling behaviour by observing which households put out a recycling container for collection. The monitoring was done on the same day as the waste collection. The monitor sat in the recycling vehicle while the crew were working and noted all the houses on the street that had placed recycling material outside the house boundary. The monitoring was repeated over three consecutive weeks: some households may not recycle weekly because of holidays or having low levels of recyclable waste. Any household that recycled at least once in the three-week period was counted as a recycler. This followed the guidance from the Waste and Resources

Action Programme, supported by the environment department, Defra (Waste and Resources Action Programme 2006).

Participation in the recycling scheme was measured for all households in the intervention and control groups at three time points: in March–April 2008 prior to the canvassing, in July 2008 after its completion, and in October 2008 to test whether households had got into the habit of recycling. Monitoring was not done on bank holidays (because services were disrupted) or during school holidays (when some households might be away). The task of monitoring participation, carried out three times, was done by a different person. None of these people were involved in any other aspect of the project and they were unaware which streets were in the treatment and control groups. The members of the recycling collection crew were aware of the research project, but did not know which streets were in the treatment and control groups.

Figure 3.1 compares the recycling participation rates of the control and canvass groups over time. At baseline, in March 2008, before the canvassing took place, the streets in the canvass group had an average participation rate of 48 per cent compared to 54 per cent of the control group. By July, immediately after the canvassing, the recycling participation rate of the canvassed streets rose to 52 per cent, a rise of 4 per cent, and participation in the control group dropped to 53 per cent, a fall of 1 per cent. The randomization of the two groups means that the streets in the canvass group are the same as those in the control group in every respect except for having been canvassed, so we should assume that – without the canvassing – the recycling rates of the canvass group would have fallen by 1 per cent, the same as the control group. Overall the short-term effect of the canvassing campaign was to raise recycling by 5 per cent (4 plus 1 per cent).

Between the baseline monitoring in March 2008 and the follow up monitoring in October, the average participation rate of the

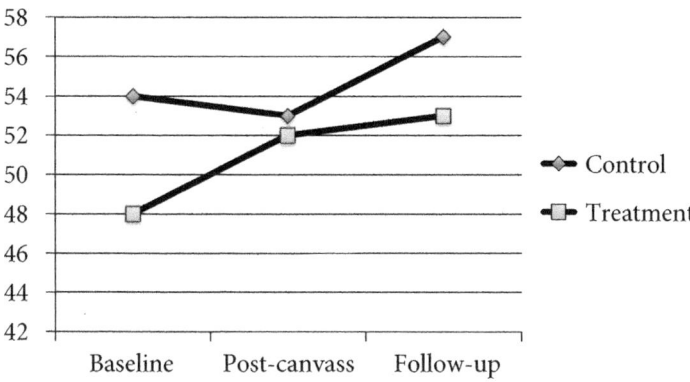

Recycling

Control
Treatment

Figure 3.1 Recycling participation rate by group

canvassed streets rose from 48 per cent to 53 per cent, a rise of 5 percentage points and the control group rose from 54 per cent to 57 per cent, a rise of 3 percentage points. So, overall, the longer-term effect of the canvassing campaign was to raise recycling by 2 percentage points (5 minus 3 per cent). The effect of the canvassing on recycling behaviour was statistically significant at the 5 per cent level when analysed using regression models (Cotterill et al 2009).

Similar canvassing campaigns conducted by the Waste and Resources Action Programme led to immediate rises in participation of 9.6 per cent in Braintree District Council, 6.5 per cent in Essex County Council, and 7 per cent in Luton Borough Council. However, none of these studies included a control group, so there is no way of knowing whether these rises were the result of the canvassing or some other factors, and none included a follow-up measure to test the impact over time (Waste and Resources Action Programme 2006). The only academic study of a canvassing campaign found an overall fall of 4 per cent, but again there was no control group (Timlett and Williams 2008).

We can sum up: a door-to-door canvassing campaign can successfully raise participation in a kerbside recycling scheme by 5 per cent. The effect is still there three months later, but is reduced to 2 per cent, showing a decline over time. This might suggest that canvassing and other promotional campaigns need to be repeated regularly to reinforce the recycling message. The canvassing had less impact on streets where recycling rates were already very high. The canvassing campaign was more successful in the most deprived neighbourhoods and in neighbourhoods with a large ethnic minority population. So, canvassing campaigns are likely to be most successful if targeted in streets with low baseline recycling rates, in relatively deprived areas, and in neighbourhoods with a high proportion of ethnic minorities.

The impact of feedback on food waste recycling

The randomized controlled trial set out to test whether feedback cards are effective in bringing about behaviour change on food waste recycling (see Nomura et al 2011, for more details of the design and results). The research was undertaken in Oldham, a former mill town in Greater Manchester. Oldham Council provides waste collection services to all households in the borough, with separate collections of garden waste, mixed recyclables, residual waste, and a weekly collection of food waste. Among the ten councils in Greater Manchester, Oldham was the first to collect food waste, and the implementation of the scheme was watched with interest by neighbouring authorities. The research was undertaken in the autumn of 2009. Oldham Council offered a food waste collection service to 89,000 households. The sample consisted of all the households covered by six separate collection rounds, located in different parts of the town: 318 streets with 9,082 households. Streets vary in size from 1 household to 229, with an average of 62 households per street. Flats and commercial properties were not included because they were not eligible for the recycling service.

The list of streets was randomly divided into two groups of equal size, one to receive feedback and the other to act as a control. The data was stratified by collection round (six rounds), recycling performance at baseline (above or below the average), and street size prior to randomization. The treatment group contained 5,009 households in 159 streets; the control group contained 4,073 households in 159 streets.

Postcards were delivered to each household in the treatment group providing feedback on how their street performed compared to the average for their neighbourhood. Giving feedback is a classic nudge. The leaflet stated: 'Did you know: X per cent of homes on A Street recycle their food waste. The average for the area is Y per cent'. It included either a smiley face (J) or a frown face (L), depending on whether the street was better or worse than the neighbourhood average, and concluded with the message: 'With your help your street could become the best recycling street in Oldham.' On the reverse were details of how to participate in the food waste scheme. The contents of the card were tailored to each street, and were produced using the data gathered by monitoring participation. The feedback postcards were delivered twice: once during the week after the first round of participation monitoring and again the week after the second round of monitoring. The feedback cards were delivered by EMERGE recycling. Households in the treatment group could receive the following possible combinations of feedback:

Smiley card at time one – smiley card at time two (smiley-smiley)
Smiley card at time one – frown card at time two (smiley-frown)
Frown card at time one – frown card at time two (frown-frown)
Frown card at time one – smiley card at time two (frown-smiley)

The participation of all households in both the feedback and the control groups was monitored. The method was similar to the previous experiment: a monitor travelled ahead of the collection crew and noted all the houses that had placed a food-waste bin outside the house boundary. The monitoring was repeated over three consecutive weeks and a household was counted as participating if they put out a container at least one week in three. The monitoring was undertaken by EMERGE recycling. Participation in the scheme was measured for all households at three time points: in August 2009 prior to the feedback campaign, in September 2009 after the delivery of the first feedback postcard, and in October 2009 after receiving the second postcard.

Figure 3.2 compares the recycling participation rate of the control and feedback groups. At baseline, before the feedback cards were sent, the streets in the treatment group had a mean participation rate of 48.1 per cent, compared to 51.5 per cent in the control group. After two feedback cards were sent, recycling participation of the treatment streets rose to 50.1 per cent, a rise of 2 per cent, and

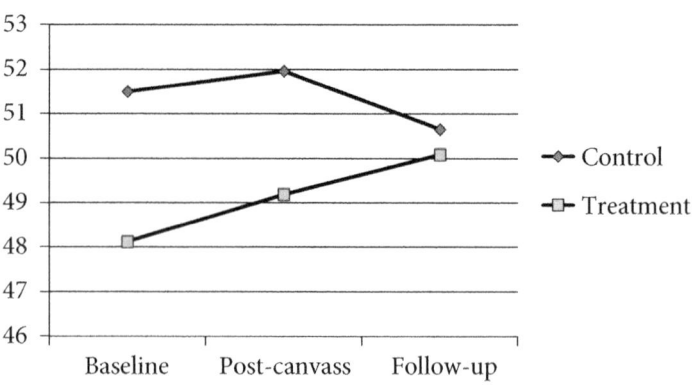

Figure 3.2 Proportion of households recycling food waste

participation in the control group dropped to 50.6 per cent, a fall of 1 per cent. The randomization of the two groups meant that the streets in the feedback group were the same as those in the control group in every respect except for having been sent feedback, so we should assume that – without the feedback – the recycling rates of the feedback group would have fallen by 1 per cent, the same as the control group. So, overall the short-term effect of the feedback was to raise recycling by 3 per cent (2 per cent plus 1 per cent). In summary, providing feedback cards to households on their street's performance raised participation in the food waste scheme by 3 percentage points, compared to a control group, and the effect was statistically significant (Nomura et al 2011). Both smiley and frown feedback were effective: positive feedback encouraged those in high-performing streets to carry on making the effort, while negative feedback persuaded those in low-performing streets to join in with the food waste collection scheme.

The only situation in which feedback was found not to be effective was with households who were already participating in the scheme. For some of the households who were already putting out their food waste, the feedback acted to discourage them from carrying on. We speculate that this is because people who were already making the effort to sort their food waste were discouraged by cards that said their street does not follow their personal behaviour.

Smaller streets were more likely to recycle and we found that feedback was more effective on smaller streets than longer streets. However, this effect was quite small. Feedback was most effective when given more than once, to reiterate the message, and when the feedback was consistent: households who received two smiley cards or two frown cards were more likely to respond than those who received mixed messages.

What are the lessons for a nudge strategy?

The two recycling experiments have the following implications for a nudge strategy. The first implication is the importance of group loyalty and identification. The findings from the food waste experiment indicate that the length of the street has an impact on recycling behaviour. People on small streets are more likely to recycle, perhaps because their behaviour is more observable to others whom they know. Secondly, the feedback cards has a greater impact on shorter streets, suggesting that there is greater group identification on smaller streets, with households being more influenced by messages about the behaviour of others when the reference group is small. However, a limitation of the nudge is that, although statistically significant, both these effects are fairly small. Overall, it seems likely from this, and other research, that household recycling behaviour is influenced by the actions of close neighbours, but the street may not be the best reference group, because streets are so variable in their size and make-up: the focus should perhaps be on the immediate circle of neighbouring properties.

The food waste experiment confirms that behaviour can be shaped by the use of relevant social or community influences. Households in both high-performing and low-performing streets were persuaded to improve or maintain their behaviour when given information on the recycling performance of their street compared to a wider neighbourhood. However, a limitation of this nudge is that feedback cards were not effective if households were already recycling their food waste at baseline: we assume that people are discouraged if they learn that they are performing better than the norm for their street. Future feedback campaigns are likely to be most effective if targeted at those whose behaviour needs to change, rather than as a way of sustaining those who are already engaged in pro-social behaviour.

The second implication of recycling research for a nudge strategy is for the discussion on choice architecture. Previous research has found that the design of the waste collection scheme is an important element in encouraging people to take part: a scheme that is easy to use, efficient, and can be trusted is more likely to be well used by residents. Citizens often regard their own behaviour change as part of a contract with expectations on both sides: if citizens are to consider changing their behaviour, they will have high expectations about the behaviour of public agencies. While this was not directly tested in this research, it was observed during the experiment that the canvassing campaign coincided with a period when the recycling collection crew was short-staffed and there was a reliance on casual staff. A minority of householders complained of missed collections, rude staff, dirty boxes, and pedantry over contamination. These households had given up on recycling altogether and had to be persuaded to restart. Canvassers felt they had to win people round who were fed up with the service, as one canvasser commented: if 'collections weren't right or something went wrong or they got disenchanted because they don't get their bin back or they are confused about how things should be sorted … we have tried to persuade them to give it another go'.

The canvassers were negotiating a contract with the householder: persuading people to recycle in expectation that the service would be better than before. By the time of the final monitoring in October 2008, a permanent and settled collection crew was in place, and the level of participation rallied to a higher level than at baseline.

These studies indicate the usefulness of adopting nudge strategies to promote recycling, but they also suggest limitations to nudge, which should be considered when designing campaigns. When using approaches based on social influences, it is important to consider what might be the most appropriate reference group, within which group loyalties may develop: the reference group may vary between individuals and may not conform to established geographic boundaries. Nudge strategies may need to be targeted, with different approaches being made to those who already participate in pro-social behaviour and those who have not yet engaged. Nudges are low-level interventions that will not automatically lead to a long-term change of habit, so they can work best if repeated regularly to reinforce the message.

Further reading

The best study is Schultz, P. W. (1998), 'Changing Behaviour with Normative Feedback Interventions: Field Experiment on Kerbside Recycling', *Basic and Applied Psychology*, 21: 25–36. For advice on how to organize a door-to-door canvassing campaign: Waste and Resources Action Programme (2006), *Step by Step Guide to Door-to-door Canvassing*, www.wrap.org.uk. For guidance on how to monitor household participation in recycling: Waste and Resources Action Programme (2010) *Improving the Performance of Waste Diversion Schemes: A Good Practice Guide to Monitoring and Evaluation*, www.wrap.org.uk. A recent systematic review of different kinds of social intentions is very useful to find out what works in this field: Varotto, A. and Spagnolli, A. (2017), 'Psychological Strategies to Promote Household Recycling: A Systematic Review with Meta-analysis of Validated Field Interventions', *Journal of Environmental Psychology*, 51: 168–88.

4

Volunteering

Why try to increase volunteering?

The idea of co-production is that public services and citizens contribute jointly to deliver positive social outcomes and sympathetic environments in which people can have creative, productive, and fulfilling lives (see, for example, Boyle and Harris 2009). Underlying recent interest in co-production across the political spectrum is a belief that 60 years of state provision of welfare, however well-intentioned, has eaten away at citizens' capacity and desire for mutuality and for self-help. These are not new ideas. William Beveridge, seen by many as the founder of the British welfare state, argued in 1948 for the importance of the 'mutual aid motive in action' and the 'philanthropic motive in action' (Beveridge 1948). He was 'keen to recognize that the state could and should have a vital and proactive role in developing policy frameworks to nurture both solidaristic and sympathetic human motivations and their capacities for expression' (Kendall 2009: 3). In Beveridge's view, the state's role was to exercise self-restraint, and voluntarism would balance the power and dominance of the state.

There have been well-documented shifts in the types of civic activity in which people engage. For some citizens, their preferences have been to use more consumer-based expressions of solidarity and philanthropy. So, new activities such as boycotting or 'buycotting' consumer goods on political or ethical grounds, or wearing badges and wristbands for causes (Micheletti 2010). However, there remains a firm interest in getting citizens to participate in co-production through active volunteering and social action of many kinds (Durose and Richardson 2016). For many policy outcomes, action by the state cannot substitute for civic acts. For example, local efforts by public sector bodies to clear up unsightly bulky refuse (like mattresses and fridges) are not a substitute for citizens choosing not to dispose of unwanted items by dumping, and preferably should involve citizens also assisting with the process through clean-up days and similar exercises. Volunteering and social action are also not easily replaced by other civic acts, such as ethical buying, which may be driven by similar sympathetic human motivations, and towards similar solidaristic ends, but which do not offer the potential for co-produced outcomes.

In this chapter we review the evidence on promoting volunteering. We refer here to volunteering as an accessible term for a wide range of social action activities, where citizens give their time and skills to directly helping a good cause. The chapter contains summaries of the various options that have been tried and a discussion of what a nudge strategy could offer. It examines a particular case and reports from a design experiment in an English local authority which attempted to facilitate volunteering by asking citizens who complain to a local authority telephone call centre to do other civic-minded acts. What do these findings imply for the challenge of promoting volunteering? By changing the choice architecture can you turn complainers into volunteers?

What do we already know? How much volunteering already exists?

There have been numerous policy interventions by public institutions, in the UK and internationally, to encourage volunteering. In the UK context, for example, despite the demise of Big Society policy with the resignation of David Cameron, and shifts in emphasis and investment, UK government policy still remains committed to volunteering. Central government has set up 'place-based social action' programmes. There has been a new phase of a Government-funded Community Organisers programme, building on the first wave of 2011–15, with a second wave for 2017–20. Youth volunteering has been a priority in UK policy. For example, 2011, the year the first edition of this book was published, saw the creation of the National Citizen Service, a national youth citizenship scheme. This volunteering programme is now overseen and funded by an independent public body, reporting to Parliament (called the National Citizen Service Trust) (Cabinet Office 2018: 43). The 2011 Localism Act, which promotes community asset ownership, is heavily dependent on volunteering, for example where volunteers are needed to manage transferred community assets.

Beyond the UK, the United Nations celebrates an annual International Volunteer Day in December, and the EU has been supporting volunteering, for example through the European Solidarity Corps. In the US, volunteering is promoted through the Corporation for National and Community Service, a federal organization which oversees volunteering through initiatives like AmeriCorps, and tracks volunteer activity levels. The National Conference for Citizenship, an organization backed by the federal government, works with different cities and states to strengthen civic life. It uses a 'civic health index' to track progress in cities, states, and nations.

As well as official central government policies and programmes, civil society has its own agenda outside of government policies, and other sectors also want to mobilize citizens' voluntary efforts. Many local governments have their own locally driven policy agendas in favour of coproduction, traditional volunteering, and other forms of social action. Private sector organizations support volunteering, for example through corporate social responsibility programmes.

How much volunteering already exists? If we take one classic measure of volunteering, the rate of formal volunteering, we can get a feel for the numbers of people participating. Other measures to take into account would be the number of hours contributed through volunteering; measures of informal volunteering (i.e. not through organizations, such as helping a neighbour); looking at who is volunteering; and differences between types of people and types of places. But just looking at headline national formal volunteering rates, there were no changes in rates of regular formal volunteering in England between 2001 and 2009, at 28 per cent (Department for Communities and Local Government 2009) and relative stability in rates between 2001 and 2016, with 2015/16 figures of 27 per cent of adult volunteering at least once a month (National Council for Voluntary Organisations 2017). These figures dropped in 2017/18 to 22 per cent for regular formal volunteering (Department for Digital, Culture, Media & Sport 2018), but this might be a result of changes in the way that data are collected. Occasional formal volunteering (i.e. volunteering through an organization at least once in the previous year) had increased between 2001 and 2009 from 39 to 43 per cent (Department for Communities and Local Government 2009). It was still at 44 per cent in 2013/14 but then gradually declined again back down to around 2001 levels, standing at 38 per cent in 2017/18 (Department for Digital, Culture, Media & Sport 2018).

Is England different from elsewhere? Looking at the US, the figures between 2002 and 2015 (Corporation for National and Community Service 2017: 2), then updated for 2017[1] fluctuate between around 25 to 30 per cent of the population volunteering through, or for, an organization at least once in a given year, with median hours in different years ranging from 38 to 52 hours per person per year. There have been concerns about a steady decline in US volunteering levels (Grimm and Dietz 2018). However, there are also some signs of possible recovery, or at least the figures change sufficiently year to year enough to put question marks over a long-term decline thesis. For example, just under a third of Americans (30.3 per cent) engaged in formal volunteering in 2017,[2] compared to previous highs of 28.8 per cent between 2003 and 2005 (Corporation for National and Community Service 2006), and a 15-year low of 24.9 per cent in 2015 (Grimm and Dietz 2018: 1).

There are some similarities between the US and the UK. The picture is similar in that there are concerns about declining rates of volunteering, but there is also a healthy core of activity with around one in four adults engaged in formal volunteering. The differences are that UK figures for proportions of people volunteering have been more stable over this period than in the US. Another difference is that the total volume of volunteering by number of hours has gone down in the UK (Office for National Statistics 2017), whereas in the US the number of hours has remained high (Grimm and Dietz 2018). UK figures are also complicated by changes in the way that data are collected, so it is hard to compare long-term UK trends (National Council for Voluntary Organisations 2018).

Reliable and consistent trend data in nearly all countries are not longitudinal and therefore do not show how many drop out and

---

1   www.nationalservice.gov/vcla [accessed 17 February 2019].
2   www.nationalservice.gov/serve/via/research [accessed 17 February 2019].

how many join in. Given a wide range in the lengths of time spent volunteering, these figures may represent many more individuals contributing over the period than is apparent. Formal volunteering levels of between one in four and one in three indicate an arguably healthy base of citizen activity, but with potential to drive up levels of volunteering.

The literature – how can volunteering be increased?

It is not immediately clear what else, if anything, could be done to raise volunteering rates. However, there are some clues in the literature. Verba, Schlozman, and Brady's study of facilitators of civic voluntarism outlines a civic voluntarism model, which sets out three drivers to stimulate volunteering: capacity, motivation, and mobilization (being asked) (Verba et al 1995). In this model, mobilizing is effective where 'people are resource-rich, have plenty of free time, and have a strong sense of efficacy' or interest already (Pattie and Seyd 2003: 446). Mobilization is predicated on sufficient capacity and motivation.

How could these ideas be translated into possible nudges to increase volunteering? The presumptions in the civic voluntarism model offered some interesting areas to test using the idea of nudge. Was there an untapped pool of unasked, skilled, and keen people who could be more effectively mobilized than through previous interventions? Could the predicates be reversed or bypassed? Was it necessary to build up or rely on pre-existing capacity and motivation, or could mobilization through a nudge develop capacity and motivation? Mobilizing is a classic nudge strategy, as it presumes citizens might already be able and willing but not activated, or could become more able and willing if activated.

Someone or something needs to be the mobilizer and do the

asking. In the original civic voluntarism model, mobilization is done through 'networks of recruitment' (Verba et al 1995: 3) and interpersonal relationships, primarily informal recruitment through friends, acquaintances, and colleagues, but also political parties. The workplace, churches, and voluntary associations act as the 'loc[i] of recruitment' (Verba et al 1995: 144). Verba et al discuss the 'non-political secondary institutions of adult life – the workplace, voluntary associations, or church' (Verba et al 1995: 369). These institutions are crucial, mostly insofar as the settings in which mobilization happens are where colleagues gather and have conversations and where 'psychological engagement' (motivation) is cultivated through debate and other cues and hooks. These settings are also where transferable skills (capacity) are acquired. Formal requests by institutions play only a small role. Recent work by the co-authors have tested whether these informal nudges can increase the giving of time, such as requests involving endorsements by celebrities or politicians (John et al 2018), the impact of social information (Moseley et al 2018), and social strategies to encourage people to stand for elected office (Ryan et al 2018).

Work by Lowndes, Pratchett, and Stoker extends the model and sets out an enhanced formal role for institutions as mobilizers in their own right, and as mobilizers of a wider group of citizens than the institutions' members or employees (Lowndes et al 2006). They propose the CLEAR framework (see Table 4.1): Can do – that is, have the resources and knowledge to participate; Like to – that is, have a sense of attachment that reinforces participation; Enabled to – that is, are provided with the opportunity for participation; Asked to – that is, are mobilized by official bodies or voluntary groups; and Responded to – that is, see evidence that their views have been considered.

Data for England in 2016/17 (National Council for Voluntary

Table 4.1   The CLEAR model

Can do – have the resources and knowledge to participate
Like to – have a sense of attachment that reinforces participation
Enabled to – are provided with the opportunity for participation
Asked to – are mobilized through public or voluntary groups
Responded to – see evidence that their views have been considered

Source: Adapted from Lowndes et al 2006

Organisations 2018) shows that the informal recruitment networks identified in the civic voluntarism model are alive and well. Of those who volunteered, 48 per cent in the Community Life survey found out about the volunteering opportunity from someone else already involved in the group or organization, and 23 per cent found out by using services provided by the group or organization. Faith networks were a route to volunteering for 19 per cent of volunteers in the survey, and 17 per cent heard about volunteer through general word of mouth. Interestingly, only 10 per cent found out about volunteering opportunities online. Where there were also gaps was in the potential ways that local government institutions could play a mobilizing role. Local government advertises local events and activities, and many contribute funding to Volunteer Bureaux. However, only 2 per cent of volunteers found out about volunteering opportunities through Volunteer Bureaux. Between 4 and 9 per cent found out about volunteering from local events and sources such as libraries, community centres, volunteer fairs, and other local events. These are very similar figures to a decade ago (Agur and Low 2009: 166).

At the same time, each local government body conducts thousands of direct transactions with citizens and service users, but does not use these contact points as mobilizing opportunities. Moreover, a high proportion of the transactions are initiated by the citizen, many because something has gone wrong with public services. The citizen or service user contacts a local authority with a one-way request for the public body to solve a problem, for example a person rings a customer contact centre direct to request that street cleaners come to their neighbourhood and remove litter from streets.

A civic request is typically not made of residents during these routine service interactions. There may well be a reciprocal civic request being made of the same citizens by the same institution, for example, to join in a neighbourhood clean-up day. But the institution's request is often made by a different department, at a different time, through an indirect route (for example, posters at a local school), and usually generates extremely low returns. When a citizen calls a local authority contact centre, the presumption by the authority appears to be that their behaviour is not civic. Yet the person being treated as a customer may be acting as a good citizen, hoping their phone call will lead to neighbourhood improvements, cleaner streets, or better neighbourhood relations. Even if a call is not orientated towards improving public goods, or influencing the institution more generally, there is still a possibility that the caller would be willing to consider making this sort of contribution, if they were asked. Therefore, the potential for co-production is often lost. But it need not be, as experimental evidence suggests (Jakobsen 2013).

What is the intervention? The nudge experiment

When citizens do get mobilized through being upset about the streets not being cleaned or bins not been emptied, the public authority can use such a situation to nudge citizens into more civic-minded behaviour. The nudge experiment was undertaken by the University of

Manchester working in partnership with a local authority. The idea was to see if voluntary activity could be mobilized more effectively. The partners agreed to change the choice architecture: the default settings of the institution – the local council in this case – were changed from one that assumed that citizens have a largely passive rule to one where they have a fuller relationship with public authorities and their communities, and would want to become volunteers. The original default setting was that routine service transactions treated service users as passive complainers and consumers. This was altered to a new default setting that any interaction was with potentially active citizens. This also required changes in the organization's cultural default settings. Seeing the callers as complaining customers suggested that the council anticipated customer hostility to being asked to volunteer. Regarding people as both consumers and potential co-producers required the council to presume people would be comfortable with being asked.

To test this out, the experiment was focused on promoting voluntary activity in two neighbourhoods in Blackburn. Callers reporting a problem or making a query to a local authority customer contact centre were asked if they wanted to get more involved in the neighbourhood. Typical reasons for calling were complaints about environmental services. After the query or complaint had been dealt with, citizens from those neighbourhoods who telephoned the contact centre were asked: 'We are currently promoting civic awareness in [your neighbourhood] and are looking for people to get involved in improving the area. We want to encourage people to take action on community issues in the area. Would you be interested in finding out more?'

Citizens who were identified as interested were split into two groups. Half of the potential volunteers were allocated randomly to an intervention group which was then encouraged – using a variety of approaches – to take further steps such as joining a local group, becoming volunteers, or changing their environmental behaviour. The other half of the volunteers were allocated to a comparison group who were sent an information pack on opportunities for citizen participation in the neighbourhood. The information pack contained information that was already publicly available and marketed to residents, and, as such, was similar to a placebo treatment.

There were two waves of the experiment. In the first, existing opportunities to participate were unchanged; what was new was the proactive approach by the contact centre, combined with a local neighbourhood officer, providing information and encouragement to the intervention group. In the second, the follow-up contact with the neighbourhood officer was supplemented by the creation of new volunteering opportunities for the intervention group. All participants were interviewed at the start of the project, and again eight weeks later, and were asked about civic activity and attitudes. These new volunteering activities were then offered to the comparison group after the data collection had been completed.

The first phase occurred in April–July 2008 in one neighbourhood. During this first phase, the intervention was tweaked in response to the research findings. Using the lessons from the first wave, the experiment was repeated in a second neighbourhood. The second phase took place between February and August 2009 in a different neighbourhood. A steering group for the project included the manager of the contact centre, the head of customer services, and three members of the council's neighbourhood team, a housing association manager, a policy manager, and the researchers. The steering group met regularly to reflect on the emerging findings from the research and decide whether the intervention should be tweaked to improve its effectiveness. The aim was to identify the most effective and appropriate way to design the intervention, both in the contact centre and in the neighbourhood.

The actual research took place in Blackburn in northwest England. The first neighbourhood was a residential area, relatively deprived in national terms, but fairly affluent compared to surrounding areas of the town. The housing was mostly owner-occupied or privately rented. The area had a high ethnic minority population, mostly of Pakistani and Bangladeshi family heritage. The area was chosen as suitable for this experiment because it had an active and welcoming community association together with a range of other potential activities. The second neighbourhood was less affluent, within the lowest 5 per cent of neighbourhoods in England, and was among the most deprived in the borough. It was a predominantly white, former council estate, now managed by a housing association. Most of the properties were social housing, with pockets of owner-occupation. Over 40 per cent of households claimed state benefits. The experiment included all telephone callers from the neighbourhood to the council's contact centre complaining about cleansing, environment, or neighbourhood services. During the second wave, calls about council tax and housing benefits were also included.

The results

There were two critical successes that suggest the potential for a nudge strategy to change complainers into volunteers. The first was that citizens welcomed the change in the choice architecture. From the start of the research, there had been some concern from local authority staff that there would be an adverse reaction from citizens to this change of approach. In particular, the contact centre managers were worried that people phoning to report problems or make complaints might be irritated by being invited to be proactive on neighbourhood issues; those reporting a problem with a local service would be angry at being asked to act themselves. Members of staff were not convinced that people would welcome a change in the nature of the relationship.

These concerns over the change in the default setting were not borne out by citizens' responses. The research tested the assumptions about citizens' preferences. The doubts of members of staff proved to be unfounded among those citizens who took part. People were happy to be mobilized by public institutions. Citizens were generally supportive, with 92 per cent across both intervention and comparison groups agreeing that the council should encourage callers to get more involved. One person spoke about the importance of the council working in partnership with members of the public:

> They [the council] are restricted in what they can do. They should work with the people to get to the bottom of it rather than tell people to ring somewhere else. We raise the same issue repeatedly and no records are kept. They probably live in the community and can benefit. We need to step back and see each other's perspectives.

The research also looked at people's motives for wanting to get involved, and found that they supported the change in default setting. People's motives did appear to be broadly concerned with public goods such as community safety or environmental conditions, and therefore could be classified as civic: most people wanted to make a difference in the area. Seven of the 30 participants in the first iteration were motivated by a principled feeling that everyone should do their bit, which is an explicitly stated belief in co-production: for example, 'I think I should be not just complaining, actually doing something' and 'If you're not making an effort you can't complain'. Where people were concerned, it was scepticism about how far the institution was making a genuine change: 'Worried it's just a token gesture'. Others were sceptical about to what extent the project could overcome barriers to participation, and argued that other citizens would not respond: 'They are flogging a dead horse' and 'it will fall on deaf ears'.

The second critical success was that the initial nudge did start to mobilize people towards volunteering. The request by the contact centre generated additional interest from citizens who had not previously been involved in volunteering, and was successful in attracting a cross-section of people in the neighbourhood. In neighbourhood one, 30 callers were recruited, including Asian women, younger people, and a large proportion of people in work. Five people had not undertaken any civic activity in the past year and a further 11 had only done limited, one-off activity. In neighbourhood two the profile was different, reflecting differences in the local population. Of the 33 callers recruited, all were white and, compared to the callers in the first location, participants tended to be slightly older. Only a quarter were in work and a third were sick or disabled or caring for a sick or disabled relative. Seventeen had not taken part in any civic activity in the past year and a further nine had only done limited, one-off activity.

However, the initial surge in interest was not translated into activity. The comparison group performed as well as the intervention group in carrying out voluntary activity, and neither group showed massive increases. The nudge was in two iterations: changing the way the authority mobilized through the contact centre, with a light-touch follow up using existing volunteering opportunities; then a second iteration which also created new volunteering opportunities. The fundamental initial shift in the default setting at the contact centre created a different citizen response. But the experiment failed to capitalize on the initial expression of interest in the follow-up intervention. There were several reasons for this. One obvious argument is that when put on the spot, people gave socially acceptable responses without being genuinely committed to considering civic action. Therefore, interest tails off. While this is always possible, there are more cogent arguments that may explain the drop-off in citizen interest.

The neighbourhood officers did not contact 8 of the 17 people in the intervention group, meaning that the intervention was flawed. More importantly, in the follow-up interviews people fed back that the voluntary opportunities offered in the first wave were not appropriate ones. For example, the types of voluntary contributions in which people expressed interest included making themselves available to present their views, or having a more in-depth dialogue with services, in order that services could better tailor, or adapt, their responses. This could include expanding the presence of police community support officers or improving parking or helping to improve the appearance of the area by reducing the amount of litter or rubbish dumping. It could include citizens helping to improve things as individuals, for example by improving their own front gardens, or by running practical community projects to help each other, such as neighbourhood watch schemes ('We should be vigilant and help each other') and projects to reduce the isolation of elderly and housebound people.

No one explicitly mentioned wanting to attend meetings or join existing community groups. Indeed, some participants had previously been put off volunteering through their experience or knowledge of these existing opportunities. However, in the first wave, the options offered to interested citizens were largely about attending public meetings or joining local community associations to help with their limited range of activities, in tightly prescribed roles. There were few options that fitted people's preferences. For example, no support was offered for garden tidying, and there were no creative ways for people to have dialogue with service providers other than the conventional routes of public meetings or individual complaints.

There was some assistance offered to those wanting to set up mutual aid and self-help community projects, but it was to transfer the job of mobilizing on to the citizen, so people were given information packs for neighbourhood watch schemes, but were not given the names of other residents who had also expressed an interest. Residents said they were uncomfortable with the level of administration involved in setting up a scheme.

The second wave of the experiment was adapted to address this, using the things citizens had said they wanted to do in order to develop new options. For those wanting to use their views more constructively to improve services, the authority then started to set up the public sector equivalent of a mystery shopping exercise (where people anonymously test a service or product). The council had previously used mystery shopping with paid staff, but wanted to extend this to citizens. People are offered training before using a script to make a series of requests of the authority, and the response is recorded using a set of criteria. Tests are made using different scenarios, from various types of citizen, with different staff and departments. Feedback is then given on how well the authority performed and on areas for improvement. However, the process of creating the scheme was a long and involved one, requiring agreement at a senior level on the timing of the mystery shopping exercise, its parameters, the script used, and feedback mechanisms, as well as organizing a relatively expensive specialist training package for the volunteers, which took place over an induction period.

For those wanting to offer help to neighbours, the authority facilitated a good neighbour scheme, through which residents could offer social support to isolated older people by means of a good morning phone call. This involved many weeks of work by the council to identify vulnerable older people who may need help, advertise the service to them and set up training in befriending for the volunteers.

Therefore, although progress was made on creating new volunteering opportunities, the delays in doing this meant that momentum was lost, and citizens' initial fears that the institutional change would not be deep enough seemed to be confirmed. The nudge did not go far enough in changing the choice architecture. Feedback from citizens suggests that mobilization would have resulted in more activity had the changes been more extensive.

Discussion – could we have improved the nudge?

Could the nudge have been improved? What would have made it a better nudge? Arguably, the experiment needed to go further by changing all aspects of the choice architecture, and doing this more quickly. The change in default setting did not extend quickly enough to volunteering options. The original intention was to offer a creative menu of voluntary options based on individuals' skills and interests. However, the institution reverted to a default setting previously hidden, which was co-production options that suited the institution and its skill set, rather than options tailored to the citizen. Participants in the first-wave intervention were offered an arguably uninspiring menu of involvement in existing neighbourhood groups and forums – easy for the authority to understand, based on an established repertoire of engagement skills, known entities, and low supervision and transaction costs – though citizens would have preferred stronger voice mechanisms, less group-reliant activities requiring additional organization, higher monitoring and transaction costs, and innovative thinking. In the language of the CLEAR model, people were not 'enabled to'; the choices we tilted people towards were not attractive or tailored enough. By the second wave, the authority had started to develop new options, but this was too slow for many of the people we had mobilized.

Another issue was that the experiment focused on changing default settings, but neglected other elements of nudging, in particular the incentives, structuring complex choices, giving feedback, and expecting error. If volunteering had been incentivized, for example through Timebanking (a scheme where volunteers earn time credits to spend later on, see www.timebanking.org) or childcare offers, this may have increased activity. There was a gap in helping practitioners and citizens structure complex choices. Both parties knew they wanted volunteering to happen, but neither was clear how best this could be done. Both had identified problems they wanted to tackle, but were unsure how to go about this. We started to help people structure these choices, first by getting local authority staff to conduct a skills audit with citizens, and then holding a workshop discussion with staff to take account of these skills and interests in developing a more extensive menu of options for citizens. Nudge includes the idea of feedback, which was used in the experiment but too late to have any real feedback effects. The authority did give feedback to people in the experiment (or 'responded to them' in CLEAR terminology) about how many other citizens had participated, and thanked them in an effort to validate citizens' efforts in coming forward. We have seen and can understand some of the gaps in the experiment in terms of nudge ideas. But as well as offering a way of interpreting our results, nudge is a potential tool for strengthening the activity. The likelihood is that a stronger nudge may have been able to extend the results further.

Further reading

The CLEAR framework is explained in Lowndes, V., Pratchett, L., and Stoker, G. (2006), 'Diagnosing and Remedying the Failings of Official Participation Schemes: The CLEAR framework', *Social Policy and Society*, 5: 281–91. The citizen perspective on volunteering is captured in Lowndes, V., Pratchett, L., and Stoker, G. (2001), 'Trends in Public Participation: Part 2 – Citizens' Perspectives', *Public Administration*, 79: 445–55. A review of citizen-sponsored efforts at community action is Richardson, L. (2008), *DIY Community Action. Neighbourhood Problems and Community Self-help*, Bristol: Policy Press. Fung, A. (2006), *Empowered Participation: Reinventing Urban Democracy*, Princeton, NJ: Princeton, University Press provides a comparative perspective on empowerment. This is updated in Fung, S. (2015), 'Putting the Public Back into Governance: The Challenges of Citizen Participation and Its Future', *Public Administration Review*, 75: 513–22. For recent work on co-production, see Durose, L. and Richardson, L. (2016), *Designing Public Policy for Co-production: Theory, Practice and Change*, Bristol: Policy Press.

5

Voting

Why is political participation important?

If the pessimists are to be believed, Britain and other democracies are experiencing a crisis of political participation, when it is very hard to engage citizens in conventional forms of politics, such as voting in local elections. Citizens appear to be turned off by political parties and politicians, and have disengaged from politics as a result. This is often seen as the result of a more privatized, work intensive, and mobile society (Putnam 2000); it may also be the result of the declining performance of democracies, which have not fulfilled citizen expectations, and where politicians have not kept their promises (Putnam and Pharr 2000). This could be the fault of the politicians, in particular their inappropriate use of public funds, highlighted, for example, by the furore over the expense claims of UK Members of Parliament in 2009. Or it might be to do with the unrealistic expectations – inevitably dashed – which citizens have of politicians (Stoker 2006). Or it could be the result of spreading feelings of anti-politics and hostility to central authority and experts (Clarke et al 2018).

In the Introduction, we alluded to the idea that there is no crisis of citizen participation, pointing to the continuing interest citizens have in politics and the large variety of citizen activities that are either continuing at similar levels or extending into new areas (Dalton 2004, Pattie et al 2005). But it remains the case that citizen participation in some forms of conventional political activities, such as voting and membership of political parties, has declined, though even here some political parties have experienced recent increases in membership. However, is there a cause for concern if democracy still seems to function in much the same way, even with fewer people as members of political parties and fewer people voting in elections? It also might not be the most direct way of addressing problems of collective action, as voting in elections does not get directly to the social, economic, and environmental problems a society like the UK faces. More people voting does not lead to more recycling (though frequent voters are more responsive to entreaties to recycle – see Bolsen et al 2014). However, there may be many reasons for increasing political participation alongside the civic acts we describe in other chapters, particularly so that collective decisions can be made by a wider group than a self-selected minority of citizens. In addition, the actions the state takes to involve citizens might lack legitimacy if many of the same people who are expected to recycle more or care more for their neighbours are not represented in the larger collective decisions. Where citizens own the policies made in their name, government seems less technocratic and manipulative when asking citizens to do more (though it is slightly paradoxical that governments manipulate political participation in order to prevent citizens feeling manipulated by government!).

What can public agencies to do to mobilize citizens? Here there are some different choices. In the think camp, the task is about using deliberative mechanisms to promote citizen interest and engagement with politics. From this perspective, the key to raising citizen interest is through creating open forums and arenas whereby citizens may debate issues and make decisions about public policy, preferably on equal terms with each other. By giving citizens a direct voice in decision-making, it is expected that citizen interest and engagement would increase. The nudge perspective says something different. It may be the case that citizens are well disposed to participate, thinking that voting in elections is a good thing, as are other forms of participation in politics, but, for a variety of reasons to do with busyness and forgetfulness, they fail to do them. What citizens need is a cue or encouragement that gets them to participate and which they appreciate. In some ways, this is similar to the canvassing argument made in Chapter 3, that citizens can be encouraged to do something civic (such as recycle their waste) by someone knocking on their doors and seeking their views on the subject.

To make this argument, this chapter first reviews the experimental literature on citizen mobilization, then reports an experiment that we carried out to mobilize citizens. It concludes by reviewing the potential of nudges to raise political participation.

What do we know about mobilizing to vote?

Voting usually draws on long-term factors that draw people into politics, such as the influence of parents and the family context. Of critical importance is socio-economic background, such as age, sex, ethnicity, and income, all of which combine to give individuals more resources for getting involved and developing an interest in politics (Pattie et al 2005). In attempting to mobilize people to vote, it is not possible – at least in the short term – to change the level of resources associated with socio-economic status, though it may be possible to tailor campaigns to take account of different socio-economic groups in society. More likely to change is the response of individuals to the strategic context in which they vote, such as the closeness of the race, which has a well-known effect on turnout. Voters go to the polls when they think the margins are close. However, it is not possible to manipulate this, except through a change to the electoral system, and that argument is beyond the scope of this book. It would be possible to manipulate the information voters get about the closeness of the electoral context, for example by deliberately informing them that a race is close. But this would raise ethical concerns and it is better to accept the electoral context as it is, and to appeal to voters' interests and their sense of duty in relation to voting.

Gerber, Green, and colleagues tested for the effects of Get Out the Vote campaigns in a series of pioneering field experiments, which show that face-to-face contact from a non-partisan source, carried out by members of a field force calling at the homes of citizens and seeking to persuade them to vote, can increase voter turnout (see Green and Gerber 2015). Further experiments find that telephoning has an impact, ranging from ineffective to positive, depending on the nature of the call. There are positive, if weaker, results for other forms of intervention, such as door postings and leafleting, none for email, and weakly positive or null, and even negative, impacts from rote telephoning (Green and Gerber 2015). Many of these results derive from single cases or from a limited number of research sites; however, the collating of these findings allows political scientists to be confident of the impacts, such as in a meta-analysis (see Green et al 2013). Although Get Out the Vote studies of this kind cannot adjudicate authoritatively on why the nudge works, the difference in impact between the types of intervention, in particular the greater success of personalized messages, implies that it is the personal and face-to-face basis of influence that has an effect, rather than the types of message received and the simple provision of information. This finding suggests a nudge needs to be personal to work.

What is the intervention?

Most Get Out the Vote experiments have been carried out in the US, which means that, even with its variety of groups and locations, it is not possible to draw conclusions about interventions in the UK context. For a greater degree of universality, interventions in non-US research sites can ascertain whether the impacts of voter mobilization interventions may be generalized comparatively. In addition, they can appraise the strength of effects discovered in the US, and find out the extent to which context matters in the efficacy of Get Out the Vote campaigns. In this chapter we report on an experiment implemented in the campaign period before the UK General Election of 5 May 2005, which compared door-to-door and telephone canvassing using the same study design (see John and Brannan 2006, 2008).

We opted for Wythenshawe and Sale East in Manchester, which had a turnout in the 2001 General Election of 48.6 per cent, much lower than the national average of 59.4 per cent. It also had a very safe majority for the sitting Labour Member of Parliament, which protected us from any allegation of seeking to influence the outcome – as well as the level of turnout – of the election in that constituency. On the other hand, a safe seat presents its own problems because, from a short-term perspective, it is not instrumentally rational for voters to go the polls if the outcome is predetermined, and this context favours justifications based on civic duty rather than those that appeal to the likely impact on outcomes. In practice, we did not find any voters in Wythenshawe who raised this problem directly.

We included in our sample the registered voters for whom we were able to obtain landline telephone numbers. We randomly selected three groups of 2,300 from the 9,976 available for the treatment and control groups. We selected one treatment group to receive the telephone call (the telephone group); the other to receive the visit (the canvassing group). We had no contact with the control group. We sent letters to everyone in the treatment groups to forewarn them of the imminent contact. In the letters we badged ourselves as a university Get Out the Vote campaign – a non-party political group supported by the McDougall Trust, interested in increasing electoral turnout. The letters advised recipients that we would be contacting them to discuss voting and provided contact details to enable recipients to register any concerns.

The door-to-door canvassing was coordinated by the Institute for Political and Economic Governance, a University of Manchester research institute. The canvassers were predominantly postgraduate students who were enthusiastic about raising electoral turnout, had a good knowledge of the research topic, and had an interest in the objectives of the project. As well as offering training and setting up procedures to ensure their safety, we devised a script for the canvassers and callers to work from, which we modified after the pilots for both canvassing and telephoning. This was intended as a guide to be used in a fairly informal conversation, rather than a text to which they should rigidly adhere. In the course of the conversation, which was planned to last up to five minutes, the callers and canvassers were instructed to ask three questions, generally speaking: Do you think voting is important? Do you intend to vote? And will you be voting by post?

However, the main purpose of the conversation was to persuade the citizen to vote, both by providing reasons that it is important and by attempting to respond to any concerns about the voting process. The reasons we provided for the importance of voting are shown in Table 5.1.

For twelve days over the two weeks prior to the General Election,

Table 5.1   The script for the telephone and door-to-door canvass

It keeps our democratic system working. If not many people voted it could threaten our democracy. Turnout has been falling in recent elections and was only 59 per cent in the last general election.

Earlier generations fought for the right to vote and in many countries people are still fighting for that right.

Voting gives you a voice and a chance to express your views about issues which affect your life. You *can* influence the outcome and politicians have to listen to communities where more people turn out to vote as their position depends on those people.

Voting is easy to do. It doesn't take much time or effort but it is your chance to make a difference.

canvassers knocked on doors, following pre-assigned routes around the sample addresses in the constituency. They conducted brief conversations with named contacts and attempted to persuade them of the merits of voting. The results were recorded on the sheets we provided. Time and resources permitting, the team carried out repeat visits if the initial attempted contact had been unsuccessful.

The telephone calls were conducted by a local survey company, Vision TwentyOne, and took place between 20 and 27 April 2005. The callers used the same script as the canvassers, thus enabling a comparison of the impact of each method. They made up to two repeat calls with a response rate of 47.8 per cent. Turning now to the telephone interviews, there was a lower response rate of 43 per cent, caused by fewer people being available or answering, as well as a higher number refusing to participate (see Figure 5.1).

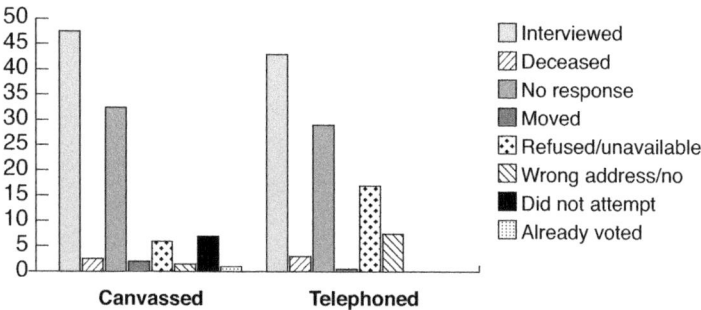

Figure 5.1 Responses to door-to-door and telephone canvassing

What did we find?

After removing postal voters and registered deceased from the three groups, checking the official marked electoral registers yielded the turnout rates for control and treatments groups, reported for canvassing in Figure 5.1.

The voter turnout figure in the non-contacted canvassing treatment group is slightly lower than the control group, which is a slight contrast to the telephone group and to US studies, which have turnout at the same rates. This difference does not affect the estimation of the treatment effect because of the procedure we adopt for its calculation.

When turning to the difference between the voting rates of the treatment and control groups, as shown in Figure 5.2, as expected we find differences from the interventions: turnout is 55.1 per cent in the canvassed group, 3.6 per cent higher than the control group at 51.5 per cent; and there was turnout of 55 per cent for telephoning, a similar figure of 3.5 per cent higher than turnout in the control group. This figure is known as the 'intent to treat' effect. We cannot, however, make inferences about the impact of the interventions from

Nudge, nudge, think, think

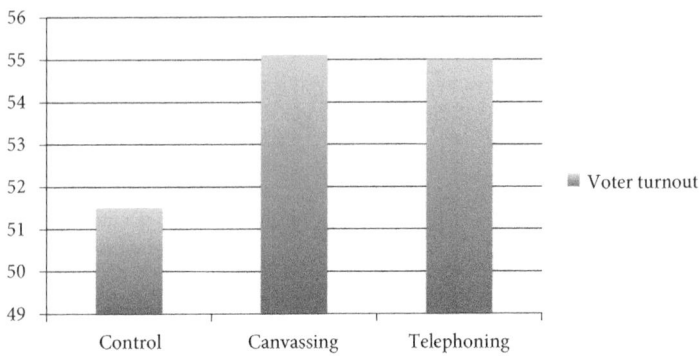

Figure 5.2 Voter turnout rates in Wythenshawe after the intervention (%)

these figures because they contain electors whom we were unable to contact. To calculate the treatment effect, we report the calculations from a well-known procedure elaborated by Gerber and colleagues (Gerber and Green 2000), who subtract the turnout rate of the control group from that of the treatment group, then divide by the contact rate. This estimates the effect of the canvassing to be 6.7 per cent and for telephoning to be 7.3 per cent. Overall the experiment was a success, as both interventions had positive, strong, and statistically significant impacts, as well as the effective implementation of the two campaigns. The treatment effect of 6.7 per cent from canvassing is in the same margins as the US studies; but the effect of 7.3 per cent from telephoning is in excess of Gerber and Green's original negligible estimates. However, more recent studies produce higher estimates closer to ours. Nickerson revises the expectations of telephoning in the Gerber and Green research by drawing attention to its extensive use in the commercial sector and the opportunities for volunteer telephone banks (Nickerson 2006). Nickerson carried out a series of experiments using volunteer telephoning that involved personalized, chatty, and informal calls, producing an average treatment effect of

3.8 per cent. Although Nickerson concludes by saying that on average 'volunteer phone calls are roughly half as effective as face-to-face meetings', the range of treatment effects is between 0.5 and 9.3 per cent, which puts the UK experiment within the upper range. In addition, our results have large standard errors because of relatively small sample sizes, which also place the estimates closer to those in the US. Nonetheless, the impact of telephoning is still high and also comparable with our canvassing effect. This experiment in the UK 2005 General Election is a successful replication of the field experiment method pioneered by Gerber and Green, both in its practical implementation and its results.

It might be argued that such effects are short-lived, but it is possible that voters who are mobilized by a campaign continue to turn out in a subsequent election. It thereby tests the extent to which they gain the habit of voting (Gerber et al 2003). The research (Cutts et al 2009) examined electoral registers for these voters in Wythenshawe for the 2006 English local elections. Descriptive statistics show that the downstream effect of the treatment was quite small at 3 per cent in 2006. But the habit effect was large. Voting in 2005 raised the probability of voting in 2006 by more than half. Regression analysis confirms the size of the habit effect. This is an important finding and shows that the effect of nudge is not just one-off, but continues into the future as citizens get into the habit of acting pro-socially.

What is the lesson?

The lesson of the 2005 experiment and the follow up, as well as that of more than 200 voter mobilization experiments done in the US (Green and Gerber 2015), is that light-touch contacts with citizens can have treatment effects of between 3 and 7 per cent, depending on the context and the type of intervention. That is, simply on the basis of a phone call or a conversation on the door step, citizens can carry out the public-spirited act of voting, which is at low cost to them, but reinforces the wider role they have as citizens. The effects are relatively modest, but it is inexpensive, making it an effective nudge form of intervention. In fact, canvassing may be just one among many ways to mobilize citizens: interventions that apply social pressure by informing neighbours of each other's turnout will increase the effect of treatments quite considerably (Gerber et al 2008). We investigate some of these interventions in the next chapter, when translated into e-petitions and donations.

The message of this chapter is that the nudge clearly works when getting citizens to participate more. The idea is that providing a cue to citizens that reminds them of their civic duty can have an impact on their behaviour. There is also a downstream effect of about 50 per cent which shows it is long lasting. The intervention we describe in this chapter is not costly: organizing a door-knock and measuring the impact cost about £18,000. But the effect of this light-touch intervention is not trivial as it can raise voter turnout by about 7 per cent. The implication of these findings is that it does not take much to alter political participation, and it may be done through changing the type of contacts between the state and citizens in the form of making personal contacts. The nudge can mobilize citizens in positive ways.

Further reading

The best review of Get Out the Vote experiments is Green, D. P. and Gerber, A. S. (2015), *Get Out the Vote! How to Increase Voter Turnout*, 3rd ed., Washington, DC: Brookings Institution Press. Also useful is Gerber, A. and Green, D. P. (2018), 'Field Experiments on Voter Mobilization: An Overview of a Burgeoning Literature', in

Handbook of Economic Field Experiments, Duflo, E. and Banerjee, A. (eds), Elsevier Science. A useful meta-analysis of GOTV experiments is Green, D. P., McGrath, M. C., and Aronow, P. M. (2013), 'Field Experiments and the Study of Voter Turnout', *Journal of Elections, Public Opinion and Parties* 23:1, 27–48.

6

Petitioning

Why study petitioning?

The last chapter reviewed some traditional ways of mobilizing citizens through a door-to-door knock or a telephone call. Even though traditional methods remain important, as the prominence of social media in the 2017 General Election campaign shows, digital forms of communication are now dominant as the ways of carrying out a whole range of personal and group activities linked to community action, and are a natural route for people to get involved in politics. Mobilization through the internet is powerful because of its ability to provide real-time feedback about what other people are doing; it may produce a kind of social pressure that encourages people to participate (Lupia and Sin 2003, Margetts et al 2015a). The internet scales up this kind of social incentive, while minimizing the cost.

In terms of politics and social action, the internet reduces the costs of participation and so should make participation an easier and more frequent occurrence. It also means that, given the large amount of information to which individuals are likely to be susceptible, the way in which information is presented may provide an opportunity for nudge. The relevant aspect of the internet is that information can be manipulated by the way it is presented on-screen. There are also technical features of the internet which allow for real-time feedback that is very hard to achieve in the offline world. This can be set up to promote interactions between citizens, for example for the purposes of deliberation, which we examine in Chapter 9. The irony this chapter seeks to confront is that, while deliberative democrats have seen the internet as a potential for citizen mobilization, in fact it may be better able to deliver discrete nudges to mobilize citizens.

From the policy-maker's point of view, there is an additional argument. The traditional forms of mobilizing are complicated to organize. It is also hard to work out what it is about mobilizing that works – is it the provision of information, or is it the personal contact, or is it persuasion? The argument of this chapter is that through the internet, where information technology is very close and in everyday reach of most citizens, there is an opportunity to reach many more citizens than face-to-face methods.

In this experiment we test the hypothesis by examining the social incentives that are at work when people are deciding whether to participate in something. Specifically, we look at how individuals use information about the participation of others as a way of making their decision about whether to participate or not. When such participation takes place online, there is a far greater possibility of the potential participant receiving real-time feedback about how many other people have participated, and this is something that someone who signs a petition in the street, or throws money into a charity collector's bucket, is unlikely to receive. Furthermore, new types of social information become available through recommendation systems (as used by Amazon to tell people about other preferences of people who have bought a certain book), reputation systems (as used by eBay to rate the trustworthiness of participants) and user feedback applications. Such applications are most prevalent in the private sector, but have high potential to be applied to political and social activity. The internet, therefore, changes the information environment in which people decide to participate (Bimber 2003, Benkler 2006).

We report on a laboratory-based and a quasi-field experiment to investigate the effect of social information in this changed environment. In both experiments, subjects were asked to sign petitions and to donate a small proportion of their turn-up fee to the cause of the petition. The experiments investigated whether seeing the numbers of other people signing (as opposed to not seeing that) influenced the willingness to sign and contribute, how the actual number of other people participating influences willingness to contribute, and the direction of that influence.

What do we already know?

Experiments provide the best way to evaluate how different kinds of social information affect participation, as the treatments can be manipulations of the kind of information on offer, something that is highly tractable with current internet technology although there is little other experimental work tackling this question. The main example is the experiments of Best, Krueger, and Ladewig, which show that the public perceives online activities (such as volunteering time, donating money, and signing a petition) to be riskier (in terms of an adverse consequence such as stolen personal information arising) than comparable offline activities, suggesting this as an explanation for low levels of online participation in comparison to offline environments and contrary to the hopes of some observers (Best et al 2007: 15). Similarly, Oostveen and van den Besselaar report experiments that test the impact on voting behaviour of the perceived security of electronic voting systems, showing that the more trusted and secure a voter perceived a technology to be, the more likely they were to vote more radically (Oostveen and van den Besselaar 2004, 2006). Xenos and Kyoung carried out a controlled test of the effects of youth-oriented political portals, finding only weak effects for exposure to such portals on self-reported cognitive engagement with election information (Xenos and Kyoung 2008). Hallam (2016) argues that the internet can help overcome the collective action problem by facilitating conditional commitment designs on Pledgebank, Kickstarter, and The Point/Groupon websites. Hale et al (2018) use the occasion of a change in the design of the UK petitions platform allowing for more feedback which shows how the gradient of participation changes from this exposure to more information mediated by the internet: some people participate much more when the social information is high, while others are discouraged when the feedback is low. Margetts et al (2015b) find that the internet allows non-charismatic leaders to kickstart collective action. Overall, there is good evidence that internet communications which promote social interaction affect political participation, often in an upward direction.

What was the intervention?

The purpose of our experiments was to test how social information provided via the internet affects collective action (see Margetts et al 2011). Does such information result in social pressure and is such social pressure maximized when numbers are small (so that an individual feels their action to be more noticeable) or large (so that an individual feels more bombarded with social pressure and other social incentives)? Our expectation was that information about the preferences of others would affect people's decision whether to incur costs in the pursuit of collective action. If people know (for example) how many people have signed a petition, we hypothesized that it would affect their willingness to sign or to incur other costs in the pursuit of the petitioned issue. We believed that in the earliest stage of a petition, there would be a very rapid joining in response to feedback information, as people would feel that their contribution would make a difference. In the later stages of the petition, we would then expect the information to have little – or even a negative – effect, as people would feel that their participation would not make much difference. At a certain point, when critical mass is reached, the information would again have a dramatically positive effect because high numbers of other signatories would exert a social pressure on individuals to sign.

The experiments tested these hypotheses by exploring the effect of being given information about the mobilization of others on any one individual subject's willingness to incur costs in supporting a collective issue. In the first lab-based experiment, 47 individuals were randomly recruited from OxLab's subject database (which includes both students and non-students from the city of Oxford). We provided both groups with a list of six petitions that were active at the time of the experiment on the petitions site of the Prime Minister (now at www.gov.uk/petition-government). First they were asked whether they agreed with the issues being petitioned for; second, they were asked to browse the internet during ten minutes in order to inform themselves about the given petition's issue; and third, they were asked whether they (a) would sign the petition on the issue and (b) whether they would donate a small proportion of their participation fee towards supporting the issue (or against the petition if they declined to sign it). Participants were divided into two groups: individuals assigned to the treatment group received information about how many people had signed the petition (petitions had varying numbers of signatories – data were drawn from real petitions so there was no deception involved), whereas those in the control group received no such information.

As we sourced the petitions from the No. 10 Downing Street website, access to it was blocked during the experiment to prevent those in the second treatment from finding this information. Participants provided socio-demographic information, attitudes, perceptions of the experiment, and levels of internet ability in a post-experiment questionnaire. They were incentivized to participate by a payment of between £12 and £15, depending upon the amount they chose to donate to the various causes. All personal information was fully anonymized and no addresses were collected.

Participants were asked to consider six petitions. These addressed the following issues (the number of signatories provided to the treatment group is shown in brackets):

1. To introduce a tax on plastic carrier bags (665,768).
2. To exert pressure on the Japanese government to halt its programme of whaling (9).
3. To create a new public holiday, the National Day of Remembrance (369,492).
4. To provide free prescriptions for asthma sufferers, unrelated to income (11).
5. To employ a policy of an opt-out system (instead of opt-in) for organ donation (1,234,117).
6. To scrap the introduction of compulsory identity cards (6).

In order to avoid using deception in the experiment, subjects were presented with existing petitions and their actual numbers of signatories. They did not actually sign the petitions during the experiment, but were provided with the opportunity to do so after its completion. All the money raised by the subjects during the experiment was donated to the respective causes by the research team after the experiment.

The quasi-field experiment used a larger subject pool: 668 people, contacted and recruited from OxLab's subject database, who participated in the experiment remotely using their own internet connection. Through a web interface we designed, participants were asked to consider six issues successively and for each: (a) to express their willingness to sign a petition supporting the issue; and (b) to donate a small amount of their participation fee to supporting the issue (or against the petition if they declined to sign it). In order to sign a petition subjects were required to provide name, email, and address. While they did not really sign the petition, this meant they had to incur some costs to support their statement. Participants could donate 20p towards every issue and the sum was then doubled by the experimenters. Individuals were randomly allocated across a control group (of 173) and a treatment group (of 495). All participants received the same six petitions but carrying different social information. In the control group, participants received no information about other people signing. In the treatment groups, people were shown two petitions in each of the following categories:

1. Petitions with a very large numbers of signatories ($S > 1$ million);
2. Petitions with a medium numbers of signatories ($100 < S < 1$ million);
3. Petitions with very low numbers of signatories ($S < 100$).

The sub-treatment groups were as follows:

Group B (164) received two 'low-numbered' petitions, two 'high' and two 'middle';
Group C (171) received two 'middle-numbered' petitions, two 'low' and two 'high';

Group D (160) received two 'high-numbered' petitions, two 'middle' and two 'low'.

In order to eliminate systematic biases of individual petitions the order in which participants were presented with the six petitions was randomized.

We incentivized the participants with a small payment (£6–£8), which varied according to the amount they chose to donate, which we paid with Amazon.co.uk vouchers. There was a pre-experiment questionnaire to establish the extent to which participants agreed (or not) with the issues in the petitions. Again, we anonymized all subject information and did not collect addresses. The petitions were as follows (with the high, medium, and low numbers provided shown in brackets):

1. National governments should put pressure on the Chinese leadership to show restraint and respect for human rights in response to protests in Tibet (High: 1,682,242, Medium: 1,189, Low: 76).
2. National governments should negotiate and adopt a treaty to ban the use of cluster bombs (High: 1,200,000, Medium: 330,000, Low: 7).
3. Governments should lobby the Japanese government to stop commercial whaling of the humpback whale (High: 1,082,808, Medium: 57,299, Low: 98).
4. Governments should support a stronger multinational force to protect the people of the Darfur region of Sudan (High: 1,001,012, Medium: 5,978, Low: 16).
5. World leaders should negotiate a global deal on climate change (High: 2,600,053, Medium: 575,000, Low: 53).
6. Governments should work to negotiate new trade rules – fair

rules to make a real difference in the fight against poverty (High: 17,800,244; Medium: 22,777, Low, 25).

Again, there was no deception. The petitions were shown in generic format (to control for the reputation effect that different web platforms would bring), yet the numbers of signatories shown to the participants were taken from existing online petitions that had been created on these issues with different numbers of signatories (low, medium, and high). The issues were all selected to be of international significance and petitions used were all drawn from across different geographical spaces and points in time (during the last three years). Again, subjects did not actually sign the petitions in the experiment, but at the end of the experiment the interface directed them to a site where they could. The research team made the donations to the causes when the experiment finished.

What did we find?

As there were six petitions in both laboratory and field, we stacked the data so as to examine the variation according to the numbers of signatories that subjects could see before signing, which yielded a total of 282 person-petitions for the laboratory and 4,008 for the field. In the initial lab-based experiment, we found that 59 per cent of petitions were signed overall: 54 per cent in the control group and 63 per cent of the treatment group (those who received information about other people signing), indicating a 9 per cent point difference between the treatment and control groups. We identified one issue (out of six) where people were significantly more likely to sign a petition if they received information that many others had signed than if they received no information. This petition was the one supporting an opt-out system for kidney donation, the only one for which the number of signatures was over a million (1,234,117), suggesting a possible hypothesis that the threshold at which social information makes a difference could be one million. Across the six petitions there was a positive correlation with the number of other signatories (for high numbers) and an individual's likelihood of signing. The numbers of subjects were too small to come to firm conclusions about the distribution of effects on people's likelihood to participate. But the identification of a distinct effect for high numbers on the propensity to sign and a weaker effect of medium numbers on propensity to donate (see below) fed into the design of the larger quasi-field experiment.

For the quasi-field experiment, 61.5 per cent of the petitions presented to the control group were signed. Of the petitions presented with low numbers, slightly less (−0.9 per cent) were signed, and for those presented with medium numbers, slightly more (+1.9 per cent) were signed. For those presented with high numbers, 66.7 per cent were signed (that is, 5.2 per cent more than in the control group), and this result is statistically significant. The percentage of participants signing each petition is shown in Figure 6.1, compared with the proportion of people signing in the control group (shown as the baseline). The figure shows clearly that for all petitions, high numbers had a positive effect. This is statistically significant for the climate change and fair-trade petitions. This effect was strongest for the petition on fair trade, which also had by far the highest number of signatories in this category (17.8 million), leading to a possible hypothesis that the effect of high numbers varied according to the magnitude of the number of other signatures. But when we tested this hypothesis we found no effect.

A stronger test for the actual willingness of a subject to support a petition is whether or not the subject would also commit to a donation. This would cost the subject real money and was a chance

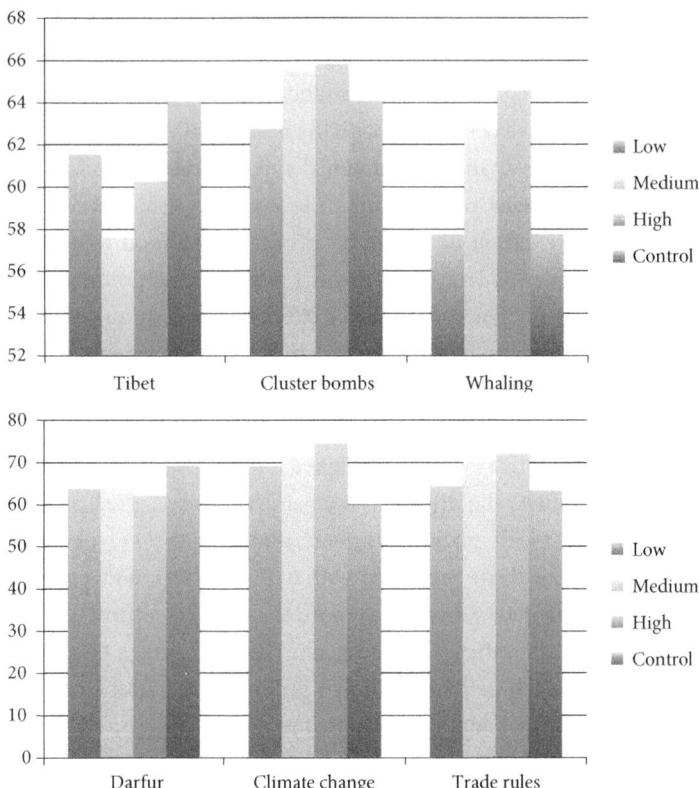

Figure 6.1 Subjects signing petitions in field experiment (by number of other signatories)

to put their money where their mouth is. On average two-thirds of those who signed a petition went on to donate. Interestingly, an as yet unexplained feature of the patterns of donation is that for each petition in the larger experiment, almost exactly two-thirds of those who signed subsequently donated, suggesting a general relationship. Even with the rather different experimental set-up and much smaller numbers in the laboratory experiment, a similar effect could be observed. Here the effect of the numbers was less clear, but low numbers had a negative effect in most cases except the petitions on whaling and on Darfur, and high numbers had a small positive effect in all but one (the petition on cluster bombs). The difference between signing and donations is interesting, possibly due to the fact that fewer people donate than sign (40 per cent versus 63 per cent). It seems that these individuals have a higher threshold for donating and are consequently less influenced by high numbers and more easily discouraged from doing so by low numbers of other signatories.

What is the lesson?

The results indicate we have found evidence that Olson's claims about social pressure in small groups could be extended in a low-cost way to large groups. Internet-enabled social information remodels the cost–benefit equation of political participation. While internet research abounds with claims of how the internet enhances political participation, empirical evidence based on causal inferences is less common (but see Hale et al 2018). These results provide insight into the influence of one type of social information – the raw numbers of other people participating – but there is potential for further investigation into the influence of other types of social information. In our experiments, subjects could only see the raw numbers of other people currently participating, rather than any information about the personality of other participants, their socio-demographic status, or their experience of past participation. Newer features of the internet allow the provision of these other types of information, particularly those associated with so-called Web 2.0 technologies based on user-generated content, which include recommendation systems, reputation systems, blogs, user feedback applications, video-sharing sites, and discussion streams such as Twitter. When used for political activity, these applications allow participants to see many other types of social information. For example, they can see other participants' comments and feedback in real time and information about how people similar to them in terms of preferences have behaved. They can see what other participants are willing to pledge, if other people also participate. These types of social information are likely to have an even greater and more complex effect on political participation. The experiments reported here should be helpful in providing a pointer for future study of the implications of these other types of social information (see Margetts et al 2015b, Hale et al 2018).

This kind of information could also inform the design of participatory initiatives, in terms of when it is good to give information and when it is not. In designing the experiment, we found a huge range of online petitions set up by non-governmental organizations and individuals, some of which gave no information at all about how many people had participated and some of which gave full information. Our findings suggest that there are circumstances where it makes sense to withhold such information (when numbers are below a million) and circumstances where it makes sense to provide it (when numbers are higher than a million), as well as circumstances where it makes no difference.

The phenomena noted in the opening paragraph of this chapter point to the changing scope and nature of mass mobilization, for example in terms of size, geographical reach, and demographic make-up. We do not make any claims about the effectiveness of these mobilizations but their significance remains as an indication of a changed environment for political participation. Understanding this changed world will be a key challenge for political science in the future. In the US, for example, the 2008 election of Barack Obama was massively affected by the accumulation of millions of small-scale activities (such as video-sharing, micro-participation in the campaign, and individual donations) with readily available information about these activities (such as video downloads, activities undertaken and donations made) shaping patterns of participation. Such activities have become routine, such as in the 2016 Presidential election and in the Brexit referendum. Such an increase in political participation is enabled by the vast reach of the internet. In this way, these experiments show the importance of the increasing automation of political activity and the capacity of the internet to provide real-time information about the participation of others.

This chapter and the previous one show that it is difficult to adjudicate between older mechanisms of personal contact and newer ones using new technology. Both are nudge and both work in our examples, with a similar magnitude of effects. But they can be distinguished. Internet nudges are much easier to achieve since they make use of an easier way to provide information than identifying and locating a citizen and approaching them individually with the information. As with other aspects of political participation – and the experiments on mobilizing it – there is an element of self-selection, but it seems internet nudges win out.

Further reading

For an account of the collective action issues raised by the internet see Margetts, H., John, P., Hale, S., and Yasseri, T. (2015), *Political Turbulence: How Social Media Shape Collective Action*, Princeton, NJ: Princeton University Press. For a general account of the internet and political engagement see Bimber, B. (2003), *Information and American Democracy: Technology in the Evolution of Political Power*, Cambridge: Cambridge University Press. Also see Graham, M. and

Dutton, R. (eds) (2019), *Society and the Internet: How Networks of Information and Communication are Changing Our Lives*, Oxford: Oxford University Press. Dunleavy, P., Margetts, H., Bastow, S., and Tinkler, J. (2006), *Digital Era Governance: IT Corporations, the State, and E-government*, Oxford: Oxford University Press, provide an argument about the benefits of e-government and how best to improve contacts between citizens and the state.

7

Giving

Why study charitable giving?

The situations in which citizens are asked to give are numerous and varied: theatregoers are asked to sponsor a seat, parents are asked by schools to give up time to help with the summer fete, and charities seek donations of money or used goods. It seems that many organizations are on the lookout for the best ways to persuade citizens to donate time, money, and other personal resources that assist the public good. Many of these examples are not controversial, but rather are widely accepted as the right thing to do: most people like to be the kind of person who gives money to charity, gives time to the local school, and helps others less fortunate than themselves. But despite good intentions, citizens are busy people, easily distracted, with many other priorities, and so there are many missed opportunities to give.

In this chapter we consider ways in which nudges can persuade citizens to give time, money, and other things for wider public benefit. This chapter starts by looking briefly at the current state of the evidence on what might encourage people to give and, in particular, focuses on two methods that can potentially promote giving: asking someone to make a pledge or commitment that they will later donate; and offering public recognition as a thank you for a donation. We describe a randomized controlled trial which tests the impact of asking for a pledge and offering public recognition on donations of books for schools in South Africa, and we review the lessons of the experiment for nudges.

What do we know about how to encourage giving?

A web of complex and overlapping issues can impact on what might encourage people to give to charitable causes and to help others. We can learn much about what leads to altruism from economics and psychology research. Motives can be divided into three broad categories: intrinsic motivation, such as pure altruism or moral preferences; extrinsic motivation, including material rewards and benefits gained by giving; and image motivation, the chance to signal to others that one is good (Ariely et al 2009). In a similar vein, a strong factor in encouraging altruism is caring about the situation of others: caring can be induced by empathy with the charity recipient and can also arise from moral beliefs. While caring about others is an important push towards giving, donors are influenced by other, less altruistic motives too, and may be dissuaded from giving, for example if to do so goes against the trends in their social group, if they lack the necessary resources, or if they just do not have the opportunity due to situational constraints or lack of awareness (Farsides 2007). People are more likely to donate if they are told beforehand that another donor has already made a substantial contribution (signalling that this is a trustworthy charity to donate to) (Huck and Rasul 2011), or that any contribution they make will be matched from another source (Huck and Rasul 2011). Transactions costs or their perception affects charitable giving (Knowles and Servátka 2015). People are more likely to donate to charity if they are regular volunteers, actively practice a religion, and if they are female, older, and have higher incomes (Saxton et al 2007, Bekkers and Wiepking 2011, Communities and Local Government 2011, Lammam and Gabler 2012). While total overall donations are highest from the richest, donors from lower income groups, on average, give a higher proportion of their income (Saxton et al 2007).

Pledging to give

One way of encouraging giving is to ask for a pledge. Practical examples of how this method is already used to promote giving include the growing number of pledge schemes that have emerged in recent years. Pledge schemes are set up by government or non-governmental organizations to invite individuals to make a public commitment to a behaviour change. Amnesty International's global campaign against violence towards women includes a series of pledge-signing events, where people pledge not to remain silent about abuse. Citizens can pledge to become more globally aware and speak up for the disadvantaged in the Global Citizen Campaign. There are a number of environmental pledge schemes, usually web-based, where individuals can sign up to one or more sustainable behaviours. Other examples are the use of pledges as part of protest campaigns, pledges to be vegetarian and local schemes like Chorley Smile, where residents of Chorley, northwest England, are asked by their local council to sign up to do things that will benefit their town.

Research from psychology suggests that in certain circum-stances people who pledge are likely to act on their good intention. Consistency is an important character trait, with people who behave inconsistently being widely regarded as unreliable and untrustwor-thy. There is strong internal and societal pressure on individuals to behave in a way that is consistent with how they see themselves.

Individuals who make a pledge to behave in a certain way can start to see themselves in a way that is consistent with that behaviour, leading to long-term change in their attitudes and behaviour. The commitment can act as a catalyst, providing the internal conviction for a new identity and leading to behaviour that corresponds with that conviction, which can last well beyond the duration of the commitment. If an individual gives a commitment that they will volunteer, vote, recycle, or not drop litter, it perhaps increases the likelihood that they will later act in a way that is consistent with those attitudes: 'When individuals feel committed to a certain type of behaviour, they will often adopt an identity that is consistent with that behaviour, the result of which frequently is long-lasting behaviour change' (Bator and Cialdini 2000: 536). Their compliance with the original commitment can be enduring, even if they are called upon to act by a different person and some substantial time later (McKenzie-Mohr and Smith 1999). Closely related to pledging are 'foot in the door' techniques: asking people to undertake a small action makes it more likely that they will later agree to a much larger request. Doing the initial small action causes the person to think of themselves as 'the kind of person who does this sort of thing, who agrees to requests by strangers, who takes action on things he believes in, who cooperates with good causes' (Freedman and Fraser 1966: 201).

Field research on whether pledging does lead to behaviour change is somewhat inconclusive. A number of studies have found that asking people to pledge can raise recycling rates, and will raise recycling at a similar rate to other alternative approaches such as incentives or persuasion (Katzev and Pardini 1987, Reams and Ray 1993, Burn and Oskamp 1996, Bryce et al 1997), but it is not clear whether it is the personal contact with the household or the pledging that changes behaviour. A report compared canvassing campaigns with and without pledges and found that the pledge made no significant difference (Thomas 2006). One experiment on giving and pledging found pledges decreased giving, with public pledges increasing the negative effect (Grolleau et al 2018). Pledges are often sought as part of a wider promotional campaign (see for example Ludwig et al 2005 on getting cyclists to wear helmets, and Geller et al 1989 on getting car drivers to wear safety belts), making it hard to distinguish whether it is the pledge or the wider campaign that gets people to change their behaviour. Asking for a prediction of whether they would vote increased the propensity of students to register to vote and then turn out to vote, compared to a control group (Greenwald 1987), but a larger scale replication study, among a broader cross-section of US residents, found that asking for a prediction had no significant effect on voting behaviour (Smith et al 2003). The likelihood of a pledge leading to long-lasting change will vary according to the nature of the pledge: change is more likely if the commitment is voluntary, made in public, and relates to an issue the pledger is already concerned about. Image concern was reported as important in experiment on blood donation by Meyer and Tripodi (2018), though this study, along with many others, reported participants not fulfilling their pledges.

Public recognition of giving

Another way of encouraging people to give is to promise them public recognition as a thank you for a donation. Practical examples of public recognition could be including the names of donor individuals and companies in brochures for public festivals and charitable events, and prominent public displays of lists of sponsors in art galleries, theatres, and community centres. Laboratory experiments indicate that donors appreciate the prestige they get from having their donations made public, and when donations are advertised in categories (for example, gold, silver, or bronze donors), people will more often give the minimum amount needed to appear in a higher category (Harburgh 1998).

Image motivation describes how citizens may be motivated by how others perceive their behaviour: when individuals are seeking social approval, they may choose to exhibit qualities that they think are widely regarded as good. Ariely and colleagues write 'People will act more pro-socially in the public sphere than in private settings' (Ariely 2009: 544). A laboratory experiment found that people were more likely to contribute to charity if their donation was made public, and these results were partially sustained in a field experiment, in which people were more likely to cycle on an exercise bike for charity if the bike was placed in a prominent public position. Interestingly, the study found that when it is made clear that there are monetary incentives to be accrued from behaving pro-socially, people are deterred from making public donations (because the signal it gives is no longer so purely altruistic) but there is not the same crowding-out effect on private donations (Ariely 2009). Get Out the Vote experiments have found that 'social pressure' mailings can increase voter turnout, either by letting people know whether or not they or their neighbours voted last time, inducing shame that their behaviour is observable to others (Gerber et al 2008) or by simply thanking people for voting in a previous election (Panagopoulos 2010). Social pressure has proved effective in improving the response of older people to a health questionnaire (Cotterill et al 2017) and encouraging charitable giving (Bekkers and Wiepking, 2011; Mason, 2015), including with low income and linguistically diverse households (Mason 2016).

What was the intervention?

We undertook a randomized controlled trial to test the effectiveness of these two nudges – asking for a pledge and offering public recognition – on charitable donations (see Cotterill et al 2013, Cotterill 2017 for the research design and results). We were interested to discover whether making a pledge encourages people to give: whether those who are invited to make a pledge are more likely to later donate a book, because they feel they have made a promise and want to see it through. We were also interested in whether households who are advised their donation will be made public are encouraged to give because their generosity will be advertised to their peers. In the spring of 2010 we organized a campaign to collect books for use in school libraries in South Africa. The research was undertaken in partnership with Community HEART, a UK registered charity formed by anti-apartheid activist Denis Goldberg, which supports local self-help initiatives in South Africa (registered charity number 1052817). Community HEART collects children's books in the UK and transports them to South Africa, where they are used to set up school libraries (www.community-heart.org.uk/projects/books/books.htm).

Population and randomization

The research was undertaken with 12,000 households in two electoral wards in Manchester, UK. One of the wards was relatively affluent and largely made up of private housing; the other was relatively deprived, with a high proportion of social rented housing. All residential properties in those two areas, both houses and flats, were included in the study. Households were randomly assigned to one of three groups of equal size: a pledge group; a pledge and publicity group; and a control group.

Intervention – a campaign for book donations

Each of the 12,000 households was sent two letters about an upcoming Children's Book Week, asking them to donate a second-hand book to help set up school libraries in South Africa. The letters were of a very simple design, on University of Manchester letterhead paper, addressed to 'The Residents'. The letters contained the same common message:

> Children's Book Week
> Sat 27th February–Saturday 6th March 2010
> Please donate a second hand book
> (in good condition, for a child of any age)
> Manchester residents are being asked to donate a book to help set up school libraries in South Africa. Millions of children in South Africa have no books and we can help by donating books we no longer want. The children's book collection is being organized by Manchester University together with Community HEART. Community HEART is a UK registered charity which supports local self-help initiatives in South Africa (registered charity no. 1052817). They collect children's books in the UK and transport them to South Africa, where they are used to set up school libraries.

After this common message, the wording of the letter was different, depending on what group the household had been allocated to:

1. Pledge group. In the first letter we asked households to 'Please pledge to donate a second hand book' by postcard, email or phone, and we enclosed a pledge card. Regardless of whether or not they returned a pledge, a few weeks later we sent a reminder letter, with details of drop-off points.
2. Pledge and publicity group. We sent two similar letters, asking for a pledge, and in addition told households that 'A list of everyone who donates a book will be displayed locally.'

3. Control group. We sent two similar letters, without the pledge or the offer of publicity.

Outcome measurement

Residents were asked to take donated books to one of six book collection points, three in each area, during Children's Book Week, 27 February–6 March 2010. We chose a variety of different drop-off points, in various locations, including two libraries, a primary school, a children's centre, a cafe, and a community centre. Residents were sent a bag to use for their donated books and each bag had a unique identifier number to allow us to track who had already given a book. Donors could choose to write their name on the bag, or to donate anonymously. We collected the book bags from the drop-off points and for each donation we recorded the donor address, the number of books donated, and the chosen drop-off point. Afterwards, to thank donors, we displayed a poster with the results and the names of book donors (excluding anonymous donors) in all the local collection points.

Were the nudges successful?

The overall response was much higher than we anticipated: a total of 7,000 books were donated. The books were very high quality and included books for all ages of children. 7.2 per cent of the control group gave books, compared to 8.1 per cent of the pledge group and 8.8 per cent of the pledge and publicity group (Figure 7.1).

The response from the pledge group (8.1 per cent of households) was higher than the control group, but the treatment effect was not statistically significant. We can conclude that asking for the pledge on its own possibly has a very small effect on donations, but does

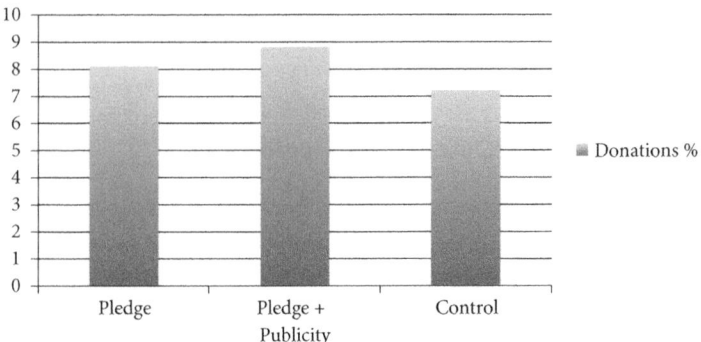

Figure 7.1 Percentage of households donating books from each treatment group

not lead to a significant increase the number of donations. But the combined approach of asking for a pledge and at the same time offering local publicity did lead to a substantial rise in donations and the difference was statistically significant. The difference between the control group (7.2 per cent of households gave books) and the pledge and publicity group (8.8 per cent of households gave books) is 1.6 per cent.

The response to the book collection was highest in: less deprived neighbourhoods; areas with a high proportion of retired residents; and areas with a low proportion of single-person households. After taking those into account, the effect of an area having high numbers of children under 16 or a high number of religious people was not statistically significant. The book collection appealed more to those in the affluent area, which had a close affinity to the university. However, we did not find any evidence that the response to the pledge and publicity interventions differed between deprived or affluent areas (Cotterill 2017), suggesting that these simple nudge interventions may appeal across income groups.

A pledge and publicity campaign could potentially be applied to other situations where citizens are encouraged to adopt civic behaviour. Examples might include:

1. a pledge to undertake environmental action such as recycling, energy saving, or alternatives to car travel, followed by publicity for those who stick to the pledge;
2. a pledge to volunteer or campaign for a cause, with a promise that a list will be displayed as a thank you to those who gave their time;
3. at the neighbourhood level, a pledge to keep to tenancy agreements, followed by publicity for those who stick to it;
4. a pledge to attend an annual workplace blood donation session, with a thank you list of donors displayed afterwards.

The book collection experiment has several implications for a nudge strategy. It is a widely held view in behavioural economics (Dawney and Shah 2005), social psychology (Cialdini 2013), and social marketing (McKenzie-Mohr and Smith 1999) that asking for a pledge increases the likelihood that individuals will later give. This is based on the premise that once someone makes a commitment they start to feel like the sort of person that behaves in that way and they don't want to appear inconsistent to themselves or others. As we saw earlier, commitments are thought to work best if they are voluntary, are made in public, relate to an issue the pledger is already concerned about and are requested as part of a wider campaign. Taking each of these in turn, in our book collection experiment:

1. Pledges were voluntary in the sense that there was no pressure or compulsion to pledge.
2. Pledges were made by sending a postcard or email, or making a phone call to a person unknown to them, who works for a

university, in the knowledge that it will be recorded. While this is not a pledge made in a public place, neither is it a purely private act.

3. We have no way of knowing whether those who pledged were already concerned about the plight of children's education in South Africa. But in the absence of any pressure to pledge, we might assume that those who pledged were either committed to the cause or were interested in off-loading used books. Certainly, many of those who pledged expressed strong sentiments towards the topic.

4. Resource constraints and the need to maintain experimental conditions prevented us mounting a significant campaign. However, as well as posting two letters on the book campaign to each household, posters advertising the collection were displayed in the six drop-off points, and the campaign was branded as part of Children's Book Week 2010.

In this book collection experiment, we found that asking for a pledge did not lead to a significant rise in book donations, over and above a general request letter. A pledge campaign of the sort we organized is not an effective way to boost charitable donations. This finding seems to correspond with many studies reported after our own that pledges often don't work.

The focus of our experiment is on whether pledge schemes are an effective tool to encourage civic behaviour, rather than whether people who pledge are more likely to give. Our research did show that there is a high correlation between pledging and acting; more than two-thirds of those who pledged went on to make a book donation. However, this simple observation that those who pledge often go on to give cannot shed much light on the relationship between pledging and giving, because if we only look at the behaviour of pledgers, without a control group, it is hard to know whether it is the pledge that makes them do it or just their disposition. It is likely that the sort of people who go to the effort of making a pledge are more disposed than others to go to a local drop-off point to donate a book.

Citizens do not act is isolation; our actions are influenced by what others do, what we think is expected of us, and how we want to be viewed by others. In particular, we care about the views of our peers. The promise of information disclosure can have a powerful effect in promoting civic behaviour, by signalling that the actions of an individual will be made known more widely (Thaler and Sunstein 2008). Research shows that people want to be thanked when they participate (Rogers 2004). Too often people do not get thanked for the good things they do in life. In the book collection experiment, the most effective request was to ask people to pledge and to tell them that their name would be posted locally, as a thank you for their donation. The combination of pledge and publicity raised book donations by almost a quarter, from 7 per cent to 9 per cent of households. Asking people for a pledge does not work on its own: it is the pledge and the promise of publicity that together have the big impact on behaviour. Our research shows that people can be spurred on to help others by the promise that their actions will be made public. Our study design does not enable us to say whether publicity without the pledge works on its own.

The response to the book collection was overwhelming: a very simple letter from a stranger on behalf of a small unknown charity to help children in a foreign country caused 1,000 people to donate a total of 7,000 books. Some people purchased new books; others gave their treasured childhood possessions including school prizes; young children were encouraged by parents to donate; and up to a dozen people went on to organize their own collections in schools, nurseries, and workplaces. This demonstrates the power of a simple request: even without the pledge or the promise of publicity 7 per cent of those who were asked chose to give.

The request is most effective if it comes from a family member or friend, but employers and faith organizations can be important mobilizers. Although it is likely that people will respond more enthusiastically to an invitation from someone close to them, mobilization by a local authority can be effective: the invitation both informs the citizen about an opportunity of which they may not otherwise have been aware and conveys that the authority values their opinion (Lowndes et al 2006, Rogers 2004). Indeed, solicitation or mobilization is the most common way of asking for charitable donations (Bekkers, 2005, Bryant et al 2003), and is successful (Bekkers, 2005, Wiepking and Maas, 2009). Policy-makers need also to be aware that too frequent requests can become a burden, lowering donations (van Diepen et al 2009). Faced with many appeals for donations, donors tend to reject appeals, and so it is sometimes difficult for small tweaks to solicitations to have an effect (Bekkers and Wiepking, 2011).

Further reading

Two general accounts of behavourial science and giving are McKenzie-Mohr, D. and Smith, W. (1999), *Fostering Sustainable Behavior: An Introduction to Community-Based Social Marketing*, Gabriola Island, Canada: New Society Publishers (especially Chapter Three, 'Commitment: From Good Intentions to Action') and Kamdar, A., Levitt, S. D, List, J. A., Mullaney, B., and Syverson, C. (2015), 'Once and Done: Leveraging Behavioral Economics to Increase Charitable Contributions', SPI Working Paper No. 025 Chicago. A review – also covering volunteering and making the case for more experiments – is Mason, D. P. (2013), 'Putting Charity to the Test: A Case for Field Experiments on Giving Time and Money in the Nonprofit Sector', *Nonprofit and Voluntary Sector Quarterly*, 42(1): 193–202. A review essay of experiments in economics is Vesterland, L. (2016), 'Using Experimental Methods to Understand Why and How We Give to Charity', in Kagel, J. H. and Roth, A. E., *The Handbook of Experimental Economics*, Volume 2, Princeton, NJ: Princeton University Press.

8

Donating

Why study organ donation?

A shortage of organ donors in many countries has made the issue of organ donation defaults and registration systems the subject of contemporary international debate (Johnson and Goldstein 2003, Abadie and Gay, 2006, Thaler and Sunstein 2008, Moseley and Stoker 2015, Thomann 2018). In the UK, for instance, which at the time of writing, with the exception of Wales, maintains an 'opt-in' system of registration, only 38 per cent per cent of the UK population as a whole was on the organ donor register in 2018, with variation across the 4 countries of the UK, ranging from 37 per cent in England to 46 per cent in Scotland (NHS Blood and Transplant 2018). The overall number of donors, while showing a significant improvement over a ten-year period, still falls short of the level needed to secure enough organs, with over 6,000 people waiting for transplants in 2018. In the US, another opt-in system, 54 per cent of the population were registered in 2017, with 114,000 people on the waiting list (US Department of Health and Human Services 2018). There is a gap between demand for organs and supply in all EU member states, and the gap is increasing in most cases (Eurotransplant 2017).

By joining an organ donor register, a citizen makes a pledge to be a potential donor if their organs can be used for transplantation after they die. The policy perspective is that we need more donors to register in order to ensure that organ supply meets demand. How can we best ask citizens to make a choice about this issue and get donation registration up to levels that will increase the life chances of those many millions who might ultimately benefit from organ transplantation?

In this chapter we begin by discussing different systems for registering organ donors, each with a different default position: the opt-out system, which assumes people are donors unless they actively choose not to be; the opt-in system, where people are assumed not to be donors unless they make a conscious choice to register; and a mandated choice system, where no assumption is made about people's preferences but they are required to choose. We then describe two experimental interventions, which used a combination of nudge and think techniques to attempt to boost numbers of registrations on the organ donor list.

Why study organ donation systems of registering?

The system for registering donors is only one factor potentially influencing whether or not people agree to be donors but research suggests that it is an important factor. Registration systems vary across the world and generally fall into one of two camps. In some countries, in order to be considered as donors, citizens must actively make this pledge during their lifetime by opting-in to an organ donor register. Informed consent or opt-in systems, at the time of writing, operate in the UK (apart from Wales), the Netherlands, Germany, Denmark, Australia, New Zealand, Japan, Canada, and the majority of US states. Citizens are asked to register on a website or by completing a form stating that they would like to become donors, or they are given the option to sign up while undertaking other registration processes, for instance passport or driving licence registration. Typically, the wording of the question in an informed consent system asks people whether they would like to become an organ donor and they simply tick the box to join up. The default position is that people are assumed not to be donors.

The other camp is where people must actively opt out if they do not wish to be donors. These are what is called the presumed consent countries and include Israel, Singapore, the Czech Republic, Poland, Bulgaria, Estonia, Hungary, Latvia, Slovenia, France, Belgium, Austria, Italy, Spain, Portugal, Greece, Cyprus, Norway, Finland, Sweden, and Wales. In these countries, citizens are given the opportunity to opt out through a variety of mechanisms, for instance through an opt-out register, a non-donor card, or during driving licence registration. In this case, the default is shifted, and people are assumed to be willing donors unless they state otherwise.

Interest in organ donation defaults is on the increase because the default position appears to matter: presumed consent countries have significantly higher organ donation rates than informed consent countries. In view of this stark contrast, many countries operating informed consent systems have begun to discuss the possibility of changing their default to assume people are donors unless they opt out. In the section below, we outline some comparative evidence on organ donor levels in countries with different defaults.

What do we already know?

Countries where people are assumed to be willing donors unless they opt out achieve organ donation rates around 25–30 per cent higher on average than countries where people are not assumed to be donors (Abadie and Gay 2006). Even when other potentially important factors such as culture, religion, and organ donation infrastructure are controlled for, presumed consent legislation has a positive and sizeable effect on organ donation rates (Abadie and Gay 2006, Rithalia et al 2009). According to one survey (Johnson and Goldstein 2003), the percentage of citizens actually signed up as donors in those countries operating informed consent systems ranges from 4 to 28 per cent. By contrast, countries with presumed consent systems achieve donor registration rates of between 86 per cent and 100 per cent. In presumed consent countries, it would seem that people don't bother opting out. For countries currently operating informed consent systems and seeking to increase their rate of organ donor registration, a change of system could help overcome the organ deficit.

From a behavioural economics perspective, shifting the default position to presumed consent makes sense. As Chapter 1 pointed out, we know that in the absence of strong incentives to change, people have an in-built propensity to maintain the status quo. Behavioural economists, psychologists, and other social scientists have demonstrated that cognitive limitations lead people to employ shortcuts or heuristics to help in their decision-making. A common heuristic in any decision is to accept the default position rather than make a choice if a default has been preselected on our behalf and there is strong evidence of this tendency (Thaler 1980, Samuelson and Zeckhauser 1988, O'Donoghue and Rabin 1999, Camerer et al 2003). The default position – or status quo – provides the rule of thumb needed when we are faced with decisions that we either want to put off for another time or find difficult to make. Moreover, from a psychological perspective, people are more concerned with losses than with potential gains (Kahneman and Tversky 1979). Where the potential gains or losses of proactively making a choice are unclear, inactivity (that is accepting the default) is often viewed as the most favourable option, costing nothing in time and effort.

Mandated choice, the more neutral alternative, does not operate in many countries, and consequently there is limited evidence about the effect of this type of system on organ donor registration rates. However, one online experiment involving 161 participants conducted in the US (Johnson and Goldstein 2003) investigated opt-in and opt-out defaults as compared to a neutral question with no default. Participants were placed in one of these conditions and asked whether, if moving to a new state, they would give their consent to become a donor. The opt-out condition generated the highest number of hypothetical donors, with 82 per cent saying yes, as compared to 79 per cent in the neutral condition and 43 per cent in the opt-in condition. This study, although based on relatively small numbers, highlights the possibility that a mandated choice system with no default could generate similar numbers of donors to a presumed consent system.

What is the debate?

Should government provide the nudge and shift choice architecture so that people are assumed to be donors unless they opt out? The main argument for change relates to the need for greater numbers of donors and, as we have already seen, presumed consent legislation appears to be positively associated with higher organ donor registrations. A second argument relates to a major problem in organ transplantation. Because of family resistance to donating relatives' organs there is a problem in converting potential donors into actual donors (Spital 1995). Presumed consent systems may help alleviate this. We know that the number of families rejecting requests for donations from their deceased relatives is lower in presumed consent countries than in informed consent countries (Abadie and Gay 2006, Thaler and Sunstein 2008). Research indicates that since the introduction of a presumed consent system in Wales in 2015 the percentage of families giving consent increased from 44.4 per cent in 2014 to 64.5 per cent in 2017 (Young et al 2017). The third argument put forward by the advocates of presumed consent is that survey evidence consistently finds that the vast majority of citizens in Western democracies are pro-donation, with figures of between 65 per cent and 90 per cent found in different surveys (Gallup Organization 1993, New et al 1994). The proponents argue that the default position should reflect the majority view. Lastly, supporters of opt-out systems have noted that opt-in systems do not provide a formal mechanism for those who wish to formally register an objection (British Medical Association 2008).

We can sum up: in informed consent countries there appears to be a gap between people's stated preferences and their actual behaviour, suggesting that failure to donate may be a simple reflection of inertia. A change of system in informed consent countries could help overcome the problems created by inertia and might better reflect the largely pro-donation views held by the general public – while also allowing those who wish to register an objection to do so more evidently.

What is the level of support for a change of system? UK-based surveys report varying levels of support for presumed consent ranging from 30 per cent to over 60 per cent (Department of Health 2008). However, opinion polls do report a general shift in public opinion towards a preference for a presumed consent system (British Medical Association 2008). Members of Parliament are in favour of a change (National Kidney Research Fund, see British Medical Association 2008), and the British Medical Association, the professional body representing the majority of doctors in the UK, advocates a system of what may be called 'soft presumed consent' (British Medical Association 2008), where people are presumed to be willing donors but where family preferences of the deceased are also taken into account. Support for this is growing in the UK, with the Welsh Assembly Government in 2015 introducing a soft opt out system of organ donor registration, and the Scottish government (2018) announcing its intentions to do so by 2021.

Despite growing interest and debate over the introduction of presumed consent systems, many countries persist with systems of informed consent, which may reflect historical traditions and cultural preferences, or could simply be an example of what public policy academics refer to as path dependency. This is a general propensity for policy-makers to continue along a path determined by existing policies that have become institutionalized through legal and administrative structures, practices, and norms. This continues until a certain set of special conditions emerges to spark change (Baumgartner and Jones 1993, Kingdon 1995). Behavioural economists might explain such policy inertia more straightforwardly as a simple case of status quo bias on the part of policy decision-makers.

However, there are valid arguments against a change of choice architecture. Potential difficulties in introducing presumed consent legislation include the risk of eroding public trust in health professionals and undermining the principle of organ donation as a gift, and there are legal difficulties too (Department of Health 2008). Possible legal problems include challenges under the European Convention on Human Rights from families not consulted on the wishes of their deceased relatives. There are also concerns that imposing new systems of presumed consent in countries that do not currently have these without first attaining widespread public support could have a negative effect on organ procurement efforts and dampen general public support for the organ donation process (Fabre 1998, Abadie and Gay 2006).

From an ethical perspective we might ask whether it is right to shift the choice architecture to make assumptions about people's preferences over an issue of such considerable importance. Organ donation is arguably a personal matter, something which relates to one's very bodily integrity and sense of self. This is a hotly debated issue, which has provoked much discussion in medical and ethics journals (Spital 1996, Fabre 1998), and in medical ethics committees (British Medical Association 2008, Cooper 2018). There is cross-national variation in the level of public support for organ donation and so the registration systems employed and stance of public authorities on the issue is likely to reflect this cultural variation (Thomann 2018).

In a mandated choice system of registration, no prior assumption is made about people's preferences, although citizens are required to state whether or not they would like to become donors. The system has advocates in some informed consent countries such as the US and the UK, where the American Medical Association and Britain's Royal College of Physicians respectively have called for trials and studies of the approach. Proponents of mandated choice suggest that the system could represent a more politically acceptable alternative to presumed consent systems while yielding similar registration levels to these systems (Johnson and Goldstein 2003, Thaler and Sunstein 2008). Others also suggest that since such a system would force individuals to decide, families would not be left with the difficult task of second-guessing a relative's wishes (Spital 1995), something which often leads them to refuse consent.

A further argument for forcing people to decide is the private and public discussion and deliberation that would be sparked. The argument is that if institutional spaces are created for people to discuss issues with one another, they may transform their views in a process of learning and deliberation, developing behaviours that are broadly civic in nature. As discussed in Chapter 1, deliberation theorists believe that certain values only come to light in a process of deliberation, critical reflection, and considered judgement. Once these values are allowed to surface, people can – and often do – transform their behaviour in line with these. Groups can create a consensus and the effect of the group itself may exert social pressure on the individuals within it. The public element of the debate, some deliberation theorists argue, should lead citizens to place greater weight on the public good than on individual self-interest (Miller 1992).

In terms of public acceptability, evidence from the UK and the US reveals some support for mandated choice amongst the general public. In a series of deliberation events involving 350 people broadly representative of the UK population, participants ranked mandated choice as amongst their most favoured registration systems (Department of Health 2008). In a Gallup survey of a representative sample of 1,002 adults in the US, 63 per cent of people stated that they would sign the organ donor register under a mandated choice system (Spital 1995). Sunstein (2016a) found a 70 per cent approval rate for a mandated organ donation choice in a survey of over 500 US citizens.

The debate over organ donor registration systems is alive and well, but there is very little experimental evidence on which system might work best in terms of generating more registrations. The Behavioural Insights Team in the UK (2013) conducted a large scale randomised controlled trial amongst people renewing their car tax or their driving licences, to examine the effects of different types of messages to promote organ donation, using nudges based on social norms, loss aversion, and reciprocity among others. Similar experimental research has been conducted in Ontario (Ontario Ministry of Health and Long Term Care 2016). Our first study took a different approach, which was to test out different defaults. We first present the results of this experimental intervention, which aimed to help reveal something about how people might respond to different default positions. We then report an experiment which compared a nudge which combined a number of different messages to a combined nudge and a think. We were interested in how many people would sign an organ donor register when they were asked in different ways.

Investigating behavioural change

The majority of experiments which have related to organ donation preferences have asked people to state their hypothetical willingness or intention to become organ donors (e.g. Johnson and Goldstein 2003, Reubsaet et al 2005, Vinokur et al 2006). Our experiment took a different approach and was instead concerned with the behavioural outcome of organ donor registration. Our aim was to investigate behavioural rather than attitudinal change or mere hypothetical willingness to change.

As we have seen, evidence from observational studies indicates that organ donation registration rates are related to the type of organ donor registration system in operation, with presumed consent countries exhibiting higher levels of registration than informed consent systems. However, as the authors of previous studies concede, confounding factors may explain part of the story. It is possible that countries with presumed consent systems also have a strong cultural preference for organ donation to begin with (Abadie and Gay 2006). Similarly, a combination of factors may play a role in addition to legislation, including the availability of donors, transplantation system organization and infrastructure, health expenditure, wealth, and public attitudes to organ transplantation (Rithalia et al 2009). Observational data therefore has its limitations. As discussed in Chapter 2, without experimental manipulation it is impossible to make causal inferences about the relationships between variables.

The 4,000 participants in our experiment were drawn from an Ipsos MORI panel and were broadly representative of the British population on key demographic variables. They were randomly allocated to one of three treatment groups: an informed consent group (effectively a control group since this represents the current system in Britain); a presumed consent group; and a mandated choice group. Presumed consent and mandated choice represent two different types of nudge. In the presumed consent group, the nudge is to change the default so that people are automatically signed up unless they opt out, while in the mandated choice group people are nudged to register by actively asking them to make a choice. Respondents in each group received an online survey on attitudes towards organ donation. The surveys were identical apart from the phrasing of the final question which asked respondents whether they would like to visit the national organ donation website to join the organ donor register. Each treatment group received a different form of words for the final survey question, reflecting one of the three registration systems or default positions in which we were interested, as shown in Table 8.1. Participants who opted to join the organ register were taken directly to the National Organ Donor Register website where they could register by completing a form. Registration rates for the three groups were tracked by the researchers in collaboration with NHS Blood and Transplant, the national organ donor registration body.

The findings provide the strongest backing for a presumed consent system where the default is that everyone is a donor, closely followed by a mandated choice system (see Moseley and Stoker 2015 for a full discussion of the study and its findings). Of the informed consent group, which served as our control group, 15 per cent (196

Table 8.1   Organ donation registration survey choices

Informed consent group (default = no one a donor)/Control group:
'Please take me to the NHS Organ Donation Website to join the National Organ Donor Register ☐ (check the box if you want to visit the site to register your name)'

Presumed consent group (default = everyone a donor)/Nudge 1:
'Please take me to the NHS Organ Donation Website to join the National Organ Donor Register ☑ (uncheck the box if you DO NOT want to visit the site to register your name)'

Mandated choice group (no default position)/Nudge 2:
'Please take me to the NHS Organ Donation Website to join the National Organ Donor Register (please answer either 'yes' or 'no') Yes ☐ No ☐'

---

of 1,334) clicked through from the survey to visit the National Organ Donor Register website. This increased to 20 per cent (265 of 1,335) when mandated choice was introduced (an increase of 5 percentage points), and to 23 per cent (300 of 1,336) when presumed consent was introduced (an increase of eight percentage points). Statistical tests indicate that there is an association between the treatment group and the number of people who clicked on the website and that this is statistically significant.

What did we find?

However, on the key behavioural outcome measure of interest, the result was much less clear. When we measured the number of people actually registering on the National Organ Donor Register website, less than 1 per cent of the total sample did so, with 0.52 per cent (seven respondents) from the presumed consent group, 0.67 per cent (nine respondents) from the mandated choice group, and 0.3 per cent (four respondents) from the informed consent group signing up. While mandated choice resulted in the greatest number of actual registrations, the registration rate across all three groups was negligible.

What is the lesson?

Based on the number of respondents clicking through to the organ donor website, the first stage of the experiment indicates that employing a default position whereby people are presumed to be donors is likely to generate the largest number of registered organ donors. This is closely followed by a no default position, where people have to make a choice. However, the extra step of having to complete on organ donor registration form online after the first stage of the experiment was enough to deter people from joining. This indicates that any system of registration needs to minimize the effort required on the part of the public. In many informed consent countries, it is common practice to provide the opportunity for people to sign the organ register when they are completing registrations for other purposes – driving licences, identity cards, and so on. In the majority of cases a simple tick box (opt-in) question is incorporated into these. We suggest that replacing an opt-in with an opt-out or mandated choice version could generate a significant increase in organ donor registrations.

As noted in Chapter 1, behavioural economists and nudgers attempt to devise strategies for behaviour change that go with the grain of human nature and our cognitive architecture, taking account of the biases, hunches, and heuristics that influence our choices. Changing the default is a way of altering choice architecture that responds to our cognitive architecture (Thaler and Sunstein 2008). By presenting certain options as the default, governments can steer people towards a socially desired choice. If individuals view the default option as reflecting policy-makers' preferences or those of society at large, this may provide them with the rule of thumb they need to help make their decision.

This experiment shows that nudging by changing the default position can work. We found significant differences in website clicks between those who were nudged and those who were not. Those who were presented with a mandated choice or an opt-out question were significantly more likely to say yes to visiting the organ donor website than those presented with the opt-in question. The legal and ethical restrictions on the experiment meant that we had to offer one further step of completing a full online organ donor registration form. While few of those clicks (from any of our treatment groups) were converted into actual organ donor registrations, the website finding is of interest in itself. While it is only a speculation, it seems plausible that the results would have been similar had the website click itself represented an actual registration.

The implication is that building a choice architecture nudge on organ donation into registration forms, such as passports and driving licences, should help to increase organ donations in countries which are currently using opt-in systems. The key is to make it as easy as possible for people to register, so signing them up while they are filling in the paperwork for something else should work. While many opt-in countries already provide this opportunity, simply changing the default position and the question wording might increase registration levels significantly.

Investigating nudge and think together

Our second experiment was constructed in order to test out nudging and thinking in one intervention, again incorporating a behavioural outcome measure of organ donor registration. The experiment sought to investigate whether a nudge in the form of an information booklet could generate increases in organ donor registrations, as compared to a booklet combined with a discussion. We considered pitting the two against one another in an all-out battle, but after much discussion felt that a think on its own seemed less likely as a viable policy intervention than a combined nudge and think. As we have noted elsewhere, deliberation requires people to absorb information before considering it. In practice, many deliberative events aiming to increase citizen participation involve presenting people with information and a series of options, and asking them to select from among these (see Smith 2009 for a review of deliberative institutions and innovations). Our hypothesis was that the information nudge would increase organ donor registration levels as compared to the control group, but that nudge and think combined would increase registration levels further still.

We recruited 179 higher education students in a UK university to take part in the experiment and they were randomly assigned to receive one of three treatments:

1. a four-page information booklet using techniques from behavioural economics to encourage registration;
2. the information booklet followed by a 15-minute group discussion on topical organ donation issues;
3. an information booklet about swine flu (placebo control).

The information nudge consisted of a four-page tailored information booklet using persuasion techniques based on behavioural economics principles (see Figure 8.1 for an excerpt from the booklet). In line with social influence theory, we included photographs and quotations from other students in support of organ donation. To

Figure 8.1 The information nudge for organ donation registration

generate a sense of peer support for the idea, the booklet highlighted that young people are one of the largest groups of people signing up to the organ donor register. It also stressed that over 90 per cent of the public are supportive of the principle of organ donation and that the number of donors is increasing daily. This was to create the sense of a social norm supportive of organ donation and to encourage participants to follow the trend. Official branding of the booklet by the UK's official organ donation body, NHS Blood and Transplant, enabled us to create the sense that the information it contained was from a credible and trustworthy source. The booklet contained the logo and website address of this body.

Celebrity endorsement with photographs and quotations was also used, drawing on information from the national organ donation website, with the selection of celebrities chosen as those most likely to appeal to a relatively young student population. In line with prospect theory, which allows us to see decisions in terms of choices between uncertain outcomes (see Chapter 1), the booklet also stressed the number of lives lost in recent years because of people waiting for organ transplants, thus emphasizing losses rather than possible life years gained through transplantation. In order to create an information-disclosure effect the booklet signalled the opportunity for people to use social networking sites and twitter to tell their friends about their decision to join the organ donor register. The booklet flagged up a real website, created by the NHS as part of its publicity campaign, which enables people to upload a personal photograph to join a Wall of Life containing photographs of registered donors. People could subsequently add a widget to their own personal social networking space (for example, Facebook) that would link to their photograph on the Wall of Life.

From a purely scientific perspective one might have wanted to isolate the effect of each of these techniques and study them separately. However, putting individual theories from behavioural economics to the test was not our purpose; rather, we wanted to design a replicable and robust intervention that could be used by policy-makers to persuade people to sign the organ donor register. We hypothesized that a nudge combining several persuasion techniques based around some of the foremost theories developed from a behavioural economics perspective could produce a reasonably strong effect on organ donor registrations.

For the think treatment, a deliberation forum was created which involved research participants taking part in small structured group discussions lasting 15 minutes. Groups consisted of three to five people and three short case studies were provided in written format for groups to consider. Each case study highlighted a topical issue related to organ donation. The issues included decision-making about organ donation by the families of deceased people, whether or not everyone should be entitled to receive an organ transplant, and the merits of different organ donor registration systems. Group discussion was led entirely by the groups themselves without the intervention of a facilitator, although researchers were present in the room to ensure that the discussions took place for the correct time period. The aim was to foster debate about controversies relating to the organ donation, to generate discussion about the merits of different types of systems, and to permit critical reflection of the issues.

The control group received an information booklet of similar length to the treatment groups but the topic was an official NHS booklet on the prevention of swine flu. The aim was to generate comparable levels of information processing to the treatment groups and to have a means of checking whether any effect was down to the actual treatments themselves rather than simply being part of a group.

After receiving their treatment, all participants completed an attitudinal questionnaire and were provided with the opportunity to join the organ donor register using an official registration leaflet. The opportunity was presented in a neutral way and it was stressed that registration was entirely a matter of individual choice. Ballot boxes were provided at various points in the lecture theatres, in which participants could post their completed anonymous questionnaires along with any completed registration forms. Alternatively, participants who chose to register could post their own registration forms directly to NHS Blood and Transplant. With the cooperation of NHS Blood and Transplant we tracked the number of students in each group signing up to the organ donor register, following up two months after the end of the experiment thus allowing sufficient time for late postal registrations. At the end of the experiment participants were told how they could de-register if they decided at a later date that they did not wish to be registered.

What did we find?

The results were somewhat contrary to expectations in that we found the information nudge to have a greater effect than the combination of an information nudge and a discussion. Our initial hypothesis was that discussion amongst citizens combined with an information nudge would have a greater impact on organ donor registration than the information nudge alone. We anticipated that the effect of discussion would be to foster commitment to the principle of organ donation.

As outlined in Table 8.2, compared to our control group, participants in the nudge group increased registration by a margin of

Table 8.2   Pre- and post-organ donor registration by group

Treatment group	Registered pre-intervention		Registered post-intervention		Total number in group	Pre–post % change
	%	No.	%	No.		
Control	34	20	64	38	59	+30
Nudge	23	14	57	35	62	+34
Nudge + think	26	15	41	24	58	+15

Table 8.3   Attitudes to organ donation

	Willingness to donate posthumously		Favourable attitude towards organ donation		Intention to register (if not already registered)	
	%	No.	%	No.	%	No.
Control	73	43	86	51	26	15
Nudge	77	48	94	58	57	35
Nudge + think	67	39	88	51	47	27

4 percentage points. Although we did see increases in organ dona-tion amongst the nudge and think group, when taking account of the control group, registrations in the nudge and think group decreased by a margin of 15 percentage points. There is a statistically significant association between treatment group and post-treatment registration rate.

The attitudinal data collected after exposure to the treatments is summarized in Table 8.3. On three attitudinal questions – willingness to donate posthumously, favourable attitudes towards organ dona-tion, and intention to register – the nudge group displayed more pro-donation attitudes than both the control group and the nudge and think group, although the association between treatment group and favourable attitudes was not statistically significant on any of the measures. On two of the three measures the nudge and think group outperformed the control group, although once again these results were not statistically significant.

What is the lesson?

The second experimental intervention suggests that nudging by itself is more effective than nudging and thinking in encouraging organ donor registration. Tailored information booklets, based around behavioural economics principles, created increases in organ donor registrations and were more effective than combined information and discussion. It seems that the added effect of discussion generates some uncertainty. We can speculate about the possible reasons underlying the result. Since the discussions themselves allowed participants to explore the complexity of the topic and reflect in more detail, this enabled them to see different sides of the issue. The discussion topics purposefully raised topical issues that participants in the other two groups are unlikely to have considered. This seems to have provoked more mixed reactions amongst participants, and a debriefing session with the research assistants who facilitated the discussion groups backs this up. For instance, groups raised controversial aspects of organ donation such as providing liver transplants to alcoholics, which may have created some negative views.

Overall, the findings indicate that an information nudge based around behavioural economics principles seems to make a difference in changing behaviour in a controversial and sensitive area of citizen behaviour. By contrast, we find that when citizens engage in relatively un-facilitated discussions about the issue, their response is quite different and behaviour is harder to shift. Our findings illustrate the dilemma facing policy-makers seeking to encourage behaviour change: should they really be nudging citizens in areas such as these that have profound implications for individual liberty? Perhaps these areas are worthy of more sustained discussion and reflection.

Behavioural economists would argue that people often fail to make active choices on these issues largely because of inertia and procrastination, suggesting that citizens just do not take the time to think the issues through. The implication of these arguments could be that a paternalistic state should help citizens make choices by providing them with a steer to guide them in the right direction. However, our research suggests that individual preferences, when

allowed more space to develop following a period of even brief deliberation, may actually be at odds with the policy-makers' priorities. A
potential implication of this is that to help citizens feel comfortable
with their choices, there should be considerable time allowed for
deliberation, education, or discussion alongside nudging. As Saward
reminds us, allowing citizens to reflect on their preferences before
making choices is part of a process of improving the democratic
legitimacy of the political systems of which they are a part (Saward
2001). Perhaps there is an argument here for allowing citizens the
opportunity to help design the nudges in order to increase the legitimacy of any changes to the choice architecture. In the case of organ
donation, a national debate or even a referendum on changing the
registration system from an opt-in to an opt-out or a mandated
choice system might be a useful way forward. This might serve to
alleviate the concerns of those who are opposed to the use of nudges
in this context.

A final point worth noting to end the chapter is that registration
outcomes were significantly higher overall for the second experiment than for our first online organ donor registration experiment,
suggesting that interventions delivered in person may hold greater
promise than online interventions. In view of the relative costs of the
two studies (with the first, the online survey, costing approximately
four times as much as the face-to-face study), interventions delivered
in person may prove a more cost-effective way of generating organ
donor registrations.

Further reading

The best overview of the evidence on presumed consent is Rithalia,
A., McDaid, C., Suekarran, S., Norman, G., Myers, L., and Sowden,
A. (2009), 'A Systematic Review of Presumed Consent Systems for

Deceased Organ Donation', *Health Technology Assessment*, 13 (26), doi: 10.3310/hta1326. For an empirical analysis of the influence of different legislative defaults on donation rates see Abadie, A. and Gay, S. (2006), 'The Impact of Presumed Consent Legislation on Cadeveric Organ Donation: A Cross-Country Study', *Journal of Health Economics*, 25: 599–620. For more detail on the mandated choice option, see Spital, A. (1996), 'Mandated Choice for Organ Donation: Time to Give It a Try', *Annals of Internal Medicine*, 125: 66–9. An example of an educational intervention aiming to increase organ donation is discussed in Quinn, M. T., Alexander, G. C., Hollingsworth, D., O'Connor, K. G., and Meltzer, D. (2006), 'Design and Evaluation of a Workplace Intervention to Promote Organ Donation', *Progress in Transplantation*, 16: 253–9. An evaluation of a recent initiative in Wales is Young, V., McHugh, S., Glendinning, R., and Carr-Hill, R. (2017), *Evaluation of the Human Transplantation (Wales) Act: Impact Evaluation Report*. Welsh Government, Statistical Research No. 71/2017, https://gov.wales/ docs/caecd/research/2017/171130-evaluation-human-transplantation -wales-act-impact-en.pdf.

9

Debating

Why study deliberation and online debating?

In defining think in Chapter 1, we highlight the claim within theoretical work on deliberative democracy that it provides the conditions under which contentious moral and political issues can be dealt with effectively. In a deliberative setting, citizens take the perspectives of others seriously, reflect on their own prejudices, and try to avoid unnecessary conflict (Gutmann and Thompson 1996). This is all well and good in theory, but does it translate into practice? Public authorities are interested in promoting deliberation amongst citizens, with democratic innovations such as participatory budgeting, citizens' juries, deliberative polling, and other such initiatives spreading across the world (Fung 2003b, Smith 2009). The provision of opportunities for citizens to deliberate about matters of public concern is perceived by policy-makers and reformers as a potential response to widespread disillusionment and disenchantment with the political process.

Whether or not particular examples of innovation have had a meaningful effect on the political process, it is undeniable that a number of public authorities are being more creative in their attempts to engage citizens. And with the proliferation of ICT, public authorities are increasingly looking to harness the internet to develop new ways of promoting deliberation amongst citizens. Internet engagement is particularly attractive to authorities because it has the potential to engage large numbers of citizens without the costs (financial and psychological) of bringing them together in the same physical space. There is the possibility of scaling up participation – and, for policy-makers in particular, numbers count when it comes to judging the legitimacy of engagement strategies.

But what happens when deliberation on controversial public policy issues goes online? Does the claim of deliberative democratic theorists, that public deliberation is particularly effective for dealing with morally contentious issues, hold in this new environment? Our experiment responds to the lacuna in social science research (in particular, experimental research) on the use of internet technologies for engaging citizens in the political process. The experiment focuses on arguably the most common form of online engagement: asynchronous discussion forums. The aim of the experiment was twofold. First, to understand the extent to which giving citizens the opportunity to debate controversial policy issues (in this case youth anti-social behaviour and community cohesion) led to changes in policy knowledge and preferences. And second, to analyse the extent to which citizens actually deliberate online and whether their interactions are inclusive and informed.

What do we know about online engagement?

Given that commentators are often quick to claim that the internet is either the saviour or the enemy of democracy, it is surprising that there is relatively little rigorous social scientific research on online citizen engagement with public authorities (rare examples include Price 2006, Neblo et al 2010). The more general literature on politics and the internet highlights a number of issues that present challenges to designing online participation and deliberation. The first is the emergence of a digital divide: not everyone has access to the internet and, once online, not everyone has the same level of proficiency in the use of new technologies. There is a concern that existing political inequalities are reinforced online, or new inequalities are created (Barber 1998, Norris 2001, Cederman and Kraus 2005). Second, even when online, most people do not suddenly become interested in politics. In other words, those people who engage in political discussions online are those who already have a high degree of political interest (EOS Gallop Europe 2002). Third, there is a concern that in the online world, people tend to be attracted to discussions that simply reinforce their already established viewpoints and prejudices: they find like-minded people and avoid those with different perspectives (Sunstein 2006, Dahlberg 2007) – the 'filter bubble' effect. Fourth, when people with different views do come together, the quality of discourse is undermined by dysfunctional emergent behaviours such as strong group polarization (Sunstein 2006, Chen 2013) and flaming (Docter and Dutton 1998, Rowe 2015). Finally, technical problems are common that make interactions difficult, such as informational cascades (Hansen et al 2013), and overload (Losee 1989), and scattered content and redundancy (Klein et al 2007). The preponderance of uncivic behaviour, most strikingly prevalent on social media platforms, offers a significant challenge to the idea that the internet can host inclusive and reasoned deliberation on morally contentious issues.

These are important insights, but they tend to be rather generic in nature: claims about internet engagement per se (see Chapter 6), rather than specific designs for engaging citizens. Recent work on internet-based forums suggests that design is crucial: generalizations about online behaviour often fail to recognize the particular characteristics of different online environments (Wright and Street 2007: 850). As Coleman argues:

> The environment and structure of communication has a significant effect upon its content; synchronous chat rooms and peer-generated Usenet groups are no more indicative of the scope for online public deliberation than loud, prejudiced and banal political arguments in crowded pubs are indicative of the breadth of offline political discussion. (Coleman 2004: 6)

For example, Janssen and Kies have argued that whether the online discussion space is real-time (chat-rooms) or asynchronous (email lists; newsgroups; bulletin boards; forums) has a substantial effect on the way that citizens interact. They argue:

> It is generally recognized that the former are spaces of encounter that attract small talk and jokes, while the latter constitutes a more favourable place for the appearance of some form of rational-critical form of debate since it allows participants to spend more time to think and justify their interventions. (Janssen and Kies 2005: 321)

Other characteristics, such as anonymity, extent of freedom of speech, form of moderation, and cognitive cues are likely to have an effect on the quality of engagement and deliberation (Manosevitch et al 2014, Santana 2014). Institutional design is likely to have a profound effect on the capacity of citizens to deliberate on morally and politically contentious subjects.

Taking an experimental approach to analysing online engagement means bringing together a random selection of citizens. This then directly connects our experiment to the developing practice of mini-publics: democratic innovations based on forms of random selection. The desire to ensure deliberations are inclusive has influenced the design of (for example) citizens' juries, consensus conferences, deliberative polls, and more high-profile citizens' assemblies

(Setälä and Smith 2018). Research on such mini-publics suggests that citizens take the opportunity to participate seriously, and frequently change their preferences in light of the provision of information and opportunities to deliberate. And there is evidence that mini-publics can deal with highly contentious issues. Consensus conferences (most prevalent in Denmark) have deliberated on new and often controversial scientific and technological developments that raise serious social and ethical concerns, for example, the use of transgenic animals in biotechnology research (Joss and Durant 1995). Deliberative polls have been run successfully in divided societies: on Australian aboriginal issues; housing, crime, and education policy towards the Roma in Bulgaria; and educational policy in Northern Ireland. They have been used to try to resolve thorny policy problems, such as decision-making on nuclear power in South Korea in 2017 (Fishkin 2018).

Aside from a couple of experiments where Fishkin and his colleagues have attempted to transfer the deliberative poll model online (Fishkin 2009: 169–75), there has still been relatively little significant experimentation with online mini-publics, particularly in relation to controversial policy issues (exceptions include Iandoli et al 2018, Neblo et al 2018). The results from online deliberative polling (ODP) indicate that the policy knowledge and preferences of participants tend to move in the same direction as for participants in offline equivalents, but that 'changes from online deliberation were less pronounced than in the face-to-face version' (Ackerman and Fishkin 2004: 117; for more detail, see Luskin et al 2006: 17–23). However, the design of the ODP exploits real-time (synchronous) technology that is unlikely to be used in practice by many public authorities due to its high cost and the requirement of specialist software and hardware. More likely, if public authorities are to make widespread use of online mini-publics they will utilize low-cost asynchronous discussion platforms with which they are already familiar. It is such a platform on which our experiment is based.

What is the intervention?

In early 2009, 6,009 members of the Ipsos MORI online panel accepted an invitation to participate in the experiment (Smith et al 2013). They were invited to complete three questionnaires over a three-week period and were told that they may be asked to engage in other online tasks during that period. On completion of the three questionnaires, participants were entered into a prize draw. The cohort of citizens was selected from Ipsos MORI's panel using quotas for gender, age, and geographical location. Given the nature of the panel, we had to accept that the sample was more educated than the general population and that, by definition, they had access to the internet. We were pleased, however, that there was a good spread of levels of internet usage (from occasional to heavy users) and that the sample was representative of the population in terms of political interest.

The 6,009 participants completed a first questionnaire and were then randomly allocated to six experimental groups. Two groups of 1,002 were invited to participate in two discussion forums. The first group started with discussions on youth anti-social behaviour; the second on community cohesion. After ten days of discussion, participants completed a second questionnaire and then swapped topics. After another ten days of discussion, participants completed a third questionnaire and were thanked for their commitment and contributions.

In designing the discussion forums, hosted on specially commissioned boards (using the phpBB 3.0x internet forum package), we included a number of features in an attempt to promote informed and respectful contributions and deliberation between participants. For example:

1. Participation was incentivized with entries into the prize draw each time participants spent ten minutes or more online.
2. New topics for discussion were added every two days and participants were sent a reminder email each time a new topic was added.
3. Participants could log-on and contribute whenever they wished.
4. When logging on for the first time, participants were greeted with a video from the then Secretary of State for Communities and Local Government, Hazel Blears, who gave her support for the project and committed herself to consider the issues raised by participants.
5. Participants were directed to the rules of discussion that stressed the importance of mutual respect to other participants.
6. Participants did not need to give background information on their gender, age, ethnicity, etc. to other participants.
7. Easily accessible background information was in what we called a 'fuel for thought' box on each page: short briefing documents and audio-visual materials, including specially commissioned videos of community representatives offering different viewpoints.
8. Visible (although relatively light) moderation prompted contributions, particularly from those who had not posted, and summarized the arguments to date.
9. Participants were able to easily report any posts that they believed offensive or to have broken the rules of discussion.

While we had advice from some quarters to use a pre-moderation strategy – that is to vet every contribution before it appeared on the site – to ensure there was no flaming, we decided against this strategy on two grounds. First, on purely pragmatic grounds we were attempting to design a process that could be easily adopted by public authorities. Pre-moderation increases costs substantially. Second, we wished to see if the combination of the other design features we had employed would encourage more civically minded behaviour on the part of participants without recourse to pre-moderation, even on highly contentious issues of public policy.

A further 2,002 participants were allocated to the two control groups: these participants only completed the three questionnaires; they had no access to the online discussion forums. This aspect of the experiment's design is essential for the inference we wish to make: that the opportunity to debate – and its practice – has effects on attitudes and knowledge.

In itself, this would represent an interesting experiment: by comparing the discussion and control groups, we are in a position to understand whether the opportunity to learn about and discuss pressing political issues online leads to changes in knowledge and policy preferences, and to observe the extent to which interactions reached the standards of informed and reasoned deliberation. But we added a twist to our experimental design. The final 2,003 participants were allocated to two information-only groups. They were treated in exactly the same way as the discussion groups with one significant exception. The boards had the same features with participants able to post comments. The difference was that they were not able to see the postings of other participants. Why did we do this? In order to investigate the added value of engaging with other participants, how important is providing the opportunity to discuss an issue compared with only receiving information for personal reflection? After all, if there is no difference, public authorities might only need to provide information and opportunities for response rather than creating more expensive discussion forums.

What did we find?

The experiment generated three significant sets of findings for those interested in think strategies: first, who participates in online forums; second, whether there are any changes in policy knowledge and preferences; and, third, the extent to which interactions can be classified as deliberative.

Who participates in online forums?

Not everyone who was invited to participate in the discussion groups took up that invitation. And not everyone who logged on to the site posted. Out of the 2,004 participants assigned to the discussion group, roughly half (1,073) logged on to the discussion board at least once during the study period, with 526 (26 per cent) contributing one or more posts. This means that around half of those who logged on did not contribute to discussions: in the online world such spectators are referred to as lurkers (Janssen and Kies 2005: 331). Having half the participants logging on and half of those posting may appear disappointing: however, given the low levels of political participation across society this could equally be seen as an impressive percentage.

Unlike offline mini-publics, where those who accept an invitation are then directly involved in interactions (they cannot escape without getting up and leaving the room!), the structure of the online world means that there is self-selection in both logging on to the discussion forum and then choosing whether or not to make a contribution. This element of self-selection may undermine the random selection, reinforcing existing differentials of participation (see, for example, Verba et al 1978). To some degree this is what happened in the experiment. An analysis of those who participated indicates that those who chose to log-on or post tended to be older and politically interested. The picture for education is more ambiguous: those who logged on tended to have higher qualifications, but this is not the case for those who posted. For the classic explanatory factors of age, political interest and, to a lesser degree, education, the traditional participation bias is felt: the online world mirrors offline differentials. But there are two important caveats that complicate the picture somewhat.

The first is in relation to gender: women were more likely to make contributions. We can speculate on why this might be the case: the asynchronous form of engagement allows women to engage in their own time rather than the inconvenient times of many public meetings; anonymity may remove barriers; the topics (social policy issues relating to youth and community cohesion) may appeal more to a female audience. Second, and surprisingly, frequency of internet use is not a significant factor. We had expected those participants with more familiarity with the online world to participate more: this was not the case.

Any change in knowledge and preferences?

In deliberative polls, Fishkin and his colleagues find fairly significant changes in policy knowledge and preferences following a period of deliberation (Fishkin 2009). Taken as a whole sample (all 6,009 participants), we find no systematic differences between control, information-only, and discussion groups. There would appear to be no added value of either providing information or opportunities to deliberate online. But this overall finding may hide differences between the significant numbers who decided not to participate, those who logged on to the site, and those who posted. More intense participation may result in differences in policy knowledge and preferences.

By comparing the whole sample with those citizens who logged-on and those who posted we can detect some, albeit modest, differences. Our analysis to date has primarily been on the youth anti-social behaviour boards. Focusing on those participants who logged on, we find no differences in knowledge or preferences when we compare results with the equivalent element of the control group. This is the case for participants in both information-only and discussion groups. However, when we focus only on those who posted on the discussion boards, then we find some modest but consistent differences in relation to policy preferences (but nothing of the order that Fishkin claims for deliberative polls).

As we see in Figure 9.1, the policy preferences of those who posted tend to move away from legal punishment and heavier policing and towards the promotion of better role models and improved monitoring of young people by adults. While there is support for such community-based intervention (over legal and policing solutions), participants are less supportive of the provision of activities or rewards for young people. These weak preference shifts only

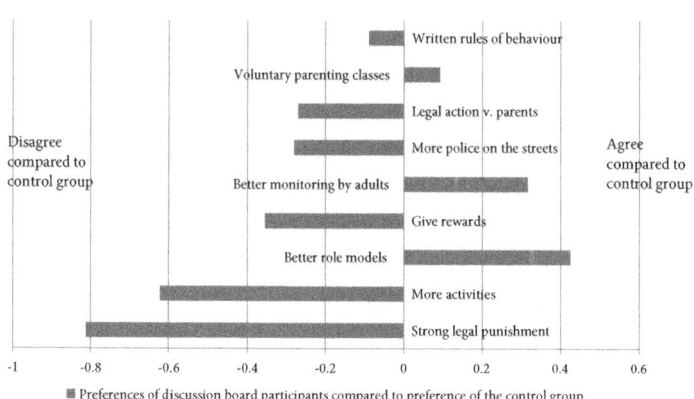

Figure 9.1 Change in preferences by policy question

occurred amongst the participants in the discussion boards, not for those in the information-only groups. But when it comes to policy knowledge, there are again no differences between the two groups. What this indicates is that participation in an online discussion forum can have a modest effect on policy preferences for those who contribute. And that it is interaction in the discussion forums, rather than increases in knowledge, that drives these modest changes. But should this interaction be understood as deliberative?

How deliberative?

The analysis to date offers some indications that the discussion forum might be less than deliberative as understood within theories of deliberative democracy (see Chapter 1). First, we have seen that the discussions that took place online are not fully inclusive, in that there is a significant amount of self-selection. This is not all in the direction of reinforcing traditional political inequalities (particularly in relation to gender), but certainly does not realize full inclusiveness. Second, while we are able to find some modest and consistent changes in policy preferences amongst those who contributed to the discussion forums, there were no changes in policy knowledge. In other words, one of the defining features of deliberation – that it is informed – is not present. Participants may know more about other citizens' views on the issues at hand, but the low level use of background materials by those who posted contributions confirms our finding.

Observing the discussions that took place online gives further insight into the extent to which interactions might be classified as deliberative. On a positive note, the fears of those who believe that internet discussion forums, by their nature, will degenerate into flaming on controversial topics are not confirmed: the two topics – youth anti-social behaviour and, in particular, community cohesion

– are controversial public issues and yet posts typically remained within the rules of discussion established for the forum. Even when contributions might be defined as disrespectful (generally towards those under discussion, not other participants), they were a long way from being overly offensive. There was no flaming and not one post was reported to the moderators for its content. In this sense an online think strategy can deal with contentious policy issues. But while interactions tended to be respectful, there was little evidence of reciprocity or reason-giving, which are significant elements of think. On the threads that we have analysed, participants tended to contribute without recognition of the contributions of others and without offering reasons to back their claims. These findings suggest that the minimal conditions were in place for deliberation, such as mutual respect, but that in actual practice deliberation was not realized.

What are the lessons?

The results of our experiment for those who wish to promote online deliberation on highly contentious issues are mixed. Most importantly they indicate that, if it is carefully designed, a large-scale online asynchronous mini-public can be successfully organized on controversial policy issues. Attention to institutional design can encourage citizens to be mutually respectful, even on challenging topics. This indicates that one of our key findings from a think experiment may actually be about nudge: those who fear that the online world will always deteriorate into flaming need to recognize that pro-civic behaviour cues can be built into the design of discussion forums. The design characteristics of any forum arguably have a significant effect on whether mutual respect will be realized.

Whether we can realistically expect online deliberation to achieve the deliberative qualities of offline mini-publics is another matter. Here public authorities face a number of challenges. First, although a random selection of participants can be invited, those who post are self-selecting. And it is this self-selecting group who experience change (albeit modest) in preferences. Second, the evidence we have provided indicates that this weak preference change is not well-informed: participants tend to go straight to the discussion thread rather than spending time reading or watching policy-relevant background materials. Forcing participants to access information before contributing to discussion threads would no doubt have further reduced participation levels. The differences here between offline and online designs are stark. Offline, we can ensure that the group is representative of the wider population; participants cannot escape being exposed to information; and facilitators can more easily encourage the more reluctant to contribute to discussions. Online, it is simply more difficult to create the conditions for deliberation: participants can decide whether to post; there is little the moderator can do to ensure an equal voice for all participants; and it is easy to avoid background information. While participants may be learning from each other, the failure to increase their policy knowledge raises the legitimate question about the extent to which online deliberation is informed.

Our experiment offers insights into the way in which online discussion forums have very different characteristics from face-to-face forums. Engagement in asynchronous discussion forums tends to be less intense, with participants choosing if and when to engage – and this has effects on the quality of interaction. We have shown that if designed carefully (with serious content, moderation, etc.), participants behave in a civil manner towards each other, even on controversial areas of social policy. However, the design did not encourage changes in policy preferences or increase in policy-relevant knowledge. This indicates the need for further experimental research that varies institutional design characteristics: is it possible to encourage more informed interactions under different sets of conditions? We should certainly not view this experiment as evidence that think does not work! After all, the forum allowed significant numbers of contributions on highly contentious topics with no recourse to flaming. That in itself shows the power of a carefully designed think strategy.

The next chapter describes a design experiment to bring the voices of the socially marginalized into the forum for making decisions.

Further reading

The online *Journal of Public Deliberation* (http://services.bepress.com/jpd) has a number of articles about online deliberation, with occasional experimental work. For organizations promoting think strategies, see the international network Democracy R&D https://democracyrd.org/, Involve www.involve.org.uk/ in the UK, and the US-based National Coalition for Dialogue and Deliberation (www.thataway.org) and the Deliberative Democracy Consortium (www.deliberative-democracy.net). *Participedia* (www.participedia.xyz) is a growing resource for information on democratic innovations. See www.scholio.net/ for a recent project testing innovative argument visualization platforms – a recent innovation. James Fishkin, the developer of deliberative polls, is now working with colleagues on using AI to scale-up facilitation online. Details of his work can be found at the Center for Deliberative Democracy (http://cdd.stanford.edu). There are a plethora of books and articles on this field: see in particular Bächtiger, A. et al (2018), *The Oxford Handbook of Deliberative Democracy*, and Elstub, S. and Escobar, O. (eds) (2019), *The Handbook of Democratic Innovation and Governance*, Chletenham: Edward Elgar.

10

Including

Why study local inclusion?

Decentralization is a common political strategy for public authorities aiming to increase citizen engagement. In theory, bringing decision-making closer to the local population reduces the costs associated with political participation because people do not have to make so much effort to attend meetings and may perceive the public authority as closer to their views and interests. However, decentralization in itself rarely manages to engage the politically marginalized as it often simply reinforces extant political inequalities.

This chapter reports on a design experiment that aims to bring the voices of the politically marginalized into the local forums recently established by a large rural local authority in the UK. One of the first activities of the forums was to consider how the authority engages the local population: the challenge of the experiment was to consider how the voices of the excluded are heard in this process. The research team worked with the public authority to develop and implement a design experiment to test whether electronic media (in this case, a DVD) could be utilized to ensure that the voices of the politically marginalized were brought into these local deliberations.

What do we know about inclusion?

Democracy rests on the principle of political equality. But studies of participation across a range of political activities provide comprehensive evidence that very few citizens actually engage regularly in political action – whether conventional or unconventional – and that participation is strongly positively correlated to income, wealth, and education (Verba et al 1978, Pattie et al 2005). Democracy's unresolved dilemma remains unequal participation (Lijphart 1997). In both elections and consultation exercises, politically marginalized social groups systematically fail to engage. This can have a significant impact on the nature of decisions: if the politically excluded are not present and able to voice their perspectives, decisions are unlikely to fully respond to their concerns (Phillips 1995: 13). While advocates of citizen participation argue for increasing opportunities for citizens to engage, there is reasonable scepticism that this will simply reinforce and amplify the existing differentials of power and influence within society (Sartori 1987: 114, Phillips 1991: 162).

In Chapter 1 we highlighted the development of democratic innovations as part of the broader think strategy: institutions specifically designed to increase and deepen citizen participation in the political process (Smith 2009). There is emerging evidence that such innovations, when carefully designed, can successfully engage those people who are politically marginalized. In the previous chapter we focused on the design of mini-publics: (near) random selection is used to ensure that all socio-economic groups are present. But there is evidence that open meetings can also be designed that reverse differentials in participation. Arguably the most celebrated is participatory budgeting in Porto Alegre. The building block of the initiative is a series of budget assemblies in which 'socio-economic inequalities did not reproduce themselves ... Much to the contrary, the household incomes of budget participants are significantly lower than those of the population as a whole … participants in the regional assemblies were poorer than the population as a whole' (Abers 2000: 122). People in poorer communities have much to gain and so participate in high numbers (Smith 2009: 43–4). This incentive to participate has not always been present as participatory budgeting has spread worldwide and, as such, existing differentials in participation have often been reproduced.

Chicago Community Policing offers another example of how careful institutional design can affect inclusion. In 1995, the Chicago Police Department began holding monthly community beat meetings in 285 neighbourhood beats across the city. In these beat meetings, police officers worked with local residents to improve public safety in the neighbourhood. Evidence suggests that in comparison to traditional forms of consultation, Chicago Community Policing attracted a significant proportion of citizens from poor and less well-educated neighbourhoods, who were able directly to influence local policing strategies (Fung 2003a, Fung 2006).

But these examples buck the trend. In both Porto Alegre and Chicago, the municipal public authority has invested heavily in community outreach programmes and offered substantial opportunities to affect the delivery of local services. As Fung argues: 'disadvantaged citizens will overcome quite substantial barriers to participate in institutions that credibly promise to reward such activity with concrete improvements to the public goods upon which those citizens rely' (Fung 2003a: 115). Most public authorities are unwilling to invest the resources necessary to build the capacity of people in marginalized communities or to restructure decision-making processes so that the direct effect of participation is felt in more effective service delivery provision. Public authorities may have good intentions and wish to hear the voices of the politically marginalized, but the forums they create often fail to motivate engagement on the part of citizens. Where public authorities develop more mundane decentralization strategies (as compared to the democratic innovations that Porto Alegre's participatory budgeting and Chicago's community policing represent), how can the voices of the politically marginalized be heard in local deliberations?

What is the intervention?

Wiltshire Council was created by the UK government in 2009, replacing a series of smaller district authorities and the county council. In recognition of the significant geographical area of the council and the differences in needs of the local communities, the council established Area Boards. These boards are made up of the local councillors from Wiltshire Council, elected representatives from town and parish councils, representatives from other local public institutions such as the police and fire service, and other community representatives. The meetings are open to local people. The aim of the boards is to influence what Wiltshire Council does in the local area and to ensure that decisions about local issues are made locally (www.wiltshire.gov.uk/communityandliving/area boards.htm).

Political leaders and officers at Wiltshire recognized the importance of hearing the voices of the politically marginalized in the process of establishing the working practices of the 18 Area Boards across Wiltshire. Members of our research team agreed to work with the Area Board Team to develop and implement a design experiment that evaluated a mechanism for including the voices of the politically marginalized in the Area Boards as they discussed the ways in which they would engage their local populations. The number of boards being established at the same time meant that a design experiment would be possible, since an intervention could be varied across geographical areas.

Wiltshire Council was not willing to make resources available for significant mobilization efforts targeted at the politically disengaged. In this sense its decentralization strategy mirrors the approach taken by most public authorities: create local forums that are open to local citizens, but with no dedicated outreach strategy beyond the usual adverts and posters. In these circumstances, how do public authorities ensure that the voices of the politically marginalized are to be heard when we know that citizens from these social groups are unlikely to attend in person?

After much discussion and negotiation, the Area Board Team and the researchers decided to focus on facilitating the perspectives of 'those who do not normally engage in formal Council mechanisms'. Board managers were to facilitate Area Board discussions on how to engage the local community more effectively, drawing on a specifically commissioned DVD that presented a range of marginalized voices: from ethnic minority groups, young people, the military, people with disabilities, and others who may not engage for reasons of disinterest, apathy, or feelings of disempowerment. The idea behind a DVD is that it could be used in very different circumstances (not just the Area Boards) and it is a cost-effective initiative that could easily be replicated by other public authorities. The experimental intervention was to be a debate at the first meeting of selected Area Boards facilitated by the relevant board manager on the question of how the board could better engage the local community. This debate would be informed by the views and ideas articulated on the DVD, challenging those present to consider the perspectives of those not in the room. The council commissioned a professional filmmaker with experience in participatory video (Lunch and Lunch 2006) to undertake the interviews; the DVD was

Table 10.1   Brief for community interviews

We are looking at how the new council for Wiltshire could engage more people more effectively in decisions which will have an effect on their lives and communities. This will be a new council that is working closely with other service providers such as Fire, the Police and Health so it really does cover lots of different aspects of local life – from community safety to roads, schools, health and emergency services. There are some really active communities in Wiltshire and we are interested in how local people and groups could be supported to work on the sort of projects and initiatives that would improve the quality of life in the area.

How are your views currently represented? Councillors are elected in each area to represent local people and the interests, priorities and issues for the community. There are town and parish councils in each area to represent these local interests. In some areas, community area partnerships have been established and also groups to represent various interests including user groups for people with disabilities, groups for older people and young people's issues groups. There are citizens' panels run by the council for residents, young people and carers. These are some of the local ways that the council has sought to engage with local people and ensure that all voices within a community can be heard.

But maybe the ways that people can participate and make their voices heard need to be improved? For example, what do you think about how you are able to engage with the council and the other service providers? Are you interested in participating? What puts you off? How could it be better? What would you like to have more of an influence over? These are some of the questions we want to look at. We will create a 20-minute film of your ideas and viewpoints which then can be shown to community groups and councillors and other interested parties to begin to challenge and develop new ways forward in engaging people.

co-produced by the board managers and the research team. The final version of the DVD consisted of different sections or chapters, each with a collection of community voices discussing aspects of engagement with the council. This structure allowed board managers to facilitate discussions around specific aspects of participation: the structure, timing, and location of meetings; and the responsiveness of the council to demands from the community.

The intervention was targeted at six Area Boards. Six further boards with reasonably similar geographical and socio-economic characteristics were selected as comparisons: in these boards, discussions about engaging the local community took place, but without the DVD (and thus the voices of the politically marginalized). Researchers attended the meetings, observing the progress of the deliberations and administering a short questionnaire to ascertain the views of attendees (councillors, officers, community representatives, and citizens) on the impact of the DVD. The design experiment involved iteration, with the Area Board Team meeting with the researchers after two board meetings to decide if the intervention needed to be adjusted.

What did we find?

The intervention had mixed results. One of the challenges of a design experiment is that it is not as decisive and discrete an intervention as a randomized controlled trial (see Chapter 2), which makes it harder to ascertain the effect of the intervention. In attempting to understand the impact of the DVD-enabled deliberation, we must try to separate out the effect of a series of unexpected practical problems.

First, board meetings were held in very different locations, some of which had poor acoustics and/or poor audio-visual equipment, making it difficult for some in attendance to hear the voices on the DVD. Second, the chairs of some boards (an elected representative) wanted other issues to be dealt with and this created long agendas and pressure on time for the discussion about community engagement. This led to a degree of frustration as the item was squeezed inappropriately. Third, some of the participants filmed for the DVD were arguably not as politically marginalized as the research team had expected. While community managers had been given the brief to introduce the professional filmmaker to 'those who do not normally engage in formal Council mechanisms', in a number of cases these were community activists who were well known to some of the councillors. Additionally, in editing the DVD, the community managers tended to privilege the voices of those who could more clearly articulate problems with engagement. The voices of more experienced community activists tended to come to the fore: an example of production values trumping democratic inclusion? An elected member in an early Area Board took exception to one of the individuals on the DVD who he had had personal dealings with, forcing a re-edit, which reduced the DVD's critical edge. But even with these practical problems that placed a challenge on the experimental conditions, the intervention generated some interesting findings.

First, the nature of the debate on community engagement in those boards that used the DVD was more extensive and considerate to the views of the politically marginalized than in those that did not. Even when the reaction from certain participants was hostile to the voices on the DVD, questions of inclusion and exclusion were explicitly raised and confronted. Where the DVD was not used, discussion of engagement was fairly superficial, with little meaningful consideration of how the politically marginalized could be more effectively engaged.

Second, the majority of participants who completed the questionnaire in the Area Board meetings where the DVD was used tended to believe that it had helped their thinking on matters of inclusion and exclusion (see Figure 10.1). There were a number of written comments along the lines that the DVD 'opened people's eyes to what the general people in the community think; real issues described by real people'; that it was 'interesting to have vox pops from people who

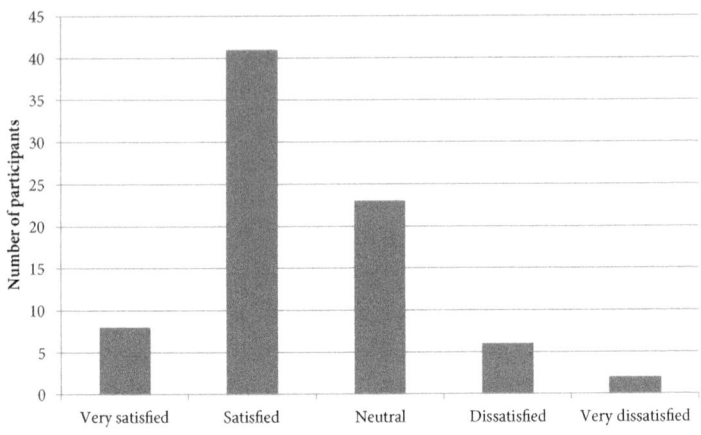

Figure 10.1 Satisfaction with the DVD (number of participants)

couldn't (wouldn't) attend a meeting in person' and that such an intervention 'acts as a starting point for debate; triggered public to talk'. The level of ambivalence ('neutral') towards the DVD appears to be related to those board meetings where there were problems with acoustics and/or the audio-visual equipment.

Third, there is evidence in at least two area boards that the DVD influenced thinking about future public engagement. One board manager planned to take the DVD into other institutions that worked at the local level:

> I think what has come out of it or what will come out of it is that there is now a will for that DVD to be taken to the partnership and to the task group. And so a question which is quite broad and which we might have talked about a little bit here and there … will now be taken on, have some more focus to it.

And, in a second area board, the DVD and the ensuing discussion led to an agreement between the local school and the board to find new ways of communicating with younger people. More widely, the DVD stimulated discussion throughout the council structures (even if in some quarters it was defensive). It certainly had an impact on the community managers themselves, one of whom stated at an iteration meeting:

> It's made me think about so many more ways to think about getting people into the meetings ... well not even into the meetings but can we get governance into the community, you know establishing governance networks in an area rather than focus on individual structures like committees. That's not what it's about – it's how we get information out to communities and how they're involved in different ways and coordinated.

Fourth, the critical nature of the voices on the DVD created resistance amongst elected representatives. While we have already discussed the problem that at least one of the people filmed on the DVD was known to one of the councillors by the phrase 'usual suspect', the negative and defensive reaction on the part of a number of councillors was certainly not all due to such personality clashes. Quite simply they were not happy about being put in an uncomfortable situation that they were not in a position to control. A number were reluctant to engage with the perspectives being voiced – on two occasions they were openly hostile. Rather than being a springboard to debate, they perceived the criticism from the politically marginalized as a direct personal attack. As one community manager asked: 'I just wonder how we're going to get those voices in if the reaction is councillors putting down their pens and folding their arms.' There appeared to be an immediate negative gut reaction on the part of some elected representatives. Such reactions are a long way from the facilitative leadership role that is being promoted for councillors in local government reform in the UK (Stoker and Greasley 2008), and indicates the extent to which those who hold a powerful position in local governance are often reluctant to loosen their grip on the political agenda.

Finally, this reaction by a number of elected members indicates the difficult position that Area Board managers are placed in. As the facilitators of this portion of the agenda, the quality of the debate rests on their skills and capacities. Creating the conditions under which all participants (in particular, elected representatives) are willing to be challenged is not an easy task – and not one that all the managers were up to. Some of this was due to time constraints and the prejudices of elected representatives present at the meeting; but in other cases, it reflected just how difficult it is to enable inclusive deliberation. This has been recognized by the council, which is now providing training in facilitation both to its Area Board managers and also to local councillors during their period of induction.

What are the lessons?

While we have witnessed the development of a number of exemplary democratic innovations that have reversed the traditional participation bias, these have required significant political and institutional commitment (Smith 2005, Smith 2009). Most public authorities do not show this level of commitment to engaging citizens in political decision-making processes, being less willing to invest the resources (financial, institutional, and political) necessary to ensure participation by the traditionally politically marginalized. Thus, we witness, for example, decentralization strategies, where public authorities create local forums open to local citizens, but without developing the necessary outreach programmes and incentive structures that enable engagement. Decentralization in itself rarely shifts the existing balance of political power (Richardson et al 2018).

Under such (mundane) conditions, the design experiment offers some evidence that audio-visual technology can be used to ensure that the voices of the politically marginalized are at least heard in such forums. Clearly one of the lessons from the production and reception of the DVD is that it is vital to ensure that those filmed are politically marginalized! Shortcuts taken by the Area Board managers in the production of the DVD (setting up interviews with known community activists) arguably undermined the overall impact of the intervention, increasing the hostility of already suspicious and uncomfortable elected representatives.

But this hostility was not just towards particular individuals on the DVD: elected representatives found the challenge that the voices on the DVD represented uncomfortable. In itself this may be a good thing: exposing the intransigence of existing political power holders. But it is not necessarily helpful in pushing forward the engagement agenda. Here the important issue is the capacity of the manager to facilitate the deliberations that interspersed the showing of sections of the DVD. The experiment exposed the limitations of a number of these managers. Facilitation to ensure inclusion is not an easy task. It is certainly not something that comes naturally to most people. And it is an undervalued element of participation exercises; a topic that receives negligible attention within democratic theory (Mansbridge et al 2006, Smith 2009: 197–8). We may be able to create tools (such as the DVD) to bring the voice of the marginalized into debates, but the conditions need to be in place such that participants in the room are willing to take these tools – and the messages they convey – seriously. Creating a forum for participation is not enough: it must be well facilitated if it is to be effective. Further experimental research is needed to better understand the determinants of effective and inclusive democratic facilitation.

Finally, the research reveals the challenging nature of design experiments. So much is out of the control of the research team:

co-production of the experiment raises significant practical (and at times political) challenges. But the rewards of such research are potentially great. The next chapter takes a further look at how institutions do in fact respond when people choose to engage.

Further reading

Information on participatory video can be found at http://insight-share.org, where it is possible to download the book *Insights into Participatory Video: A Handbook for the Field*. The idea for the DVD intervention was to some extent influenced by the issue books produced for community meetings (or study circles) by the independent organization Everyday Democracy in the US, www.everyday-democracy.org. For more on the range of democratic innovations being institutionalized across the world, see Smith, G. (2005), *Beyond the Ballot: 57 Democratic Innovations from Around the World*, London: Power Inquiry, the user-generated platform *Participedia*, www.participedia.net, and references in the previous chapter. Recent studies of participatory videos include Tremblay, C., Jayme, B., Openjuru, G., and Jaitli, N. (2015), 'Community Knowledge Co-creation Through Participatory Video', *Action Research*, 13(3): 298–314, and Ham, van der A. J., Kupper, J. A., Bodewes, A. J., and Broerse. J. E. W (2013), 'Stimulating Client Involvement and Client–provider Dialog Through Participatory Video: Deliberations on Long-term Care in a Psychiatric Hospital', *Patient Education and Counseling*, 91(1): 44–9.

11

Linking

Why institutions are critical for citizen behaviour

If they are to be successful, nudge and think interventions need ways of linking citizens and political representatives in central and local government. Thinking makes more sense if the ideas that citizens come up with are reviewed, judged, and preferably acted upon by policy-makers. It is also possible to imagine situations where nudges work better with links, too. Some of the nudges described in this volume aim to get people involved in making decisions jointly with decision-makers, or to petition, lobby, or complain. Why participate if no one is listening?

The institutional links between citizens and government provide a framework for citizen participation. Institutions have, in many cases, frustrated citizens' ability to be citizens, and therefore institutional reform is vital. Many decision-makers themselves want to be more responsive. Concern continues, for example in the UK in the form of periodic inquiries, commissions, and calls for action (Department for Communities and Local Government 2007, House of Commons Communities and Local Government Committee 2013, Copus 2014).

While the experiments and other research in this volume suggest there is untapped citizen potential, this can be hard to realize from the ways in which institutions frame the debate, how they create structures, and how they respond to citizens. Examples from everyday life are easy to come by: citizens can see where institutions promise choice and quality in public services but deliver long waits in doctors' waiting rooms, where their questions about rapidly changing populations have been suppressed, where they are asked to come forward with opinions but ignored when their views are unsolicited, or that warnings about climate change come from the same politicians and civil servants who approve decisions to build new homes on flood plains.

Nudge strategies are themselves premised on the idea that institutions could create stronger forms of citizenship if they dealt with people as they are, which is often more sympathetic or willing than institutions presume, but possibly less straightforwardly rational, more social, and more emotional. Think strategies are a tool for debating how far institutional frameworks could, or should, intervene to shape people's behaviour, what choices citizens are willing to make or are prepared to accept from governments. The issue is whether institutions can operate their frameworks for civic behaviour in a creative enough way to match the sophistication of citizens.

There are many encouraging signs that formal decision-makers, particularly in local institutions, understand the need for change in their relationships with citizens (Department for Communities and Local Government 2007, Mangan et al 2016, Tjoa 2018, Walker and Lawson 2018). Although the desire may be there, reform is extremely hard; some of the inherent characteristics of institutions arguably militate against reform (John 2014).

Chapter 4 described some of the difficulties in persuading a public institution to tailor volunteering opportunities to better match citizens' preferences and interests. This chapter takes the discussion further, and looks at relationships between citizen groups and decision-makers within local institutions. We review existing evidence on the lack of responsiveness by institutions to citizens' attempts to be civic; then we look at how nudge and think can help develop more responsive institutions. We present an experiment on testing for the responsiveness of local councillors to a citizen-interest group lobby.

Literature – what are the gaps in institutional responsiveness?

The literature on the quality of institutional framing makes for depressing reading. Broadly, since the mid-1960s, public trust in government and political institutions has been decreasing in all of the advanced industrialized democracies (Dalton 2004). Political trust is closely related to how far citizens feel institutions are accountable and respond to their needs and preferences. The Rockefeller Fund has a grant programme specifically designed to enhance institutional responsiveness because of perceived gaps (see www.rffund.org/programs/institutional-accountability-and-individual-liberty).

In the UK, the leaders of institutions have previously misunderstood the needs and demands of citizens across a huge range of fundamental topics: citizens' preferred identities; preferences for participation in decision-making; preferences for where they live and with whom they share their neighbourhoods (Durose et al 2009). Historically, the culture of English local government has been described as: 'inward-looking, silo-based, resistant to change and challenge and more concerned with a self-serving attachment to a particular model of delivery than thinking what would produce the best outcome for people in the locality' (Improvement and Development Agency 2009: 8).

There is some evidence that more could be done to link local government to concerns at the local level, and convince more of the public that local government is listening and responding to citizens' ideas. Citizens and institutions need to be in dialogue with each other – or at least connect together – if institutions are to have a chance of responding to citizen views. Just over half (56 per cent) of respondents in one reputable survey in England felt that their council acted on the concerns of local residents either 'a great deal' or 'a fair amount' (Local Government Association 2018a: 13). Although this figure 'represents a significantly lower proportion than 12 previous rounds' of this survey (Local Government Association 2018a: 13), the figures between 2012 and 2018 hover around the three-fifths mark (Local Government Association 2018b: 13), which is 'towards the lower end of the satisfaction scale' (Local Government Association 2018b: 12).

Responsiveness is a key measure, regardless of whether citizens actively attempt to influence decisions or not. However, it has also been the case that citizens remain unconvinced of their ability to be heard by local decision-making institutions. For example, only around one in four (26 per cent) in England in 2017–18 felt able to influence decisions that affected their local area, although more (around three-fifths) felt it was important to be able to have this influence (Department for Digital, Culture, Media & Sport 2018: 13). Broadly there has been little change in the perception of influence over several years, with earlier surveys also showing around one in four or one in five saying they had an influence over locally relevant decisions (Newton 2010: 36).

Lack of responsiveness, and perceived gaps in responsiveness, can have a knock-on effect for citizen behaviour. Gerber and Phillips argue (from a US perspective) that:

> When institutions are more responsive (i.e. when they produce policy outcomes that reflect the changing preferences of the median or some

other important group of voters), political actors can achieve their policy goals within an existing institutional regime. When institutions are less responsive, some actors may prefer to circumvent status quo institutions and replace them with new ones. (Gerber and Phillips 2002: 2)

In 2008, a UK practitioner-developed framework on the ability of community groups to influence decision-making was produced after:

> it became glaringly apparent to us that there was no point in focusing solely on 'developing;' communities which are empowered and empowering, if the agencies they are trying to connect with are shutting them out and behaving in disempowering ways. This stark realization kick-started the research [with] a focus on assessing and increasing public agencies' openness to influence. (Changes n.d.)

Local councillors' perceptions of their roles help give useful context for some of these perceived gaps in responsiveness. In a major comparative study across 16 European countries, on average, over half (57 per cent) of the councillors in the study described themselves as 'trustees' (Karlsson 2013: 99). That is, in a critical situation in the council, they would vote according to their own convictions. Only 15 per cent said that in such a situation, they would act as 'delegates' and vote according to the opinion of the voters. The remainder (28 per cent) would choose according to the opinion of the party group (Karlsson 2013: 99). While these possible roles are all legitimate, the classic (and centuries old) debates on whether politicians are trustees or delegates increase the challenges of linking.

There are many areas of mutual miscomprehension. In the Republic of Ireland in 2018, a survey commissioned by the statutory body overseeing local government found that knowledge of the council and awareness of the services provided was generally low, with just 4 per cent saying they 'know a great deal' about their council. The majority know 'just a little' (51 per cent) about their council (Ipsos-MORI 2018: 8). In line with this lack of knowledge, the majority do not feel informed by their local council about what the council does, and under a third (29 per cent) agreed that the council was transparent (Ipsos-MORI 2018: 15). Results for England have seen a statistically significant decline between 2013 and 2018 in people 'feeling informed' by their local council (Local Government Association 2018a). Misunderstandings and lack of awareness are arguably compounded by a lack of direct contact between local councillors and their constituents. For example, it has been suggested that 'the overwhelming proportion of Britons have had no contact whatsoever with their elected, or non-elected, officials in the past 12 months at all levels of government (Warman 2018: 9). These results chime with previous data for England on the high proportions of people who knew nothing at all about their local members, had never met any of their local councillors, or did not know the name of their local councillor (Local Government Association 2008: 14).

There is also potential for change in mutual misunderstanding. Local councillors have been frustrated at citizens' lack of awareness about their roles and constraints. Councillors are concerned about public perceptions held of them – about their powers, functions, abilities, and responsibilities (Copus 2014). Councillors have experienced tensions over confused expectations of them, battles over what they have perceived to be a downgrading of their role, and occasional public hostility in the face of their desire to perform public service (Copus 2014).

In the face of this rather depressing picture, there are some positives on which different relationships could be built. Local political representatives are trusted by the public to make local decisions. When asked which individuals were most trusted to make decisions about how services are provided in one's local area, 70 per cent of respondents in England selected 'local councillors', compared to 'members of parliament' (13 per cent) and 'government ministers' (5 per cent) (Local Government Association 2018a: 9–10). Public trust in local councils in England has been far greater than trust in Parliament when it comes to making decisions about how services are provided in local areas. Asked who respondents most trusted when it came to local decision-making, their 'local council', 'the government', or 'neither', 72 per cent said their 'local council', 14 per cent said 'the government' and 13 per cent said 'neither', figures which were consistent with all other rounds of polling from 2012 (Local Government Association 2018a: 14–15).

Local councillors hold to the idea of responsiveness. Around 70 per cent of councillors in one English study believed the most important thing they do is listening to the views of local people (Kettlewell and Phillips 2014: 9), and this figure was similar between 2004 and 2013: 64.8 per cent believed that representing local residents' views to the council was the most important thing that they do as a councillor (Kettlewell and Phillips 2014: 9).

Another positive is that many councillors have favourable attitudes towards participation in local democracy. For example, in a European-wide study of local councillors, 81.8 per cent agreed that it is important citizens participate before decisions are made by representatives, and 65 per cent were in favour of active and direct participation by citizens (Sweeting and Copus 2013: 121).

How does responsiveness relate to citizen participation?

Some citizens are active despite a lack of responsiveness on the part of public authorities, and have high levels of motivation, or, some may argue, irrational behaviour. They could be described as persistent at the very least, given how little impact they feel they have through their unpaid activity. One research study (Newton et al 2010) showed that being civically active or engaged in public debate does not necessarily produce satisfied and empowered citizens who feel their efforts are taken seriously. The study showed that amongst people active in their communities, only a third (35 per cent) believed they could influence decisions, while 56 per cent of those who had been involved said that they could not, although this is higher than people who are not involved (35 per cent compared to 23 per cent) (Newton 2010: 36). The main reason for these findings appears to be that people did not perceive changes to be happening as a result of their involvement, although we do not know whether these people started off more dissatisfied, and became involved in decision-making because they were already unhappy with decisions that had been made.

However, for some citizens, the marginal gains to be made from their potential involvement are off-putting enough to stop them becoming active. Other research shows that there is a feedback effect on citizen attitudes and participation from poor responsiveness: 'The biggest deterrent to participation of all was citizens' perception – or experience – of a lack of council response to consultation' (Lowndes et al 2001: 452). For larger jurisdictions, writers have argued that cross-national variations in political membership are not so much related to social or attitudinal differences between these countries' citizens, and are explained to a great extent by the structure of the political system of each nation (Morales 2009).

In the UK, other evidence indicates a correlation between poor local government responsiveness and low levels of citizen participation (Barnes et al 2003). More responsive local authorities were correlated with higher levels of participation, although the direction of causation is unclear. The Newton et al study examined the problem of making a causal inference in more detail, looking at why citizens did or did not feel they had influence over local decisions (Newton 2010). Institutional responsiveness to citizens was critical, for example, to whether citizens felt that local public services acted on the concerns of local people. The study showed that 34 per cent of the variance of feelings of influence was explained by whether people felt that local public services acted on the concerns of local people (Newton 2010: 31). Residents judged that local public institutions were responsive in several different ways: if they listened and heard what residents had to say; if they fed back on the outcomes of decisions; and if they made decisions people felt the majority agreed with. Feelings of influence were also linked to whether agencies had delivered on promises. Broken promises decreased trust in institutions.

Links to nudge and think

An investigative audit of the practice of public authorities in engaging their citizens in local decision-making and consultative processes (Lowndes et al 2006) identified the challenge of linking at the local level. The task was to ensure that formal and elected representatives draw upon the insights and understandings of a wide range of citizens. This research developed the diagnostic tool, CLEAR (discussed in Chapter 4). The implication of the argument is that participation is most effective when citizens have the resources to participate, are mobilized and enabled. Most importantly for our discussion on linking, the R in CLEAR stands for 'responded to':

> The 'responded to' factor is simultaneously the most obvious but also the most difficult factor in enhancing public participation. But it is also the factor most open to influence by public policy-makers. Leadership and decision-making arrangements – in political and managerial domains – play an important role in determining whether groups of

citizens are able to gain access to those with power, whether decision makers have a capacity to respond and whether certain groups are privileged over others in terms of the influence they exert. (Lowndes et al 2006: 289)

Several of our experiments aimed to facilitate deliberation with citizens and to nudge them to behave more civically. But we did not want to ignore the institutional role. Our experiments were not premised on the idea that institutions were perfectly designed, with effective engagement structures and processes in place simply waiting for an apathetic citizenry to be mobilized into action. We understood that citizen activity is a two-way process, and that people's negative experiences of engaging with the large, unwieldy, and sometimes stubborn and paternal, bureaucracies of power could have a significant part to play in their unwillingness to be mobilized. Could we turn the tables? What if similar nudge and think techniques could be applied to institutions to enhance their ability to respond?

The experiment

The Building Links project tested out different ways that community organizations could approach local councillors, get their attention, and win support for their work (see Richardson and John 2012). How can both sides work together on relevant local issues and problems? How could citizen organizations lobby decision-makers? The aim was to see which, if any, was the more effective approach. We asked other questions. Do councillors find it hard to judge between different demands made on them? Can communities help with this by getting their message across more effectively?

The study was a randomized controlled trial, where the units were local politicians (councillors) in English local government. We recruited eight community groups, spread across the country in eight different local authorities. Each group had a real local issue they wanted to tackle, but all were keen to make stronger connections to their local councillors. We selected the authorities on the basis of the availability of a comparable and willing interest group to do the intervention, and actively recruited groups in different places in order to get variations in political control and location. The sample size was 248 councillors. This was based on a total of 496 councillors across all eight local authorities in the experiment. We randomly selected half of the councillors in each authority to make up the sample, as we felt an approach to all councillors, in a round-robin style, would be counter-productive to our lobby.

The intervention was that each of the community groups sent letters to the randomly selected councillors in the sample in their local council. There were two differently worded letters, and each councillor received just one: that is, half the sample received letter A, and the other half letter B, which meant that a quarter of all the councillors in that authority received each kind of letter. There was no control group, as the response from councillors not receiving a letter would have been difficult to measure. Both letters asked for help with the same problem, but one approach was based on the literature on how to campaign and lobby, and the other was not. Studies show there are several factors that contribute to an effective lobby, of which eight key ones are that:

1. the lobbying material comes from a credible source;
2. it frames the issue in a way that is consistent with lobbyists' values and goals;
3. it offers the policy-maker private or costly information that would otherwise be difficult for the policy-maker to gather;
4. it summarizes and processes a mass of publicly available information in a way that clarifies the implications for the policy-maker;

5. it contains emotive or symbolic appeals to commonly held values;
6. it outlines how current policy approaches lead to negative outcomes;
7. it outlines how an alternative approach would promote shared policy goals;
8. and it has a clear set of recommendations or makes a clearly articulated demand of the policy-maker.

The experiment incorporated the eight factors considered by the literature to form an effective lobbying letter. This created the two treatments: weak and strong. Letter A was designed to be the weak treatment. It contained weak, un-evidenced, and not locally relevant versions of five of the eight factors in effective lobbying. It did not contain three of the eight factors. It had only one reference to a request, which was weak and unclear. Letter B was designed to be the strong treatment. It contained strong, evidenced, and locally relevant versions of all the factors in effective lobbying. There were three references to a clear request and two references to all other factors.

We measured the results by (a) the number of replies to each of the two letters and (b) the helpfulness of the replies. Ultimately the best measure of quality would be that the lobby succeeded. Following the lobby, some of the groups saw progress, for example, a participatory arts organization was awarded a £0.25 million contract to provide services, and a carers network was invited to local authority strategic planning meetings for the first time. However, while positive for the groups, these outcome variables cannot be considered to be direct results of the intervention. Although concrete and observable outcomes like these are attractive for the research, they are decisions much further down the chain of decision-making and are the result of a complex mix of institutional factors not attributable solely to the treatment. A successful outcome to the lobby was not necessarily within the gift of all of the individual councillors.

The initial response by telephone, letter, or email was used in the analysis as the outcome variable. Both treatments contained a set of generic requests as a basis for outcome measurement: 'We would very much appreciate the opportunity to collaborate. Please could you let us know: your position on [the relevant local issue]; and how you would like to take this issue forward?'

However, this causes an issue for the analysis of quality of response in that any verbal response to a request can be considered suspect. The analysis dealt with these issues by creating a coding framework that allowed for a series of different types of response from the same individual in order to see if a response was backed up by other (seemingly) helpful actions or comments, or if they were just empty phrases. A coding framework for the quality and content of the responses was created based on the generic request combined with the nature of the actual responses received. The coding framework covered: quality of help overall; a statement that the issue was not the councillor's responsibility or remit; the suggestion of other contacts without a direct referral; a direct referral to a civil servant/ officer or relevant committee; a direct referral to a fellow councillor; willingness to take up the issue; the offer or occurrence of further discussion; a comment on the issue; an offer of personal support to the group for their lobby; willingness to meet or met in person; and the giving of information about party policy. The responses were then blind-coded by two researchers who had not been involved in the experiment and had no knowledge of which group the councillor was in.

What did we find?

Overall, 18.5 per cent of councillors responded. There was considerable variation according to local authority, ranging from 4.2 to 30.6 per cent. The weak letter, the one not based on the lobbying literature, had a slightly higher level of response and more helpful responses. The stronger letter based on the literature had a 16.0 per cent response. The more general letter based on the literature had a 21.0 per cent response. Therefore, the weak letter with its information-low and emotion-poor approach yielded a higher response – of 5 percentage points – than the strong letter with its information-high and emotion-rich approach. The difference is not statistically significant, however, and the conclusion must be that the type of letter did not make a difference in the replies overall.

The number of responses is only one outcome. The quality of the responses is also clearly critical; fewer but constructive and supportive responses from appropriate decision-makers may be of more benefit to the interest groups than a larger number of non-committal or unhelpful answers from politicians not in a position to assist. Using the data from the qualitative coding of the helpfulness of the replies, we probed the structure of these responses with factor analysis (a statistical procedure that reduces a large number of responses to a few common factors). Helpful responses included councillors expressing a willingness to meet, and offering face-to-face follow-up discussions, or positively signposting the lobbyist on to colleagues if the issue would be better dealt with by someone else. Less helpful and dismissive responses included councillors stating it was not their remit or responsibility and the letter writer needed to go elsewhere, without positively signposting the lobbyist on to colleagues or referring them elsewhere, or even, in many cases, offering a relevant name to the writer. The regression analysis (see Richardson and John

2012) shows that the extent to which people passed the letter on to another person in the council was more influenced by the better letter than the one with less information.

Conclusion

The core idea we were testing was that decision-makers within public institutions could be nudged to be more responsive. Our nudge was to present local politicians with a lobby from groups they were largely unaware of, and that did not have relationships with councillors. The strong letter was information-rich, and attempted to offer politicians with intelligence, not only on the salience of the local issue to be tackled, but also information about the legitimacy of the community group and their potential contribution to joint problem-solving with the local authority. This was based on a wide and robust literature, which indicated that informational lobbying was an effective tactic. Unfortunately, this was not the case in our experiment. What is striking is that there was no difference between the supposedly weaker and stronger letters. What is also noticeable is the low level of response to either of the letters from community groups. These groups were lobbying their locally elected representatives to seek their help on what they see as a genuine local issue.

Indeed, follow-up research talking directly to councillors shows that they suffer from information overload, and find it hard to manage demands made on them; they feel overwhelmed by irrelevant paperwork and demands, and unable to influence their own bureaucracies in order to create change (Richardson 2013). Demands on local politicians have substantially increased in recent decades. Another possible explanation of the responses may be that a rise in the number of internal organizational and party-political demands has left less time to represent the people who voted them in, or process lobbying requests from unknown bodies. It suggests that UK local politicians may still be suffering from a perception of themselves as having weak status and low power. This might also explain our other finding, that the treatment encouraged politicians to pass the letter on to another person, possibly of higher status, in the council.

Follow-up research for this project found that local councillors felt overwhelmed by irrelevant paperwork and demands, and unable to influence their own bureaucracies in order to create change (Richardson 2013). Other research in northern Europe has also found that it may be hard to change the way local councillors see their roles, because of established attitudes, existing organizational practices, and prevailing cultures in local government institutions (Vabo et al 2018). However, this does not take away from the fact that so few replied, whether to dismiss the claim being made on them, to request a less cognitively demanding letter, or even to explain the limitations they faced. Under these circumstances it is hard for the community groups doing the lobbying not to feel that their institutions do not value them and their contributions.

The literature, and our experiment, reveal the extent of the gap between citizens and local representatives but also how hard it will be to close that gap. It may be the case that weaknesses in linking show the limited possibilities of both nudge and think strategies – as effective policies need citizens to feed back to decisions. The evidence indicates that some urgent work, such as training, is needed to develop the capacity of local elected members as community leaders. It suggests that more work is needed to build relationships between community organizations and local members. Local authorities could manage their communications with councillors to allow members to focus on their priorities.

Linking

Beyond these small-scale local practical measures, there is a bigger challenge: how to address the more fundamental cultural and organizational framing issues. The process of engaging citizens needs to be complemented with a reform of government to make those in power better able to listen to and work with citizens and community groups. This is particularly critical at the level of local government, where the people who are seen by citizens as decision-makers feel very disempowered themselves.

Further reading

There are a number of experimental studies of lobbying, the earliest being Chin, M. L., Bond, J. R., and Geva, N. (2000), 'A Foot in the Door: An Experimental Study of PAC and Constituency Effects on Access', *Journal of Politics*, 62: 534–49, followed by Bergan, D. E. (2009), 'Does Grassroots Lobbying Work? A Field Experiment Measuring the Effects of an e-mail Lobbying Campaign on Legislative Behavior', *American Politics Research* 37: 327–52. A useful survey of what are called 'elite experiments' is by Grose, C. (2014), 'Field Experimental Work on Political Institutions', *Annual Review of Political Science*, 17(1), 355–70. After the notable study by Butler, D. M. and Broockman, D. E. (2011), 'Do Politicians Racially Discriminate Against Constituents? A Field Experiment on State Legislators', *American Journal of Political Science*, 55(3): 463–77, there is a meta-analysis of experiments testing the responsiveness of legislators and officials to citizen contact: Costa, M. (2017), 'How Responsive are Political Elites? A Meta-analysis of Experiments on Public Officials', *Journal of Experimental Political Science*, 4(3): 241–54. There is also an accessible guide to the policy-focused debates (in a UK context but applicable elsewhere) in Mangan, C., Needham, C., Bottom K., and Parker, S. (2016), *The 21st Century*

Councillor, Birmingham, UK: University of Birmingham. Further resources from the *21st Century Public Servant* and *21st Century Councillor* are available on the project website, https://21stcenturypu blicservant.wordpress.com/

12

Summary of key findings

In the earlier chapters of this book we showed how public agencies can encourage citizens to contribute more to society. We have examined a wide range of activities through which citizens can make that contribution including voting, volunteering, petitioning, taking part in debates on policy issues, recycling, and donating. We have detailed a similarly broad range of interventions that public agencies and other bodies can carry out such as canvassing, giving feedback, making direct requests of citizens, involving them in debate, and inviting them to make pledges. We have used research tools of the highest quality – randomized controlled trials and design experiments – to test our claims. We have provided evidence of what works and of what works better. With this evidence at their fingertips, policy-makers are better equipped to select effective interventions that involve citizens in public life and, as a result, improve policy outcomes.

We build on a long body of work by the many academics who have argued that citizens are central to public policy-making and implementation. Hirst was prescient: he made the case for associative democracy as an alternative to more state-controlled forms of rule (Hirst 1993). Citizens are able to participate in locally based associations, which can sustain a more decentralized pattern of politics. Scholars working on research with the label social capital have also stressed the positive role that individuals play in forming beneficial social networks. Clusters of social capital play a role in sustaining positive policy outcomes and maintaining the quality of government (Putnam 1993, Putnam 2000). Halpern, in his review of the literature, assembled a large amount of observational evidence, finding that there is such a relationship between social networks/trust and desired policy outcomes occurring across many policy fields, such as crime, health, and education (Halpern 2005). His later book argues that societies have a large amount of hidden wealth in the form of stocks of social cooperation and intelligence, which policy-makers can tap into if only they know how to (Halpern 2010). The social capital research and policy programme has led to a large number of applications to policy problems, such as in rural areas (Pisani et al 2017) and health (Kawachi et al 2008).

There have been many case studies of how policy might be improved by involving citizens more. Fung, for example, examined the participation experiments of cities in the US whereby citizens have sought to use new decision-making forums to influence the political agenda and to achieve social policy objectives such as the reduction of crime (Fung 2003b, Fung 2006). Brannan, John, and Stoker brought together the evidence from a selection of policies in the UK that involve the citizen directly, such as tenant initiatives and crime on housing estates (Brannan et al 2006). They found that citizen action can – in the right circumstances – overcome the bias of institutions that often limit political and citizen participation. Sirianni made a cogent argument for involving citizens in a new partnership with state institutions (Sirianni 2009). He provided many examples of collaborative governance from the US, and developed a set of principles policy-makers could follow. Smith reviewed the evidence about democratic innovations that have emerged across the world, and which shows the many varieties of these experiments, such as participatory budgeting, citizens' assemblies, and experiments in e-democracy (Smith 2009). Richardson collected examples from a hundred community groups of do-it-yourself community action in the UK, showing how citizens can deliver interventions themselves without much help from government (Richardson 2008). There is much comparative research and evidence collected on the phenomenon of civic-tech, that is using technology online to generate civic capacity, with good case study evidence (Silva 2013). Research on citizen involvement in public services co-production continues in many reviews and syntheses (e.g. Fung 2015, Durose and Richardson 2016, Pestoff 2019).

These reviews and studies – often using valuable research designs, such as case studies or analyses of observational data – have provided persuasive arguments that there is potential for citizen mobilization. But, in our view, they lack the killer evidence to make their cases compelling, particularly concerning what government and other agencies can do to foster change. In this volume we offer our own unique solution to this problem: randomized controlled trials. They can provide conclusive evidence of what works because of their ability to demonstrate convincingly whether an intervention was successful or not, and because they provide the genuine counterfactual of what would have happened without the intervention. The trials we have presented in this book show what is possible. Added to this we have insights from two more qualitative studies using design experiments, which we deployed to examine more intensive and complex interventions (see the Appendix for the summary of the methods of the experiments).

Our message is that public interventions do make a difference. All our experiments worked – to a greater or lesser extent – in stimulating citizen behaviour and/or changing attitudes. There is much that public agencies can do to get citizens involved with policy. We believe that citizens are willing to do more and they do not need that much encouragement to get there. We are aware of the constraints in increasing participation that many critics have pointed out. We know that a small minority of citizens do most of the volunteering, and many of these people live in affluent areas (Mohan 2011). Most people either lack the interest or the capacity to get involved. It is true we found that more affluent areas were more susceptible to our experiments, such as the book donation experiment (Chapter 7), but we also found that poorer areas responded positively as well. In our volunteering experiment (Chapter 4) we found that people from a range of backgrounds came forward. We uncovered a similarly diverse set of responses to our intervention in our recycling experiments (Chapter 3). Contrary to usual expectations, we found the canvassing campaign was more successful in the most deprived neighbourhoods and those places that have a large ethnic minority population.

Conventional methods of recruitment often tend to deploy the personal social networks of activists. These people often recruit people similar to themselves. If public organizations bypass these networks and ask randomly selected people directly, unsurprisingly we get a more representative group of participants. Indeed, John (2009) found that citizen governance forums, in contrast to the traditional political activities of petitioning and protest, tend to recruit participants who are younger and are members of ethnic minorities. Similar evidence has been uncovered concerning participation in other forms of carefully designed democratic innovations (Smith 2009). In short, in spite of the constraints on expanding social and political participation, there is much that government can do to involve citizens from a wider social background than the ones who already take part in existing forms of citizen involvement.

With our experiments testing out nudge and think, we found that the nudge experiments, on the whole, worked. We could knock on citizens' doors to encourage people to recycle their household waste and to vote in elections (Chapters 3 and 5); we could give them feedback too on how well they were doing so as to encourage even greater recycling of their food waste (Chapter 3). When citizens are given due credit for their contribution, we can get them to pledge to make donations to charity (Chapter 7). Critically for the nudge approach, we found that mandated choice works almost as well as opting out (Chapter 8). Defaults work just as Thaler and Sunstein say they do (Thaler and Sunstein 2008). As a result, we can say to policy-makers that they have a set of information-based tools of government that structure how citizens receive a signal or a cue, and can encourage them to volunteer, participate in politics, or do good in the community.

Nudge is, of course, not a panacea. The first issue is that nudge interventions tend to have weak effects, which is not particularly surprising because these interventions are light-touch in character. The experiments show an uplift of participation of between 1 and 9 percentage points. This falls short of the transformation of public policy outcomes that many might see as essential for dealing with current policy problems. On the other hand, the nudges are relatively cheap to implement. Our local nudges cost about £10,000 to administer, which is a small amount of money even in an age of fiscal austerity, and turns into a reasonable cost for each extra item of waste recycled, books donated, organs promised, and so on. Even the larger experiments were not very expensive, such as the online donations experiment at £22,000. The online deliberation was more expensive at about £100,000, but this was a national sample and represented our commitment to investigate think as much as we investigated nudge.

It could also be argued that if governments were to provide some of the nudges themselves, and with more institutional or rule-based changes alongside the information provision, we might expect a much larger effect. But – and this is the second limitation (or advantage depending how one sees it) – the nudger needs to be believed and this is a constraint in an era of large-scale distrust of government and public officials right across the world. Nudges work precisely because government is not so directly involved. People trust a message when it is from a reliable third-party source rather than from government itself. One of the ironies of our findings is that policymakers can learn from our work that nudges are effective but also that they may find it hard to nudge by themselves. Public officials may find it advantageous to work with other partners in delivering nudge interventions at a local level. Such local experiments can complement a nationally rolled out programme. They show how innovations can work best when government is at one step removed from the general public and is not nudging them individually.

The third limitation is that the range of possible interventions may be limited to those aspects of behaviour where people have already made up their minds and are willing to act. This may leave out a range of other behaviours that are more controversial and that may require a great deal more effort to change. Examples are recycling, which is already widely perceived as a good thing to do, and organ donation; the issue in these cases is that while most people agree with the ideas of recycling and organ donation, many do not act. This gap becomes even more important when the nudges address issues of public controversy and require citizens to engage in larger and more profound changes than the ones with which we presented them. This provides a justification to our use of think, which may be appropriate precisely in those contexts where there is not a settled point of view.

It is likely that nudge may not have a long-term effect and this is its fourth limitation. Certainly, we do find that people learn how to change behaviour and observe a downstream effect. There is an effect through habit, but this decays over time. In the Get Out the Vote study it did so by as much as 50 per cent, and there was a similar level of fall-off in the canvassing/recycling intervention. Of course, this criticism needs to be considered fairly. All interventions have a time-limited nature, so the effectiveness of nudges needs to be assessed alongside the effectiveness of other interventions, such as public funding, for example, which also reduces in impact once the investment has been made (such as with an urban regeneration project). The mistake, in our view, would be to see the nudge being undertaken in isolation from other policies and without considering the views of citizens themselves. As we argue below, nudges work best when seen as part of the local policy process – part of the necessary interaction between policy-makers and citizens. This would imply that nudges should be repeated and varied by these local agencies, as they learn from experience. And it was this creative process of using nudges that our design experiments attempted to reproduce. In this way, the time-limited nature of nudges is not a disadvantage because public agencies and other partners are continually using a wide range of time-limited strategies to improve public policy.

The fifth limitation stems from the collaboration needed to implement nudges involving public agencies. The messiness of everyday policy-implementation means that it takes a lot of effort to get a nudge off the ground, to get partners to work together and to get the details right. Not all of our nudges worked in all respects, as we saw with the volunteering design experiment using a call centre (see Chapter 4). This is the real world of policy implementation, which can be very distant from the pronouncements of government or the mission statements of glossy white papers. This very messiness, however, should not be seen as a disadvantage, but can be used to harness local energy and enthusiasm, as we explain below.

The limitations to nudge should not be used to decry our results – far from it. But they should encourage policy-makers to think about the appropriate conditions for introducing nudges, to know when and where they are going to be effective, perhaps alongside other interventions. The limitations also argue for a potentially more profound information tool to be considered, one that might lead to more long-term, systematic changes in citizen behaviour. This tool is discussion and deliberation – what we call think. Our results show considerable potential for this institutional reform. For example, the design experiment in Wiltshire with councillors (see Chapter 10) demonstrates that you can introduce into local government forums the voices of those who do not usually participate and this can shift the perceptions of those involved. The online experiment (Chapter 9) shows that you can engage large numbers of people on controversial topics such as youth anti-social behaviour and the implications of greater ethnic diversity of neighbourhoods. They are able to debate these issues without recrimination and without falling out.

But there are some limitations to think, too. First, think can fail when it asks people to engage in more tricky moral choices. With organ donation, when people were asked to deliberate as well as being nudged, there was a weaker effect than produced by the nudge alone. The process of deliberation appeared to firm up participants' doubts, if nothing else. This could be a good thing if reflection is the goal, but the assumption that further thought will lead automatically to the policy-maker's desired end needs careful consideration.

The other limitation is that digital means of communication may not be the best medium to encourage the majority of citizens to change their attitudes, although those who selected into the youth anti-social behaviour debates did change their views (see Chapter

9). The attitudes of many remained the same in spite of people being willing to sign into an experiment, being presented with information about these controversial and topical issues, having the chance to post their own views and to see the posts of others. It might be said that perhaps our intervention was not strong enough – that there was not enough on the discussion forum for citizens to engage in or that it did not have the potential to transform citizens. It may be the case that deliberating online can be challenging because of the nature of the online environment, which means that participants are not forced to pay attention to information and it is more difficult to encourage exchanges of views. The big attraction of the online environment is the number of people it can engage, but challenges exist in designing online interventions that encourage civility and cooperation and are thus more fully deliberative. We believe that our online deliberation has as many lessons for nudge as for think by highlighting the importance of institutional design, which can encourage citizens to be mutually respectful, even when debating controversial policies and issues. It is possible that pro-civic behaviour cues can be built into the design of online discussion spaces.

In the short term, there is a better case for using the internet as a site for nudge than for delivering think interventions. Our experiment on e-petitions achieved a significant shift in behaviour with much less of an intervention than the deliberation (see Chapter 6). The e-petition participants simply saw the number of other people participating, in what must be have been an almost subliminal experience compared to the vast number of videos, links to information posts, and email reminders we offered in the online deliberation. The design possibilities of the internet and the large numbers of users involved allow policy-makers to make minor modifications to the design of the interface between the citizen and the state – for example in providing feedback and in framing information – and to expect significant behaviour change as a result of these nudges. With the current level of technology and its increasing use, the potential of the internet for both nudge and think is increasingly being tapped.

But in spite of the online revolution, face-to-face interventions still have traction, both for think and nudge. Thus, many of our interventions were old-fashioned in their method of delivery. Consider doorstep-canvassing, for instance, as used with our voting (Chapter 5) and recycling experiments (Chapter 3). This gets results through the personal touch of the canvasser meeting face-to-face with a local resident. Deliberation in a community setting in Wiltshire delivered positive outcomes too (Chapter 10). Even when not face-to-face, the same effect can be achieved by talking to potential volunteers on the telephone – as we found in our call centre experiment (Chapter 4). Reading a printed booklet was an effective nudge in our student organ donation experiment (Chapter 8), an old-fashioned kind of intervention compared to the internet posts and blogs we created. Moreover, the other ancient form of communication of getting a letter in the post is also powerfully effective in reaching a large range of citizens, as we found in our book donation experiment (Chapter 7) and our feedback intervention on food waste (Chapter 3). This is especially important as there is no national database of email addresses and not everyone has access to the internet. In spite of the valuable results we achieved in our online deliberation and organ donation experiments, we cannot routinely rely on survey companies to collect names for us, as we did for those experiments. In the end, that group was a self-selected minority of people who gave their names to be on survey lists. Thus, a range of techniques is needed to deliver nudge and think, with each one having its advantages and disadvantages.

Overall, we think policy-makers need to recognize that nudging and thinking are complex processes, and context may be the factor that determines where one may be appropriate and not the other. We think that policy interventions could use elements of both nudge and think, partly because they resemble each other. If done in a sensitive manner, both can involve some reflection and some debate, even if that is limited as it was in our doorstep-canvassing experiment, where citizens wanted to have a conversation with the canvassers while they were being nudged. Many of our nudges (and some of our thinks) took place in a local context, where third-sector parties and local government itself were willing to engage with experiments. Deciding what to nudge and implementing it can involve much discussion and think, as does examining reaction to the nudges and responding to the lessons learned with new local policies. This form of local interaction was built into our design experiments, such as the call centre and decentralization experiments, but also affected how we delivered and reported nudges over recycling and donations. In this way, a devolved and locally appropriate version of nudge, where the intervention becomes part of the learning process and where there is sufficient decentralization of power, allows a range of actors to shape local policy-making – citizens, local associations, third sector organizations, and local authorities all play a role.

Looking at it this way we can challenge one of the biggest criticisms of nudge – that it takes away citizen freedom by being manipulative – a charge that is levelled because nudge is thought to work at subliminal level rather than in the open process of democratic debate (Anderson 2010). Nudge may even be criticized as another instance of the nanny or bossy state, which is keen to tell citizens what to do without allowing much reflection or reaction from citizens themselves. An extreme version of nudge would see a central agency collecting all the evidence, a nudge version of the National Institute for Clinical Excellence reviewing many hundreds of trials and then rolling out nudge interventions across the country, and in so doing implementing a science of behaviour change. We do not subscribe to this vision – we think there is a more locally focused alternative where public agencies and citizen-based organizations can experiment with interventions and can judge what is best for their local area. In this way, the nudge and think can coexist together in more localized and experimental political culture and practice.

Seen in this way, nudge and think help drive change at a local level, though we are not naive about the structural obstacles to achieving social change, given social inequalities in British society and its neighbourhoods. But our experiments show that interventions tailored in the right way can partially overcome some of the obstacles. We strongly believe that the reform agenda of civic engagement using nudge and think cannot be brushed aside by reference to citizen apathy or the inevitable inequalities of political participation. In fact, our positive results and broad base of involvement point in the opposite direction.

The big question, in our view, is whether central and local public agencies are ready to respond to the energy of citizen-based activism. A locally based nudge-think experimental culture in public agencies implies that they, too, respond to signals from citizens themselves as well as producing them. But we had some indication that it may be public authorities that are at fault rather than apathetic or unwilling citizens. In three of our experiments, we found it was elected officials or bureaucrats that provided the main obstacles to change. In the phone experiment when citizens called to make a complaint to the council (Chapter 4), we asked them to volunteer. We found citizens were willing, but the council could not find them appropriate things to do and so these potential volunteers gave up. In Wiltshire, it was the councillors who reacted badly to hearing the voice of the excluded in their local board meetings (Chapter 10). Similarly, we found in our lobby experiment that fewer than one in five councillors responded to a community lobby, which was well reasoned and on a matter of local interest (Chapter 11). If the politicians and bureaucrats are not going to respond to citizen concerns, what is the point in stimulating citizens to get more involved? In this sense, it is the policy-makers as much as citizens who should be nudged and who need to learn how to think.

13

Epilogue:
the future of nudge and think

The first edition of the book came out in 2011, which seems like a very different era to 2019, the publication date of this second edition. The original edition introduced a set of policy experiments that were innovative at a time when governments in developed democracies were rediscovering this method of evaluation. Nudge was in its infancy, as it was only three years since the publication of the seminal, eponymous book (Thaler and Sunstein 2008). The Behavioural Insights Team (BIT) had just been founded in 2010 and had not even started doing the experiments it later became so famous for, such as on court fines (Haynes et al 2013). It published its encomium for trials only in 2012 (Haynes et al 2012). The wave of nudge units and behavioural initiatives and reports had to wait until the mid-2000s to get going in earnest (John 2019). Think has had a longer genesis. In the UK, a period of experimentation with democratic innovations took place under the 'New' Labour government of 1997–2007, but it was still a relatively novel idea in the minds of policy-makers in 2011. As shown in the updated discussions of policy and practice in the previous chapters and references to new waves of sectoral studies, the ideas we identified in 2011 have bedded down and become institutionalized. If we wanted to pat ourselves on the back, then we could say we published *Nudge, nudge, think, think* at the start of an upswing of interest in nudge and think, and also in a period when randomized controlled trials were being increasingly used as a key tool of evaluation.

In 2011, it would be fair to say that the large developed economies had produced parties and leaders who were prepared to work with the existing sets of institutions and standard operating procedures, which included the established bureaucracies and public bodies. These bureaucracies and institutions are supported by extensive networks and other bodies that promote research findings and offer guidance to decision-makers in making choices about public policy. What has been called the practice of evidence-based policy (Davies and Nutley 2000) of course goes back to the nineteenth century, when governments started to use science and social science in the formulation of policies and their evaluation. Such an approach relies on governments being ready to listen to evidence even if they also have party-political objectives to meet; it also depends on a wider culture where expertise is valued and aspects of politics and government are made in this context. When parties tack to the centre and away from strong ideological positions, they can more readily embrace this neutral and pragmatic way of making public policy. Both nudge and think may be thought of as part of this wider process of consensus politics where politicians are searching for new ideas and more effective means of implementing policy as a way to take their parties beyond old politics, such as state control for the left and too much adherence to markets for the right. This agenda attracts leaders of political parties of different stripes to the project of modernization in its many forms.

By 2019 the climate of consensus and support for technocratic policy-making no longer appears to be so secure, when newly elected politicians seem less likely to automatically back the mainstream point of view. Expert views appear to be more contested and seen by some as part of an establishment advancing its own interests in the guise of scientific knowledge. Social forces that were latent in earlier years have been unleashed and entered the mainstream of politics. This is partly about the rise of anti-politics, where citizens question politicians for their self-interested motives (Clark et al 2018), although this need not necessarily involve challenging expertise. Increasing polarization on the left and right (Hopkins and Sides 2015) has led to the emergence of new leaders on both sides who do not subscribe to consensus politics. The implication of polarization is that debates proceed through partisan lenses, leading to partisan information-processing in which evidence and factual argument may play less of a role in political debate than they may have done before. Experts seem to have lost their ascendency in assessing public problems and in proffering solutions, perhaps linked to the failure to anticipate the recession of 2008 and the association of economists with the pre-crash regulatory regime.

The other relevant dimension is the rise of populism. Such anti-establishment thinking was a key factor in the Trump campaign and the Brexit vote in 2016 (Eatwell and Goodwin 2018). The US and UK are key countries where behavioural public policy has been most fully adopted, yet they are the very same places that appear to have shifted most markedly away from the technocratic underpinnings of such an approach. Nudge relies on politicians standing back and letting experts put forward new ideas, then using randomized controlled trials to make the policy or implementation choice. Such a relaxed approach might be seen as normal for a politician like the former UK Prime Minister David Cameron, who was often pragmatic in office and wanted the Conservatives to lead new policies to rebuild society and stay in government. Such an approach also fitted with the style of the Obama Presidency, which led from the centre in a restrained and pragmatic way, and had close links to academics (Obama had a background in a law faculty and he employed Cass Sunstein as an advisor).

Today's leaders, elected on waves of populism, might seem no longer so attracted to behavioural public policy, which may be tainted by association with the East Coast liberal elites at Harvard, MIT, and other institutions and foundations, and where policy changes need to appeal to a core set of voters and their instincts. It is no surprise then that President Trump abolished the US equivalent of the Behavioural Insights Team, the Social and Behavioral Sciences Team, on assuming office in January 2017, though it might have reflected a general hostility to federal regulation rather than nudge on its own. (Much of the work of the US nudge unit has been trans-ferred to the Office of Evaluation Sciences (https://oes.gsa.gov), so remains within federal government if not in the White House.) The UK government is bogged down trying to respond to Brexit, so is less attentive to the tweaking agenda of nudge. The changes of leadership in Italy to the populist right, German Chancellor Angela Merkel's decision to stand down from office, and the troubles facing President Emmanuel Macron in France all point to the weakness of the centre and the vulnerability of technocratic policy-making, the supportive environment of behavioural public policies.

Think might also be hard to carry out in a more contentious age of ideology and anti-politics. Think relies on the idea that we can develop respect and understanding across lines of difference through debate and, like nudge, that evidence can be brought to bear to solve disputes and come to agreed positions. Where politicians are entrenched, they might be less willing to commission delibera-tive processes where they have no control over the outcomes. Think relies on openness on the part of politicians, who need to listen and act on the views ascertained in deliberations and town halls.

But if polarized politicians may not be interested in nudges, they might not oppose them either, as nudges are more often related to implementation and longer-term needs of policy-makers. There is good reason to believe that much of nudge and think can still operate in different ideological contexts, both of left and right, as it is relatively neutral with respect to ends or policy goals. A government led by a left-wing leader like Jeremy Corbyn could use nudge to help implement its public policies, just as it could use think to encourage debates about its policy choices and their legitimacy. Despite some academic criticism that nudge ignores structural inequalities and could lead governments to neglect more fundamental approaches to addressing public policy problems (Leggett 2014), we argue that it has the potential to help tackle inequalities, such as in health, through targeted changes in choice architectures, when used in combination with other policy tools rather than as a substitute. Think strategies can be used effectively to address uncomfortable policy choices, whether they are faced by a left-of-centre or a right-leaning government. After all, many think mechanisms, such as citizen juries, are designed to work precisely when there is political controversy rather than the reverse. Moreover, in trying to introduce more controversial policy choices, more attention needs to be given to implementation, including the ways that policy targets are likely to react. This will require different ways of working, in which think interventions might help build broader acceptance for a more radical political project.

One key point is that the changes to politics are much more gradual and less transformative than might be thought from reading headlines and focusing on election and referendum results. It is possible to focus on the events of 2016 too much and forget that many centrist politicians remain in place in the UK. Trump by no means leads his own party and the Democratic Party controlled the House of Representatives from 2019. When considered in a world context, with the full range of countries and governments (John 2019), and considering the role of the private sector in delivering many policies, there is still substantial interest in nudge and in deliberative mechanisms such as mini-publics and deliberative polls. We also need to consider the role of agencies at a remove from government and the contribution of regional, state, and local governments, as well as international agencies. In many countries much policy is delegated to subnational politics, such as to the US states, where research and policy innovation commonly works from the bottom up. There is considerable scope for experimentation at the sub-national level and roles for policy entrepreneurs.

The trend towards polarization is gradual and by no means uniform. Anti-politics goes back many decades and is quite ambiguous and variegated, with citizens not always giving up on state action (Stoker and Hay 2017). It is also focused on politicians, not so much on the experts and the bureaucrats who commission nudges and thinks. There is a considerable amount of survey evidence that shows continuing public support for nudge (Sunstein et al 2018), even if that support is in part partisan-conditioned, especially in the US. Surveys show that professionals and even professors still remain trusted by the vast majority of respondents (MORI Veracity Index 2018, www. ipsos.com/ipsos-mori/en-uk/advertising-execs-rank-below-politicia ns-britains-least-trusted-profession). The changing attitudes and attachments of voters outside the US is complicated and show how party systems are adapting rather than necessarily polarizing in response to contentious politics (Whitefield and Rovny 2018).

The movement in favour of nudge and think has been established, with the former showing a normal pattern of diffusion (John 2018) with a more gradual adoption of nudges and nudge units that appear through the 2010s. Instead of being relegated as a fashion, popular just in the Anglo-American democracies, nudge is in the mainstream in most kinds of jurisdictions across the world. Moreover, think has become more institutionalized over time and used as a more regular component of policy-making across the world (Setälä and Smith 2018, Smith 2018). Trends toward adopting new policy instruments of governance started and achieved momentum as far back as the 1980s, as governments looked for new ways of delivering policies and engaging with citizens, while command and control and top-down implementation no longer seemed to work (Salamon 1989). The intellectual innovation behind behavioural economics goes back to the 1960s and 1970s, as do debates on participatory democracy that foreshadowed the development of deliberative democracy. The adoptions of nudge and think have been powerful phenomena, having been introduced over a long time alongside many other changes to public policy and public management. They have bedded down, do not show signs of abating, and are adopted by many governments and agencies across the world. The use of randomized evaluations shows no sign of slowing down either. Partly for this reason, in this chapter we review developments in randomized evaluations, nudges, and thinks to show how strong these linked phenomena are, which supports our belief that the research and policy agendas are moving ahead in ways that are just as strong if not stronger than we thought in 2011.

But we would not be true to our original mission if we did not think that more progress could be made, in particular in the realm between think and nudge, and in showing links between the two. We are alert to the potential weaknesses of nudge in particular for being too top-down and technocratic, and for wishing to limit the autonomy of individuals. In fact, nudge's weakness in this respect is think's strength, in that think involves embracing the autonomy of the individual in making choices. But think has problems scaling up to a larger population, which we discussed with our online experiment in Chapter 9. So, how to get the best of both worlds? We offer a proposal in the final part of this chapter, nudge plus. This is not just a merging of the insights of nudge and think, a kind of best of both worlds, but relies on re-thinking the cognitive foundations of human behaviour which affect how we design nudge policies and condition what we can expect from think.

The progress of randomized evaluations

In Chapter 2, 'Testing', we made the case for the more frequent use of randomized controlled trials because of their superiority in generating causal inferences about policy ideas. Other methods suffer from the familiar problem of endogeneity, which is where there might be a confounding variable that affects both the outcome and influencing variables, that limits the ability to make a valid inference. All methods have strengths and weaknesses, but the advantages of trials in testing out new ideas for policy interventions, especially nudges, but also thinks and deliberations, are very strong.

In the past, policy-makers were reluctant to adopt trials as methods of evaluation, at least outside health. Part of the reason for this was that the early adoption of trials in social policy was very complex, such as the Negative Income Tax trials in the 1960s, which suffered from implementation problems (see Munnell 1987). But over time there has been a more gradual diffusion of the use of trials and greater knowledge about how to implement them, especially in social policy in the US with three decades of social experimentation (Greenberg et al 2003, Greenberg and Schroder 2004). Trials were adopted by the federal and state governments despite changes in partisan control at each level. The UK has also been an important site for work and welfare experiments, strongly influenced by the US experience, such as the Restart programme, which tested for the importance of the mandatory interview with job seekers (White and Lakey 1992). It was followed by a series of trials in the 1990s (Greenberg and Schroder 2004). The Labour government elected in 1997 also used trials to evaluate employment and regeneration policies, in particular its New Deal programme, which required clients to participate in employment searching (see Walker et al 2006).

Building on this gradual development, the 2000s saw the growing use of trials, particularly in the US (see John 2017), for example, trials on education subsidies (see Angrist et al 2002, 2006). Congress tied randomized evaluation to the release of federal funds in the US Education Sciences Reform Act of 2002. Partly as a result, Baron finds 90 education studies using trials carried out from 2002 to 2013 (Baron 2013). There has been an upswing in the trials commissioned since 2008, for example of the Reading Recovery programme, the Success for All programme for education of students in elementary schools and the impact of the Teach for America programme (Baron 2013: 127). Under the Obama presidencies (2009–17), evidence and analysis came to be taken much more seriously by the US government (Haskins and Margolis 2015).

One additional area of expansion has been in the development field, in particular in the evaluation of aid programmes, with centres of activity at research organizations including Abdul Latif Jameel Poverty Action Lab and Innovations for Poverty Action, formed in 2003. These experiments have been large scale, such as Olken et al's (2014) performance management experiment in Indonesia. Trials have now become widely established as a method of evaluation by economists in this field (see Duflo 2006). These studies have involved close collaborations with policy-makers, such as donor governments or aid agencies that deliver the interventions.

BIT has been a pioneer of trials, which were promoted by its 2012 report *Test, Learn, Adapt* (Haynes et al 2012). For example, the team evaluated work/welfare programmes and applied behavioural insights to their operation (see Behavioural Insights Team 2015). Partly as a result of the team's efforts, the British government has been adopting trials more regularly, such as to test if vouchers would help the growth of small and medium sized enterprises (Behavioural Insights Team 2015). The most prominent example was Her Majesty's Revenue and Customs (HMRC), which initiated a large number and range of trials from 2012. These usually reminded taxpayers using a social norm or other behavioural cue (Hallsworth et al 2017). HMRC has a behavioural unit that runs trials across a range of functions and processes at regular intervals. The UK government set up a Cross-Government Trial Advice Panel (see www.gov.uk/governm ent/publications/cross-government-trial-advice-panel-role-and-me mbership). The 2018 update report of the panel was confidently enti-tled *The Rise of Experimental Government*, which indicates the per-ception by the policy and research community that a step change in the culture of experimentation had already happened (Cabinet Office and Economic and Social Research Council 2018). The docu-ment states: 'Recent years have seen government departments make use of experimental methods in a growing range of policy areas, including energy, the environment, housing, and social care'. Since 2015, the panel has assisted 52 projects across 18 departments and public bodies. The report draws on a case study of a trial on building integrated communities through English language provision, which also shows how trials have moved beyond transactional activities to more general policy development. Overall, trials by government agencies and partners in the UK have matured over time. Naturally, more progress is needed in standards of reporting and the replica-tion of research findings, but there are signs that the practitioners of these trials are aware of these challenges and seek to address them (Sanders et al 2018).

The other part of our methodological toolkit is design experiments, which we sought to make more widely visible as they were confined to education research. There have been embryonic signs of design experiments being considered to strengthen citizen participation. For example, the network #notwestminster and the Centre for Public Scrutiny have been promoting 'design experiments for local democracy' and refer to our work (see https://notinwestminster. wordpress.com/design-experiments-for-local-democracy). Despite this, it would be fair to say that these have not appeared as regular features of evaluation. It was always a less easy task than to advocate trials, which have had considerable momentum and legitimacy, as they go back to the 1920s and have a secure foundation in medical evaluations. But it is also fair to say that the design idea has become very strong in the movement for policy or design labs, which engender close examination of policies issues from the ground up, and like our design experiments, are about thinking through and modelling the design of policies through close observation. This design approach has become more commonly adopted across Europe, in what are sometimes called policy innovation labs (McGann et al 2018), and is leading to a new form of experimental government. For example, in April 2018, the Policy Lab was officially launched by the Open Policy Making team in the UK Cabinet Office using design principles. The basic ideas linked to design experiments remain very much alive as an approach to current policy-making.

The triumph of nudge

The period since 2011 has seen the maturation of nudge or behavioural public policy as a key tool of governance, which is accepted by policy-makers across the world, backed up by evidence from the use of experiments as has been discussed. During Obama's presidency (2009–17), behavioural science informed several policy measures, in part inspired by Cass Sunstein's presence in the administration (Sunstein, 2014). In the UK, BIT used insights from behavioural studies to launch initiatives across a range of policy fields (Halpern 2015, John 2018). In 2016, the federal level of government in Australia established the Behavioural Economics Team of Australia (www. dpmc.gov.au/domestic-policy/behavioural-economics), building on earlier initiatives at the state level. The Netherlands has also seen the influence of behavioural public policy across government (Feitsma 2018).

The international arena has seen the influence of behavioural science. The World Bank (2015) published a report in praise of behavioural change and created a Global Insights Team (www.worldbank. org/en/programs/gini) that uses psychology and behavioural insights to improve social outcomes. Both the Organisation for Economic Co-operation and Development (www.oecd.org/env/tools-evaluat ion/behavioural-experimental-economics-for-env-policy.htm) and the EU (European Commission, 2016) have shown an interest in collecting cases studies of successful behavioural change and nudge policies. There is no doubt that there is considerable momentum behind nudge that shows no sign of abating.

In the early phase of the policy programme a number of empirical criticisms of nudge were commonly articulated (e.g. Marteau et al 2011). Many of the interventions were mainly focused on large routine transactions between public agencies and the public, such as tax reminders, court fines, and other communications, usually paper letters or SMS messages. These initiatives have the advantage of demonstrating that nudge interventions can make a practical and financially beneficial contribution to good governance, but they

appeared to lack ambition. However, this was because the circumstances of launching a new programme of work may have encouraged a focus on the need to demonstrate proof of concept that could
in the future be relaxed. The search for quick wins led to the adoption of policies whose value could be readily shown. But there was
nothing in principle against nudge policy extending its range. Nudge
became well adapted to focus on rights (social rights/entitlements,
such as the right to vote, right to stand for election, right to complain,
right to take up benefits or tax advantages, and right to switch utility
supplier or banks); and there are applications that help to maximize
individual wellbeing (not just societal utility), such as healthy-eating
nudges which benefit individual as well as societal health.

Recent reviews of nudge applications show this increase in
range (Loewenstein and Chater 2017, Organisation for Economic
Co-operation and Development 2017). Benartzi et al's (2017) assessment of the costs and benefits of nudging provides evidence of cost
savings across a range of interventions categorized by security in
retirement, education, energy, health, job security, programme
integrity and compliance, and home affairs. Chetty (2015) discusses a
more pragmatic turn in the use of behavioural insights, with applications to a range of policy tools in fields such as retirement savings,
labour supply, and neighbourhood choice. Oliver (2013) argues that
behavioural science can be used more extensively across the tools
of government, using the term 'budge' for less libertarian interventions, which integrate behavioural insights into regulatory measures.
Some of the most exciting interventions of recent years have indeed
combined both a nudge and an item of regulation at the same time,
such as making taxes more salient to consumers (Chetty et al 2012).
Bhargava and Loewenstein (2015) argue that stronger application
of nudges to regulatory policies is where future opportunities lie.
Other applications are to decision-making in government, where

behavioural biases can be addressed through interventions. This topic is the focus of the new academic field (Grimmelikhuijsen et al 2017). BIT published a study which reviewed the evidence for behavioural biases in political decision-making and set out a new research agenda in this regard (Hallsworth et al 2018). Sanders et al (2018) reiterate the claim about the maturation of nudge and the new opportunities for further research and policy development. The authors argue that scaling up behavioural interventions, the behaviour of government, social diffusion, nudging organizations, and addressing thorny problems are new opportunities for behavioural researchers and policy-makers to address.

One important development is the growth of local interest in nudges, which links to our argument in the previous chapter about the potential for bottom-up nudges, taking advantage of the diversity of local areas and different kinds of democratic authorization as one way to counter the top-down orientation of much behavioural public policy. For example, BIT set up 'Behavioural Insights Team UK: North', which has close links to local authorities and has pioneered local trials, such as the Working Well programme in Greater Manchester to help people back into work (Behavioural Insights Team 2017: 34–7). There are a number of local tax trials, some run by BIT, others by different partnerships (John and Blume 2018). Another local example of nudging is encouraging disability parking permit holders to renew online at Essex County Council (John and Blume 2017). The Local Government Association has set up its own behavioural insights programme with a scheme for funding. Several of our original trials were conducted in partnership with voluntary sector organizations, and there is clearly a role for greater involvement of community groups in developing and implementing nudges (Cotterill et al 2012).

Progress continues in nudge policy and, as the 2017 report from BIT claims, there are signs that the scope and range of interventions is expanding, with 'a gradual shift to more complex behavioural challenges' (Behavioural Insights Team 2017: 4). The range of countries and governments willing to use insights from nudge is also increasing. One option would be to let this expanded programme develop and learn from experience. Governments setting the choice architecture of citizens to help them make better decisions might at first sight seem a benign undertaking. But as the reach of nudge expands, the potential for scepticism increases as we consider who determines the framing, with what level of awareness from citizens and to what ends? In spite of the policy successes, there is still a worry that the use of behavioural science manipulates citizens to make choices that go against their own interests. The danger is that the legitimacy of nudge is thus undermined in the long run. We suggest that there may be some role for linking think to nudge, which can help respond to some of the criticisms about the manipulative potential of nudge.

The institutionalization of think

As with nudge, think has seen an expansion of activity since the first edition of the book. The area where this is most obvious is in the application of deliberative mini-publics, which bring together randomly selected citizens to consider evidence on a particular area of policy and come to a recommendation. Such mini-publics come in a variety of designs, ranging from deliberative polls that include hundreds of citizens through to smaller citizens' juries (Setälä and Smith 2018). Since the 1990s, James Fishkin (2018) has been involved in the organization of numerous deliberative polls across the world, providing evidence that mini-publics can be used across different political contexts and policy issues. The pre- and post-survey methodology that deliberative polls employ has made them a particular focus for experimental research, much of which has concentrated on behavioural aspects of deliberation. Australia and Canada have been the countries where mini-publics have been most widely adopted, with NewDemocracy and MASS LBP (respectively) playing key entrepreneurial roles in persuading politicians about the value of deliberative processes and delivering successful projects. In 2018, MASS LBP ran its fiftieth long-form deliberation. The US has also been a site of innovation. Originating in Oregon and now spreading to other states, the Citizens' Initiative Review involves a randomly selected citizens' panel reviewing evidence on forthcoming initiative ballots and providing recommendations to all households on the veracity of arguments as part of the ballot brochure.

Arguably the step-change in the practice of mini-publics has been driven by the Irish use of citizens' assemblies to deal with controversial constitutional and policy issues. The Convention on the Constitution (which was an innovative mixed assembly comprised of randomly selected citizens and politicians) recommended changes to the constitutional status of same sex marriage, which was passed in a referendum in 2015. This was followed by the Citizens' Assembly (this time constituted by randomly selected citizens only), which recommended changes to the constitutional status of abortion and which, once again, was passed in a national referendum in 2018. Not surprisingly, these high-profile uses of citizens' assemblies raised the profile of deliberative practices internationally.

The Irish experience certainly had a positive influence in the UK, where the use of mini-publics had not captured the attention of politicians to the same extent as in other countries. The Citizens' Assembly on Brexit (Renwick et al 2018) held in 2017 provided an opportunity to show that citizens were willing and able to discuss complex and controversial issues such as the type of Brexit deal that should be agreed between the UK and the EU. While this was an academic-led experiment and had little substantive influence on the Brexit process, it provided proof of concept in the UK context. This experience directly led to the Citizens' Assembly on Social Care, sponsored by two select committees, where there is clear evidence that citizens' recommendations influenced the final report. In Northern Ireland, a further Citizens' Assembly on Social Care was organized in 2018 by a range of civil society organizations to show how a different, more consensual politics could be realized. The launch of the Innovations in Democracy Programme by the Department for Digital, Culture, Media & Sport, sees six to eight local authorities supported in running citizens' assemblies and a campaign for deliberative democracy by the RSA (Royal Society of Arts, Manufactures and Commerce) and Involve also launched in 2019, indicates the extent to which the profile of mini-publics has been raised in the UK in the last few years.

It would be a mistake to assume that all the development in think strategies is related to deliberative mini-publics. Other participatory designs which promote deliberation amongst citizens have also proliferated. Most prominent is participatory budgeting (PB), a set of practices that has travelled from Brazil across the world. While much of what is termed PB is often a pale comparison to the early examples in Brazil, which often led to significant redistribution of resources to poorer communities, citizens across the world are engaged in debates about the distribution of budgets. Large cities such as New York and Paris run high-profile PBs, and the Scottish government is committed to seeing all councils embed PB processes. Whereas deliberative mini-publics typically empower citizens to make policy recommendations, PBs empower citizens to decide directly on how resources should be distributed locally. More broadly there is growing interest in how public officials can engage citizens more effectively – the 'deliberative bureaucrat' (Boswell and Corbett 2018) – for example in planning processes (Puustinen et al 2017).

One of the challenges of think strategies – in particular deliberative mini-publics – is their relative size. Politicians are not always convinced by the relatively small numbers involved, which also limits their potential for broader changes to citizen behaviour. While there is extensive evidence that the efficacy of participants increases, broader social effects (beyond decision-making) are limited. This is one of the reasons why the potential for scaling up deliberation online is so enticing. Our own work on online deliberation (Chapter 9) was one of the first to explore systematically and experimentally the deliberative potential of online activity. The work by Neblo and colleagues (2018) on the 'Connecting to Congress' project indicates the importance of experimentation as part of thinks. Funded by the National Science Foundation and Harvard's Ash Institute for Democratic Governance and Innovation, the project aims to improve dialogue between citizens and their representatives and to look at the effects of these interactions. The online town halls, composed of randomly assigned, representative samples of constituents, discussed controversial issues of immigration policy and terrorist detainee policy. Evidence suggests improvement in democratic outcomes such as political trust. The potential of argument visualization platforms to curate massive online interactions is generating a great deal of interest. A number of innovative argument visualization platforms are beginning to emerge and gain purchase (Gürkan et al 2010, Tang 2016, Iandoli et al 2018). While interesting work is emerging on how to curate online deliberation, this remains an area where the democratic potential is still to be exploited.

Many of the developments in think are not directly linked to fostering wider changes in citizen behaviour, which is the focus of this book. While there may be links between dialogue over policy choices that lead to behaviour changes, this is a more tortuous route than the direct impact of nudge. The question for the rest of this chapter is whether there is a middle way between think and nudge that can take advantage of citizen empowerment in think and the potential for wide behaviour change in nudge.

Linking nudge and think: nudge plus

The key dilemma of relying too much on nudge is that it suffers from lack of consent and a concern that it is too manipulative. It is possible that nudge focuses too much on limiting the cognitive demands on citizens and places too much reliance on the state to consider what is best in the absence of citizen reflection (Button 2018). But is it necessary to be so negative about the cognitive capacity of citizens in comparison to policy experts? We argue that by revisiting the cognitive foundations of nudge it is possible to come up with a way forward rather different to the assumptions of behavioural economics. Nudge policy can then be freed to take a different direction, which relies less on a collection of desirable modifications and more on broader cognitive foundations so that citizens can be nudged to think rather more about their choices but in ways that correspond with their world views.

Nudge might appear to rely on automatic processes – 'system one' in Kahneman's (2011) scheme – which tends to reinforce the idea of experts deciding the best course of action and then rolling this out on unsuspecting citizens. We argue that this might apply to some nudges but not to all of them, and that indeed many nudges do require citizens to think and reflect. A simple reminder to attend an appointment does demand some reflection. Many interventions that start with a nudge require a degree of think from the individual. In practice, a lot of nudges are not as automatic as they first appear. Commitment devices, for example, often require the citizen to consider a change in behaviour. Such a view is shared by other nudge scholars, who classify some nudges as 'system two' nudges (Hansen and Jespersen 2013, Sunstein 2016a).

The recognition that many nudges involve reasoning provides the basis for a broader argument: the need to revisit the cognitive assumptions that underlie nudge. We agree that citizens reason – in the sense that they have reasons for doing what they do but that those processes of reason are framed by the bounds of their cognitive capacity and the environment in which they are located (Lupia et al 2000). Thinking is a flawed process, but we should not assume that people are unable to come up with the answers that are right for them. As Gigerenzer (2007: 4) argues: 'what seem to be limitations of the mind can actually be its strengths … More information, even more thinking, is not always better, and less can be more.' Gigerenzer and colleagues have developed this perspective by offering the concept of ecological rationality, which can be summarized as the idea that human reasoning is adaptive rather than logical in its motivation (Goldstein and Gigerenzer 2002). The best type of reasoning is the one that is most suited to the environment or task with which we are faced.

We propose that designers of nudge recognize that citizens are not always cognitive misers but are also capable thinkers. Many effective nudges, whether they admit it or not, already incorporate some citizen reflection and deliberation: we propose building on and using that wider cognitive palate in the interventions that policymakers use and in the ways they approach citizens. There is also good evidence to suggest that nudges do not need to rely on automatic processes, that thinking about the nudge does not undermine its effectiveness (Loewenstein et al 2015, Kroese et al 2016, Bruns et al 2018).

A programme of nudge plus would meet the charge of paternalism head on by looking not only to experts or governments to lead behaviour change but rather by giving citizens the space and capacity to make changes to their lives (John 2018, John and Stoker 2019). Examples include development commitment devices as part of behaviour change, or using Cognitive Behavioural Therapy (CBT) to encourage people to think slow when considering, for example, employment choices (Heller et al, 2017). Nudge plus links to other kinds of intervention, such as giving citizens 'boosts' to consider information choices in medicine for example (Hertwig 2017), or a prompted choice in organ donation.

We offer nudge plus as an enhancement to the current range of nudge policies. Nudge plus builds on the reflective component that is already implicit in many nudges. It encourages slow thinking at times, so that individuals can reflect on the messages that governments give them from time to time. There is a recognition that the nudger needs to design interventions with these long-term considerations in mind, such as giving citizens the boosts they need to make decisions, or personalizing nudges. While nudge plus fall short of full citizen control of policies, and still places responsibility for their design in the hands of bureaucrats and politicians, it is based on having a conversation between citizens and those who represent the state and government, which acknowledges the democratic foundation of public policies and the autonomy this should entail.

Beyond nudge plus, there is more that can be done to bring think into nudge policy. Nudges, especially those that entail less reflection (the system one nudges) and/or are recognized as potentially politically controversial, should be subject to discussion and scrutiny by citizens themselves. Transparency in nudging is something that we, in this book and elsewhere (John et al 2009, Moseley and Stoker 2013), and Thaler and Sunstein themselves have argued for (Thaler and Sunstein 2008, Sunstein 2016b). We suggest that governments should always be open about the policy instruments they are using, and doing this in the context of developing nudge interventions will inevitably lead to more 'thinking' about nudge. Thinking – in particular the use of deliberative mini-publics – can be used at the inception stage of nudges, in deciding not only what form nudges should take but which issues they should be applied to (or not).

Concluding comments

The research agenda on nudge and think has come a long way in the ten years since we first made the pairing (John et al 2009). Our subsequent experiments, reported in earlier chapters, are examples of good practice and offer a set of findings that test out nudge and think. The research and policy agendas have moved ahead considerably since that time, with behavioural public policy becoming secure as both a policy tool and a research programme. Think continues to offer important value for citizen involvement, as shown by the continuing interest in sponsoring citizen assemblies and town halls. But it is fair to say that the two realms are still far apart in terms of policy-makers' agendas and the programmes of research communities, in spite of our earlier attempts to bring nudge and think together in a dialogue about decentralization and bottom-up policy-making. There are some signs that nudge is moving more in the think direction, such as Sunstein's work on educative nudges, where he argues for the importance of human agency with nudge (Sunstein 2017b). The deliberative turn has been increasingly concerned with the behavioural context of policy-making and its institutional framing. But we think the link could go further, hence our programme of nudge plus. We will have to see whether nudge and think will get closer over the next ten years.

Note on results from the experiments

This appendix provides a summary of the results from our experiments. Differences in the unit of analysis and study design prevent a uniform measure of effect size, which may be comparable across the interventions. However, these figures summarize the percentage shifts the intervention achieved or give a qualitative assessment in the case of the design experiments.

Table A1.1   Effects of the experiments

Chapter & topic	Intervention	Effect of the intervention in comparison to a control group	Nudge or think
Chapter 3 Recycling experiment 1 (household recycling)	Canvassing	5% increase in recycling (immediate); drops to 4% increase (3 months later)	Nudge
Recycling experiment 2 (food waste)	Feedback	3% increase in recycling	Nudge

Chapter 4 Volunteering	Asking	Initial surge of interest but no change in volunteering levels	Nudge
Chapter 5 Voting	i) Telephone calls ii) Canvassing	i) 3.5% more votes ii) 3.6% more votes	Nudge
Chapter 6 Petitioning	Social information	i) 9% more petitions signed in lab study ii) 5.2% more petitions signed in field study	Nudge
Chapter 7 Giving (books)	i) Pledging ii) Pledging & publicity	i) 0.9% more donations (non-significant) ii) 1.6% more donations	Nudge
Chapter 8 Organ donating experiment 1 (information & discussion)	i) Information ii) Information & discussion	i) 4% increase in registrations ii) 15% decrease in registrations	Nudge v. Nudge & think
Organ donating experiment 2 (choice architecture)	i) Presumed consent ii) Mandated choice	i) 8% increase in registrations ii) 5% increase in registrations	Nudge & think
Chapter 9 Debating (online experiment)	i) Discussion forums & information ii) Information only	i) Modest opinion shifts in policy preferences; no changes in policy knowledge ii) No change	Think

Chapter 10 Including (DVD)	DVD portraying views of politically disengaged groups	Discussions with DVD generated debate, where decision-makers were more considerate of disengaged groups; DVDs influenced Area Boards' thinking about future engagement but created some resistance amongst councillors	Think
Chapter 11 Linking (letters to councillors)	i) Weak letter ii) Strong letter	i) 21% response from councillors ii) 16% response from councillors (no control group in this study)	Nudge

Glossary

Behavioural economics   A branch of economics that stresses the cognitive influences and limits on human behaviour. By stressing the use of judgement and heuristics, it is thought to depart from the classic rational model of decision-making.

Control group   One of the groups randomized as part of a randomized controlled trial. The control group does not get the intervention so may be used as a base from which to compare the impact of the intervention in the treatment group.

Counterfactual   A piece of information or inference that shows what would have happened in the absence of an intervention or event.

Experiment   A method of research where the group of people, or the area receiving the intervention or treatment, is randomly different from a control group or between treatment groups. This includes natural experiments and randomized controlled trials.

External validity   The extent to which research findings may be generalized to other cases.

Hawthorne effect   The impact on the results of research caused by an adjustment or improvement in the behaviour of people because they are being studied.

Glossary

Inference   Asserting a relationship between two variables.

Internal validity   The extent to which research findings represent the actual causal relationship.

Interrupted time series   A method for finding out whether a population, or an area that gets an intervention, improves when compared to a comparison group. It performs time series analysis on the two groups to see if one group's outcomes change at the point of, or shortly after, the intervention.

Intervention   The means by which an agency seeks to change behaviour or outcomes in a population. In an experiment, the treatment group receives the intervention.

Observational data   Data collected through observing the subjects of interest rather than from an experiment that seeks to manipulate the outcomes.

Randomized controlled trial   An experiment where the units of observation are randomized into two or more groups, with one as the control group and the others as the treatment group or groups, or are randomized between treatment groups.

Significant   A shorthand for statistically significant, that is, that the researcher can be confident with a minimum level of risk (5 per cent) that an independent variable affects a dependent variable in a regression, or there is an association or correlation between two variables in a table.

Treatment group   One of the groups randomized as part of a randomized controlled trial. The treatment group gets the intervention so may be used to compare values of the control group or another treatment group so as to evaluate its impact.

References

Abadie, A. and Gay, S. (2006), 'The Impact of Presumed Consent Legislation on Cadeveric Organ Donation: A Cross-Country Study', *Journal of Health Economics*, 25: 599–620.

Abers, R. (2000), *Inventing Local Democracy: Grassroots Politics in Brazil*, Boulder, CO and London: Lynne Rienner.

Ackerman, B. and Fishkin, J. (2004), *Deliberation Day*, New Haven, CT: Yale University Press.

Agarwal, S., Chomsisengphet, S., Mahoney, N., and Stroebel, J. (2013), 'Regulating Consumer Financial Products: Evidence from Credit Card', Working Paper, NBER.

Agur, M. and Low, N. (2009), *2007–08 Citizenship Survey: Empowered Communities Topic Report*, London: Department for Communities and Local Government.

Akerlof, G. and Shiller, R. (2016), *Phishing for Phools: The Economics of Manipulation and Deception*, Princeton, NJ: Princeton University Press.

Allcott, H. and Kessler, J. B. (2015), 'The Welfare Effects of Nudges: A Case Study of Energy Use Social Comparisons', Working Paper No. 21671, NBER.

Anderson, J. (2010), 'Review: Richard Thaler and Cass Sunstein: *Nudge: Improving Decisions about Health, Wealth, and Happiness*', *Economics and Philosophy*, 26: 389–406.

Angrist, J. D., Bettinger, E., Bloom, E., King, E., and Kremer, M. (2002), 'Vouchers for Private Schooling in Colombia: Evidence from a Randomized Natural Experiment', *American Economic Review*, 92(5): 1535–58.

References

Angrist, J. D., Bettinger, E., and Kremer, E. (2006), 'Long-Term Educational Consequences of Secondary School Vouchers: Evidence from Administrative Records in Colombia', *American Economic Review*, 96: 847–62.

Ariely, D., Bracha, A., and Meier, S. (2009), 'Doing Good or Doing well? Image Motivation and Monetary Incentives in Behaving Prosocially', *American Economic Review*, 99: 544–55.

Askew, R., John, P., and Liu, H. (2010), 'Can Policy Makers Listen to Researchers? An Application of the Design Experiment Methodology to a Local Drugs Policy Intervention', *Policy and Politics*, 38: 583–98.

Bächtiger, A., Dryzek, J., Mansbridge, J., and Warren, M. E. (eds) (2018), *The Oxford Handbook of Deliberative Democracy*, Oxford: Oxford University Press.

Barber, B. (1998), 'Three Scenarios for the Future of Technology and Strong Democracy', *Political Quarterly*, 113: 573–89.

Barnes, M., Stoker, G., and Whiteley, P. (2003), *Developing Civil Renewal: Some Lessons from Research*, ESRC Seminar Series, Swindon: ESRC.

Barnhill, A. (2014), 'What is Manipulation?', in C. Coons and M. Weber (eds), *Manipulation: Theory and Practice*, New York, NY: Oxford University Press, 50–72.

Baron, J. (2013), *Randomized Controlled Trials Commissioned by the Institute of Education Sciences Since 2002: How Many Found Positive Versus Weak or No Effects*, http://coalition4evidence.org/wp-content/uploads/2013/06/IES-Commissioned-RCTs-positive-vs-weak-or-null-findings-7-2013.pdf [accessed 17 February 2019].

Bator, R. and Cialdini, R. (2000), 'The Application of Persuasion Theory to the Development of Effective Proenvironmental Public Service Announcements', *Journal of Social Issues*, 56: 527–41.

Baumgartner, F. R. and Jones, B. D. (1993), *Agendas and Instability in American Politics*, Chicago, IL: University of Chicago Press.

Behavioural Insights Team/Cabinet Office (2013), *Applying Behavioural Insights to Organ Donation: Preliminary Results from a Randomised Controlled Trial*, London: Behavioural Insights Team.

Behavioural Insights Team (2015), *The Behavioural Insights Team Update 2013–2015*, London: Behavioural Insights Team.

Behavioural Insights Team (2017), *Update Report 2016–17*, www.bi.team/publications/the-behavioural-insights-team-update-report-2016-17/ [accessed 17 February 2019].

Bekkers, R. (2005), 'Participation in Voluntary Associations: Relations with

References

Resources, Personality, and Political Values', *Political Psychology*, 26(3): 439–54.

Bekkers, R. and Wiepking, P. (2011), 'A Literature Review of Empirical Studies of Philanthropy: Eight Mechanisms that Drive Charitable Giving', *Nonprofit and Voluntary Sector Quarterly*, 40(5): 924–73.

Benartzi, S., Beshears, J., Milkman, K. L., Sunstein, C. R., Thaler, R. H., Shankar, M., and Galing, S. (2017), 'Should Governments Invest More in Nudging?', *Psychological Science*, 28(8): 1041–55.

Benkler, Y. (2006), *The Wealth of Networks: How Social Production Transforms Markets and Freedom*, New Haven, CT: Yale University Press.

Bergan, D. E. (2009), 'Does Grassroots Lobbying Work? A Field Experiment Measuring the Effects of an e-mail Lobbying Campaign on Legislative Behavior', *American Politics Research*, 37: 327–52.

Best, S. J., Krueger, B., and Ladewig, J. (2007), 'The Effect of Risk Perceptions on Online Political Participatory Decisions', *Journal of Information Technology and Politics*, 4: 5–17.

Beveridge, W. (1948), *Voluntary Action: A Report on Methods of Social Advance*, London: George Allen and Unwin.

Bhargava, S. and Loewenstein, G. (2015), 'Behavioral Economics and Public Policy 102: Beyond Nudging', *American Economic Review*, 105(5): 396–401.

Bimber, B. (2003), *Information and American Democracy: Technology in the Evolution of Political Power*, Cambridge: Cambridge University Press.

Bolsen, T., Ferraro, P. J., and Miranda, J. J. (2014), 'Are Voters More Likely to Contribute to Other Public Goods? Evidence from a Large-Scale Randomized Policy Experiment', *American Journal of Political Science*, 58: 17–30.

Boswell, J. and Corbett, J. (2018), 'Deliberative Bureaucracy: Reconciling Democracy's Trade-off Between Inclusion and Economy', *Political Studies*, 66(3): 618–34.

Boyle, D. and Harris, M. (2009), *The Challenge of Co-Production*, London: Nesta.

Brannan, T., John, P., and Stoker, G. (2006), *Re-energizing Citizenship: Strategies for Civil Renewal*, Basingstoke: Palgrave Macmillan.

Braybrooke, D. and Lindblom, C. (1963), *A Strategy of Decision*, New York, NY: Free Press.

British Medical Association (2008), 'BMA Briefing Paper – Presumed Consent For Organ Donation, UK', *Medical News Today*, 14 November.

Brown, A. (1992), 'Design Experiments: Theoretical and Methodological

References

Challenges in Creating Complex Interventions in Classroom Settings', *Journal of the Learning Sciences*, 2: 141–78.

Bruns, H., Kantorowicz-Reznichenko, E., Klement, K., Luistro Jonsson, M., and Rahali, B. (2018), 'Can Nudges be Transparent and Yet Effective?', *Journal of Economic Psychology*, 65: 41–59.

Bryant, W. K., Jeon-Slaughter, H., Kang, H., and Tax, A. (2003), 'Participation in Philanthropic Activities: Donating Money and Time', *Journal of Consumer Policy*, 26(1): 43–73.

Bryce, W., Day, R., and Olney, T. (1997), 'Commitment Approach to Motivating Community Recycling: New Zealand Kerbside Trial', *Journal of Consumer Affairs*, 31: 27–52.

Burn, S. M. and Oskamp, S. (1986), 'Increasing Community Recycling with Persuasive Communication and Public Commitment', *Journal of Applied Social Psychology*, 16: 29–41.

Butler, D. M. and Broockman, D. E. (2011), 'Do Politicians Racially Discriminate Against Constituents? A Field Experiment on State Legislators', *American Journal of Political Science*, 55(3): 463–77.

Button, M. E. (2018), 'Bounded Rationality Without Bounded Democracy: Nudges, Democratic Citizenship, and Pathways for Building Civic Capacity', *Perspectives on Politics*, American Political Science Association. doi: 10.1017/S1537592718002086.

Cabannes, Y. (2004), 'Participatory Budgeting: A Significant Contribution to Participatory Democracy', *Environment and Urbanization*, 16: 27–46.

Cabinet Office (2011), *The Magenta Book: Guidance Notes for Policy Evaluation and Analysis*, London: Cabinet Office, www.gov.uk/government/publications/the-magenta-book [accessed 22 November 2018].

Cabinet Office (Halpern, D., Bates, C., Mulgan, G. and Aldridge, S. with Beales, G., and Heathfield, A.) (2004), *Personal Responsibility and Changing Behaviour: The State of its Knowledge and its Implications for Public Policy*, London: Cabinet Office

Cabinet Office (2018), *Civil Society Strategy: Building a Future That Works for Everyone*, London: Cabinet Office.

Cabinet Office and Economic and Social Research Council (2018), *The Cross-Government Trial Advice Panel: Update Report on the Activities and Impact of the Trial Advice Panel in its First Three Years*, www.gov.uk/government/publications/the-cross-government-trial-advice-panel-update-report [accessed 9 January 2019].

Camerer, C., Issacharoff, S. Loewenstein, G., O'Donoghue, T., and Rabin,

References

M. (2003), 'Regulation for Conservatives: Behavioral Economics and the Case for "Asymmetric Paternalism"', *University of Pennsylvania Law Review*, 151(3): 1211–54.

Cederman, L.-E. and Kraus, P. A. (2005), 'Transnational Communication and the European Demos', in R. Latham and S. Sassen (eds), *Digital Formations: IT and New Architectures in the Global Realm*, Princeton, NJ: Princeton University Press.

Changes (n.d.), 'Community Empowerment stories', http://changesuk.net/themes/community-empowerment/stories [accessed 9 January 2019].

Chen, H. M. (2013), 'Group Polarization in Virtual Communities: The Case of Stock Message Boards', iConference 2013 Proceedings (pp. 185–95), http://hdl.handle.net/2142/36051 [accessed 9 January 2019].

Chetty, R. (2015), 'Behavioral Economics and Public Policy: A Pragmatic Perspective', *American Economic Review*, 105(5): 1–33.

Chetty, R., Friedman, J. N., Leth-Petersen, S., Nielsenm T., and Olsen, T. (2012), 'Active vs. Passive Decisions and Crowdout in Retirement Savings Accounts: Evidence from Denmark', www.nber.org/papers/w18565 [accessed 17 February 2019].

Chin, M. L., Bond, J. R., and Geva, N. (2000), 'A Foot in the Door: An Experimental Study of PAC and Constituency Effects on Access', *Journal of Politics*, 62: 534–49.

Chivite-Matthews, N. I. and Teal, J. (2001), *1998 British Social Attitudes Survey: Secondary Data Analysis of the Local Government Module*, London: Department of the Environment, Transport and the Regions.

Choi, J., Laibson, D., Madrian, B., and Metrick, A. (2003), 'Optimal Defaults', *American Economic Review*, 93: 180–5.

Cialdini, R. B. (2007), *Influence. The Psychology of Persuasion*, New York, NY: Collins Business.

Cialdini, R. B. (2013), *Influence: Science and Practice*, Needham Heights, MA: Allyn and Bacon.

Clarke, H., Kornberg, A., McIntyre, C., Bauer-Kaase, P., and Kaase, M. (1999), 'The Effect of Economic Priorities on the Measurement of Value Change', *American Political Science Review*, 93: 637–47.

Clarke, N., Jennings, W., Moss, J., and Stoker, G. (2018), *The Good Politician: Folk Theories, Political Interaction, and the Rise of Anti-Politics Paperback*, Cambridge: Cambridge University Press.

Cobb, P., Confrey, J., diSessa, A., Lehrer, R., and Schauble, L. (2003), 'Design Experiments in Educational Research', in A. Kelly (ed)., *Educational Researcher*, 32: 9–13.

References

Coleman, S. (2004), 'Connecting Parliament to the Public via the Internet: Two Case Studies of Online Consultations', *Information, Communication and Society*, 7: 1–22.

Collins, A. (1992), 'Towards a Design Science of Education', in E. Scanlon and T. O'Shea (eds), *New Directions in Educational Technology*, Berlin: Springer Verlag.

Collins, A., Joseph, D., and Bielaczyc, K. (2004), 'Design Research: Theoretical and Methodological Issues', *Journal of the Learning Sciences*, 13: 15–42.

Communities and Local Government (2011), *Community Action in England: A Report on the 2009–10 Citizenship Survey*. London: Communities and Local Government.

Conly, S. (2013), *Against Autonomy: Justifying Coercive Paternalism*, Oxford: Oxford University Press.

Cooper, J. (2018), 'Organs and Organisations: Situating Ethics in Organ Donation after Circulatory Death in the UK', *Social Science & Medicine*, 209: 104–10.

Copus, C. (2014), *Report to the Communities and Local Government Committee Select Committee: Councillor Workshops: Councillors on the Frontline*, Leicester: de Montfort University.

Corporation for National and Community Service (2006), *Volunteering in America 2006: National, State, and City Information*, Washington, DC: Corporation for National and Community Service.

Corporation for National and Community Service (2010), *Volunteering in America 2010: National, State, and City Information*, Washington, DC: Corporation for National and Community Service.

Corporation for National and Community Service (2017), *2017 State of the Evidence Annual Report*, Washington, DC: Corporation for National and Community Service.

Costa, M. (2017), 'How Responsive are Political Elites? A Meta-analysis of Experiments on Public Officials', *Journal of Experimental Political Science*, 4(3): 241–54.

Cotterill, S. (2014), *Randomised Controlled Trial: The Effect of Asking for a Pledge on Charitable Donations*. SAGE Research Methods Cases, London: Sage.

Cotterill, S. (2017), 'The Influence of Population Characteristics on Household Response to a Charity Book Collection Based on Pledges and Social Pressure', *International Journal of Nonprofit and Voluntary Sector Marketing*, 22 (1): 1–6, https://doi.org/10.1002/nvsm.1572.

References

Cotterill, S. and Richardson, L. (2010), 'Expanding the Use of Experiments on Civic Behavior: Experiments with Local Governments as Research Partners', *Annals of the American Academy of Political and Social Science*, 628: 148–64.

Cotterill S., Howells K., Rhodes S., and Bower, P. (2017), 'The Effect of Social Pressure on Retention in a Longitudinal Health Questionnaire: An Embedded Randomised Controlled Retention Trial', *Trials*, 18: 341–7.

Cotterill, S., John, P., Liu, H., and Nomura, H. (2009), 'Mobilizing Citizen Effort to Enhance Environmental Outcomes: A Randomised Controlled Trial of a Door-to-Door Recycling Campaign', *Journal of Environmental Management*, 91: 403–10.

Cotterill, S., John, P., and Richardson, L. (2013), 'The Impact of a Pledge Campaign and the Promise of Publicity: A Randomized Controlled Trial of Charitable Donations', *Social Science Quarterly*, 94(1): 200–16.

Cotterill, S., Moseley A., and Richardson L. (2012), 'Can Nudging Create the Big Society? Experiments in Civic Behaviour and Implications for the Voluntary and Public Sectors', *Voluntary Sector Review*, 3(2): 265–74.

Cronqvist, H. and Thaler, R. (2004), 'Design Choices in Privatised Social-Security Systems: Learning From the Swedish Experience', *American Economic Review*, 94: 424–8.

Cronqvist, H., Thaler, R., and Yu, F. (2018), 'When Nudges Are Forever: Inertia in the Swedish Premium Pension Plan', *AEA Papers and Proceedings*, 108: 153–8.

Cutts, D., Fieldhouse, E., and John, P. (2009), 'Is Voting Habit Forming? The Longitudinal Impact of a GOTV Campaign in the UK', *Journal of Elections Public Opinion and Parties*, 19: 251–63.

Dahlberg, L. (2007), 'Rethinking the Fragmentation of the Cyberpublic: From Consensus to Contestation', *New Media and Society*, 9:827–47.

Dalton, R. (2004), *Democratic Challenges, Democratic Choices: The Erosion of Political Support in Advanced Industrial Democracies*, Oxford: Oxford University Press.

Davies, H. T. O., and Nutley, S. M. (2000), *What Works? Evidence-based Policy and Practice in Public Services*, Bristol: Policy Press.

Dawney, E. and Shah, H. (2005), *Behavioural Economics: Seven Principles for Policy Makers*, London: New Economics Foundation.

Department for Business and Skills and Cabinet Office (2014), *Growth Vouchers Trial Protocol*, London: Department for Business and Skills

References

and Cabinet Office, www.behaviouralinsights.co.uk/wp-content/uplo ads/2015/07/bis-14-561-growth-vouchers-programme-trial-protocol.pdf [accessed 9 January 2019].

Department for Communities and Local Government (2007), *Representing the Future: The Report of the Councillors Commission*, London: Department for Communities and Local Government.

Department for Communities and Local Government (2008), *Communities in Control: Real People, Real Power*, Cm. 742, Norwich: The Stationery Office Limited.

Department for Communities and Local Government (2009), *Citizenship Survey: 2009–10 (April–June 2009), England Statistical Release*, 9, London: Department for Communities and Local Government.

Department for Digital, Culture, Media & Sport (2018), *Community Life Survey 2017–18 – Statistical Release*, London: Department for Digital, Culture, Media & Sport.

Department of Health (2008), *Organs for Transplants: A Report from the Organ Donation Taskforce*, London: Department of Health.

diSessa, A. (1991), 'Local Sciences: Viewing the Design of Human-Computer Systems as Cognitive Science', in J. Carroll (ed.), *Designing Interaction: Psychology at the Human-Computer Interface*, New York, NY: Cambridge University Press.

Docter, S. and Dutton, W. (1998), 'The First Amendment Online: Santa Monica's Public Electronic Network', in R. Tsagarousianou, D. Tambini, and C. Bryan (eds), *Cyberdemocracy: Technologies, Cities and Civic Networks*, London: Routledge.

Dolan, P., Hallsworth, M., Halpern, D., King, D., and Vlaev, I. (2010), *Mindspace: Influencing Behaviour Through Public Policy*, London: Institute for Government.

Dolan, P., Hallsworth, M., Halpern, D., King, D. Metcalf, R., and Vlaev, I. (2012), 'Influencing Behaviour: The Mindspace Way', *Journal of Economic Psychology*, 33: 264–7.

Druckman, J., Green, D., Kuklinski, J., and Lupia, A. (2006), 'The Growth and Development of Experimental Research in Political Science', *American Political Science Review*, 100: 627–36.

Duflo, E. (2006), 'Field Experiments in Development Economics', in R. Blundell, W. Newey, and T. Persson (eds), *Advances in Economics and Econometrics: Theory and Applications*, Ninth World Congress, Cambridge: Cambridge University Press.

Dunleavy, P., Margetts, H., Bastow, S., and Tinkler, J. (2006), *Digital Era*

Governance: IT Corporations, the State, and E-government, Oxford: Oxford University Press.

Durose, C., Greasley, S., and Richardson, L. (2009), *Changing Local Governance, Changing Citizens*, Bristol: Policy Press.

Durose, C. and Richardson, L. (2016), *Designing Public Policy for Co-production: Theory, Practice and Change*, Bristol: Policy Press.

Eatwell, R. and Goodwin, M. (2018), *National Populism: The Revolt Against Liberal Democracy*, London: Pelican Books.

Ebeling, F. and Lotz, S. (2015), 'Domestic Uptake of Green Energy Promoted by Opt-out Tariffs', *Nature Climate Change*, 5(9): 868–71, doi: 10.1038/nclimate2681.

Elstub, S. and Escobar, O. (2019), *The Handbook of Democratic Innovation and Governance*, Cheltenham: Edward Elgar.

EOS Gallop Europe (2002), *Flash Eurobarometer 135: Internet and the Public at Large*, Brussels: EOS Gallop Europe.

European Commission (2016), *Behavioural Insights Applied to Policy Application to Specific Policy Issues and Collaboration at EU Level*, Conference and Workshop report by the Joint Research Centre (JRC), Brussels: European Commission.

Eurotransplant (2017), *Annual Report 2017 Eurotransplant International Foundation*.

Fabre, J. (1998), 'Organ Donation and Presumed Consent', *The Lancet*, 352: 150.

Farsides, T. (2007), 'The Psychology of Altruism', *The Psychologist*, 20: 474–7.

Fearon, J. (1998), 'Deliberation as Discussion', in J. Elster (ed.), *Deliberative Democracy*, Cambridge: Cambridge University Press.

Feitsma, J. N. P. (2018), 'Brokering Behaviour Change – The Work of Behavioural Insights Experts in Government', *Policy and Politics*, Advance View.

Festinger, L. (1957), *A Theory of Cognitive Dissonance*, Stanford, CA: Stanford University Press.

Fishkin, J. (2009), *When the People Speak: Deliberative Democracy and Public Consultation*, Oxford: Oxford University Press.

Fishkin, J. S. (2018), *Democracy When the People Are Thinking*, Oxford: Oxford University Press.

Frederick, S., Loewenstein, G., and O'Donoghue, T. (2002), 'Time Discounting and Time Preference: A Critical Review', *Journal of Economic Literature*, 40: 351–401.

Freedman, J. L. and Fraser, S. C. (1966), 'Compliance without Pressure:

References

The Foot-in-the-Door Technique', *Journal of Personality and Social Psychology*, 4: 195–202.

Fryer Jr, R. G., Levitt, S. D., List, J., and Sadoff, S. (2012), *Enhancing the Efficacy of Teacher Incentives through Loss Aversion: A Field Experiment* (No. w18237), National Bureau of Economic Research, doi: 10.3386/ W18237.

Fung, A. (2003a), 'Deliberative Democracy, Chicago Style: Grass-roots Governance in Policing and Public Education', in A. Fung and E. O. Wright (eds), *Deepening Democracy*, London: Verso.

Fung, A. (2003b), 'Survey Article: Recipes for Public Spheres: Eight Institutional Design Choices and their Consequences', *Journal of Political Philosophy*, 11: 338–67.

Fung, A. (2006), *Empowered Participation: Reinventing Urban Democracy*, Princeton, NJ: Princeton University Press.

Fung, A. (2015), 'Putting the Public Back into Governance: The Challenges of Citizen Participation and Its Future', *Public Administration Review*, 75: 513–22.

Fung, A. and Wright, E. (2003), *Deepening Democracy: Institutional Innovations in Empowered Participatory Governance*, London: Verso.

Gallup Organization (1993), *The American Public's Attitude toward Organ Donation and Transplantation*, Princeton, NJ: Gallup Organization.

Geller, E. S., Kalsher, M. J., Rudd, J. R., and Lehman, G. R. (1989), 'Promoting Safety Belt Use on a University Campus: An Integration of Commitment and Incentive Strategies', *Journal of Applied Social Psychology*, 19: 3–19.

Geng, S. (2016), 'Decision Time, Consideration Time, and Status Quo Bias', *Economic Inquiry*, 54: 433–49.

Gerber, A. S. and Green, D. P. (2000), 'The Effects of Canvassing, Telephone Calls, and Direct Mail on Voter Turnout: A Field Experiment', *American Political Science Review*, 94: 653–63.

Gerber, A. S. and Green, D. P. (2012), *Field Experiments: Design, Analysis, and Interpretation*, New Haven, CT: Yale University Press.

Gerber, A. and Green, D. P. (2018), 'Field Experiments on Voter Mobilization: An Overview of a Burgeoning Literature', in E. Duflo and A. Banerjee (eds), *Handbook of Economic Field Experiments*, Amsterdam: Elsevier, North-Holland.

Gerber, A. S., Green, D. P., and Shachar, R. (2003), 'Voting May be Habit-forming: Evidence from a Randomised Field Experiment', *American Journal of Political Science*, 47: 540–50.

References

Gerber, A. S., Green, D. P., and Kaplan, E. H. (2004), 'The Illusion of Learning From Observational Research', in I. Shapiro, R. M. Smith, and T. Masoud (eds), *Problems and Methods in the Study of Politics*, Cambridge: Cambridge University Press.

Gerber, A. S., Green, D. P., and Larimer, C. W. (2008), 'Social Pressure and Voter Turnout: Evidence from a Large-scale Field Experiment', *American Political Science Review*, 102: 33–47.

Gerber, E. R. and Phillips, J. H. (2002), 'Land Use Policy: Institutional Design and the Responsiveness of Representative Government', Paper presented at the Midwest Political Science Association Annual Meeting, Chicago, April.

Gerring, J. (2006), *Case Study Research: Principles and Practices*, Cambridge: Cambridge University Press.

Gigerenzer, G. (2007), *Gut Feelings: The Intelligence of the Unconscious*, New York: Viking Press.

Gigerenzer, G. (2015), 'On the Supposed Evidence for Libertarian Paternalism', *Review of Philosophy and Psychology*, September, 6(3): 361–83.

Glaeser, E. (2006), 'Paternalism and Policy', *University of Chicago Law Review* 73(1): 133–56.

Glennerster, R. and Takavarasha, K. (2013), *Running Randomized Evaluations. A Practical Guide*, Princeton, NJ: Princeton University Press.

Goldin, J. (2015), 'Which Way to Nudge? Uncovering Preferences in the Behavioral Age', *Yale Law Journal,* 125(1): 226–70.

Goldin, J. and Lawson, N. (2016), 'Defaults, Mandates, and Taxes: Policy Design with Active and Passive Decision-makers', *American Law and Economics Review* 18(2): 438–62.

Goldstein, D. and Gigerenzer, G. (2002), 'Models of Ecological Rationality: The Recognition Heuristic', *Psychological Review*, 109(1): 75–90.

Goodin, R. (2004), 'Heuristics of Public Administration', in M. Auger and J. G. March (eds), *Models of a Man: Essays in Memory of Herbert A. Simon*, Cambridge, MA: MIT Press.

Graham, M. and Dutton, W. H. (2014), *Society and the Internet: How Networks of Information and Communication are Changing Our Lives*, Oxford: Oxford University Press.

Green, D. P. and Gerber, A. S. (2002), 'Reclaiming the Experimental Tradition in Political Science', in H. Milner and I. Katznelson (eds), *State of the Discipline*, vol. 111, New York, NY: Norton.

Green, D. P. and Gerber, A. S. (2003), 'The Underprovision of Experiments

References

in Political Science', *ANNALS of the American Academy of Political and Social Science*, 589: 94–112.

Green, D. P. and Gerber, A. S. (2015), *Get Out the Vote! How to Increase Voter Turnout*, 3rd ed., Washington, DC: Brookings Institution Press.

Green, D. P., McGrath, M. C., and Aronow, P. M. (2013), 'Field Experiments and the Study of Voter Turnout', *Journal of Elections, Public Opinion and Parties*, 23(1): 27–48.

Greenberg, D. H., Linkz, D., and Mandell, M. (2003), *Social Experimentation and Public Policy Making*, Washington, DC: Urban Institute Press.

Greenberg, D. H. and Schroder, M. (2004), *The Digest of Social Experiments*, 3rd ed. Washington, DC: Urban Institute Press.

Greenwald, A., Carnot, C., Beach, R., and Young, B. (1987), 'Increasing Voting Behavior by Asking People if they Expect to Vote', *Journal of Applied Psychology*, 72: 315–18.

Grimm, R. T., Jr. and Dietz, N. (2018), *Where Are America's Volunteers? A Look at America's Widespread Decline in Volunteering in Cities and States*, Research Brief: Do Good Institute, University of Maryland.

Grimmelikhuijsen, S., Jilke, S., Olsen, A. L., and Tummers, L. (2017), 'Behavioral Public Administration: Combining Insights from Public Administration and Psychology', *Public Administration Review*, 77(1): 45–56.

Grolleau, G., Mateu, G., Sutan, A., and Vranceanu, R. (2018), '"Facta non verba": An Experiment on Pledging and Giving', *Journal of Economic Psychology*, 65: 1–15.

Grose, C. R. (2014), 'Field Experimental Work on Political Institutions', *Annual Review of Political Science* 17(1): 355–70.

Grose, C. R. and Russell, C. A. (2009), 'Avoiding the Vote: A Theory and Field Experiment of the Social Costs of Public Participation', Working Paper, Nashville, TN: Vanderbilt University.

Gürkan, A., Iandoli, L., Klein, M., and Zollo, G. (2010), 'Mediating Debate Through On-line Large-scale Argumentation: Evidence From the Field', *Information Sciences*, 180(19): 3686–702.

Gutmann, A. and Thompson, D. (1996), *Democracy and Disagreement*, Cambridge, MA: Belknap Press.

Hale S., John P., Margetts H., and Yasseri, T. (2018), 'How Digital Design Shapes Political Participation: A Natural Experiment with Social Information', *PLoS ONE* 13(4): e0196068.

Hallam, R. (2016), 'How the Internet Can Overcome the Collective Action Problem: Conditional Commitment Designs on Pledgebank, Kickstarter, and The Point/Groupon Websites', *Information Communication & Society*, 19(3): 362–79.

Hallsworth, M., Egan, M., Rutter, J., and McCrae, J. (2018), *Behavioural Government: Using Behavioural Science to Improve How Governments Make Decisions*, London: The Behavioural Insights Team.

Hallsworth, M., List, J., Metcalfe, R. D., and Vlaev, I. (2017), 'The Behavioralist as Tax Collector: Using Natural Field Experiments to Enhance Tax Compliance', *Journal of Public Economics*, 148: 14–31.

Halpern, D. (2005), *Social Capital*, Cambridge: Polity.

Halpern, D. (2010), *The Hidden Wealth of Nations*, Cambridge: Polity.

Halpern, D. (2015), *Inside the Nudge Unit*, London: W. H. Allen.

Ham, A. J. van der, Kupper, F., Bodewes, A., and Broerse, J. E. W. (2013), 'Stimulating Client Involvement and Client–Provider Dialog through Participatory Video: Deliberations on Long-term Care in a Psychiatric Hospital', *Patient Education and Counseling*, 91(1): 44–9.

Hansen P. G. and Jespersen, A. M. (2013), 'Nudge and the Manipulation of Choice: A Framework for the Responsible Use of the Nudge Approach to Behaviour Change in Public Policy', *European Journal of Risk Regulation*, 1: 3–28.

Hansen, P. G., Hendricks, V. F., and Rendsvig, R. K. (2013), 'Infostorms', *Metaphilosophy*, 44: 301–26.

Harburgh, W. T. (1998), 'What Do Donations Buy? A Model of Philanthropy Based on Prestige and Warm Glow', *Journal of Public Economics*, 67: 269–84.

Harder, M. K., Woodard, R., and Bench, M. L. (2006), 'Two Measured Parameters Correlated to Participation Rates in Kerbside Recycling Schemes in the UK', *Environmental Management*, 37: 487–95.

Hargreaves-Heap, S. (2013), 'What is the Meaning of Behavioural Economics?', *Cambridge Journal of Economics*, 37(5): 985–1000.

Haskins, R. and Margolis, G. (2015), *Show Me the Evidence: Obama's Fight for Rigour and Results in Social Policy*, Washington DC: Brookings Institute Press.

Hayek, F. (1943), *The Road to Serfdom*, Chicago, IL: University of Chicago Press.

Haynes, L., Service, O., Goldacre, B., and Torgerson, D. T. (2012), *Test, Learn, Adapt: Developing Public Policy with Randomized Controlled Trials*, London: Cabinet Office.

Haynes, L., Green, D. P., Gallagher, R., John, P., and Torgerson, D. J. (2013), 'Collection of Delinquent Fines: An Adaptive Randomized Trial to

References

Assess the Effectiveness of Alternative Text Messages', *Journal of Policy Analysis and Management*, 32: 718–30.

Heller, S. B., Shah, A. K., Guryan, J., Ludwig, J., Mullainathan, S., and Pollack, H. A. (2017), 'Thinking, Fast and Slow? Some Field Experiments to Reduce Crime and Dropout in Chicago', *Quarterly Journal of Economics*, 132(1): 1–54.

Hertwig, R. (2017), 'When to Consider Boosting: Some Rules for Policymakers', *Behavioural Public Policy*, 1(2): 143–61.

Hirst, P. (1993), *Associative Democracy: New Forms of Economic and Social Governance*, Cambridge: Polity.

Homonoff, T. A. (2013), 'Can Small Incentives Have Large Effects? The Impact of Taxes versus Bonuses on Disposable Bag Use', Industrial Relations Section, Princeton University Working Paper No. 575, http://arks.princeton.edu/ark:/88435/dsp014q77fr47j [accessed 17 February 2019].

Hopkins, D. J. and Sides, J. (2015), *Political Polarisation in American Politics*, New York, NY: Bloomsbury Academic.

House, J. S. (1981), *Work, Stress and Social Support*, Reading, MA: Addison-Wesley.

House of Commons Communities and Local Government Committee (2013), *Councillors on the Frontline. Sixth Report of Session 2012–13*, London: The Stationery Office Limited.

Huck, S. and Rasul, I. (2011), 'Matched Fundraising: Evidence from a Natural Field Experiment', *Journal of Public Economics*, 95: 351–62.

Iandoli, L., Quinto, I., Spada, P., Klein, M., and Calabretta, R. (2018), 'Supporting Argumentation in Online Political Debate: Evidence from an Experiment of Collective Deliberation', *New Media and Society Journal*, 20(4): 1320–41.

Improvement and Development Agency (2009), *In Shape for Success? Chief Executives' Perspectives on Achieving Culture Change in Local Government*, London: Improvement and Development Agency.

Ipsos-MORI (2018) *National Oversight and Audit Commission Local Authority Satisfaction Survey 2018*, NOAC Report No 18, London: Ipsos-MORI.

Jakobsen, M. (2013), 'Can Government Initiatives Increase Citizen Coproduction? Results of a Randomized Field Experiment', *Journal of Public Administration Research and Theory*, 23: 27–54.

Janssen, D. and Kies, R. (2005), 'Online Forums and Deliberative Democracy', *Acta Politica*, 40: 317–35.

References

John, P. (2009), 'Can Citizen Governance Redress the Representative Bias of Political Participation?', *Public Administration Review*, 69: 494–503.

John, P. (2011), *Making Policy Work*, London: Routledge.

John, P. (2014), 'The Great Survivor', *Local Government Studies*, 40: 687–704.

John, P. (2017), *Field Experiments in Political Science and Public Policy*, New York, NY: Routledge.

John, P. (2018), *How Far to Nudge: Assessing Behavioural Public Policy*, Cheltenham: Edward Elgar.

John, P. (2019), 'The International Appeal of Behavioural Public Policy: Is Nudge an Anglo-American Phenomenon?', *Journal of Chinese Governance*, doi: 10.1080/23812346.2019.1576264.

John, P. and Blume, T. (2017), 'Nudges that Promote Channel Shift: A Randomized Evaluation of Reminders for Disability Badges', *Internet and Policy*, 9(2): 168–83.

John, P. and Blume, T. (2018), 'How Best to Nudge Taxpayers? The Impact of Message Simplification and Descriptive Social Norms on Payment Rates in a Central London Local Authority', *Journal of Behavioral Public Administration*, 1(1), https://doi.org/10.30636/jbpa.11.10 [accessed 17 February 2019].

John, P. and Brannan, T. (2006), 'How to Mobilise the Electorate: Lessons from the University of Manchester "Get Out the Vote" Experiment', *Representation*, 42: 209–21.

John, P. and Brannan, T. (2008), 'How Different are Telephoning and Canvassing? A Get Out the Vote Field Experiment in the UK 2005 General Election', *British Journal of Political Science*, 38: 565–74.

John, P. and Stoker, G. (2019), 'Rethinking the Cognitive Foundations and the Role of Expertise in Behavioural Public Policy: A New Prospectus', forthcoming, *Policy and Politics*.

John, P., Fieldhouse, E., and Liu, H. (2011), 'How Civic is the Civic Culture? Explaining Community Participation Using 2005 English Citizenship Survey', *Political Studies*, 59: 230–52.

John, P., James, O., Moseley, A., Richardson, L., Ryan, M., and Stoker, G. (2018), 'The Impact of Peer, Politician and Celebrity Endorsements on Volunteering: A Field Experiment with English Students', *Journal of Nonprofit & Public Sector Marketing*, doi: 10.1080/10495142.2018.1526743.

John, P., Sanders, M., and Wang, J. (2014), 'The Use of Descriptive Norms in Public Administration: A Panacea for Improving Citizen Behaviours?' SSRN: https://ssrn.com/abstract=2514536 [accessed 17 February 2019].

John, P., Smith, G., and Stoker, G. (2009), 'Nudge Nudge, Think Think: Two

References

Strategies for Changing Civic Behaviour', *The Political Quarterly*, 80(3): 361–70.

Johnson, E. J. and Goldstein, D. (2003), 'Do Defaults Save Lives?', *Science*, 302: 1338–9.

Johnson, E. and Goldstein, D. (2013), 'Decisions by Default', in Eldar Shafir (ed.), *Behavioral Foundations of Policy*, Princeton, NJ: Princeton University Press, 417–27.

Jones, B. (2001), *Politics and the Architecture of Choice*: *Bounded Rationality and Governance*, Chicago, IL: University of Chicago Press.

Joss, S. and Durant, J. (1995), *Public Participation in Science: The Role of Consensus Conferences in Europe*, London: Science Museum.

Jowell, R. (2003), *Trying it Out: The Role of 'Pilots' in Policy-Making*, London: Cabinet Office.

Kahneman, D. (2011), *Thinking, Fast and Slow*, London: Penguin.

Kahneman, D. and Tversky, A. (1979), 'Prospect Theory: An Analysis of Decisions Under Risk', *Econometrica*, 47: 313–27.

Kahneman, D., Knetsch, J. L., and Thaler, R. H. (1990), 'Experimental Tests of the Endowment Effect and the Coase-theorem', *Journal of Political Economy*, 98: 1325–48.

Kamdar, A., Levitt, S. D., List, J. A., Mullaney, B., and Syverson, C. (2015), 'Once and Done: Leveraging Behavioral Economics to Increase Charitable Contributions', SPI Working Paper No. 025 Chicago.

Karlsson, D. (2013), 'Who Do the Local Councillors of Europe Represent?', in Egner, B., Sweeting, D., and Klok, P. J. (eds) (2013), *Local Councillors in Europe*, Urban and Regional Research International Volume 14, Germany: Springer: 97–119.

Katzev, R. D. and Pardini, A. U. (1987), 'The Comparative Effectiveness of Reward and Commitment Approaches in Motivating Community Recycling', *Journal of Environmental Systems*, 17: 93–114.

Kawachi, I., Subramanian, S.V., and Kim, D. (2008), *Social Capital and Health*, New York, NY: Springer.

Kendall, J. (2009), *The Value of Volunteering in Europe in the Noughties*, Birmingham: Third Sector Research Centre.

Kettlewell, K. and Phillips, L. (2014), *Census of Local Authority Councillors 2013* (Local Government Association Research Report), Slough: NFER.

King, G., Keohane, R., and Verba, S. (1994), *Designing Social Inquiry*: *Scientific Inference in Qualitative Research*, Princeton, NJ: Princeton University Press.

References

Kingdon, J. (1995), *Agendas, Alternatives and Public Policies*, New York, NY: Harper Collins.

Klein, M., Cioffi, M., and Malone, T. (2007), 'Achieving Collective Intelligence via Large-scale On-line Argumentation', ICIW, http://cci. mit.edu/publications/CCIwp2007-01.pdf [accessed 20 August 2014].

Knowles, S. and Servátka, M. (2015), 'Transaction Costs, the Opportunity Cost of Time and Procrastination in Charitable Giving', *Journal of Public Economics*, 125: 54–63.

Kroese, F. M., Marchiori, D. R., and Ridder, D. T. D. (2016), 'Nudging Healthy Food Choices: A Field Experiment at the Train Station', *Journal of Public Health*, 38, 133–7.

Kuran, T. and Sunstein, C. R. (1999), 'Availability Cascades and Risk Regulation', *Stanford Law Review*, 51(4): 683–762.

Laibson, D. (1997), 'Golden Eggs and Hyperbolic Discounting', *Quarterly Journal of Economics*, 112: 443–77.

Lammam, C., and Gabler, N. (2012), *Determinants of Charitable Giving: A Review of the Literature*, Fraser Institute, www.yumpu.com/en/docu ment/view/21076729/determinants-of-charitable-giving-a-review-of-the -fraser-institute [accessed 8 January 2019].

Leggett, Will (2014), 'The Politics of Behaviour Change: Nudge, Neo-liberalism and the State', *Policy and Politics*, 42: 3–19.

Lijphart, A. (1997), 'Unequal Participation: Democracy's Unresolved Dilemma', *American Political Science Review*, 91: 1–14.

Local Government Association (2008), *The Reputation of Local Government*, London: Local Government Association.

Local Government Association (2018a), *Polling on Resident Satisfaction with Councils: Round 21*, London: Local Government Association.

Local Government Association (2018b), *Polling on Resident Satisfaction with Councils: Round 19*, London: Local Government Association.

Loewenstein, G. and Chater, N. (2017), 'Putting Nudges in Perspective', *Behavioural Public Policy*, 1(1): 26–53.

Loewenstein, G., Bryce, C., Hagmann, D., and Rajpal, S. (2015), 'Warning: You Are About to be Nudged', *Behavioral Science and Policy*, 1(1): 35–42.

Losee, R. M. (1989), 'Minimizing Information Overload: The Ranking of Electronic Messages', *Journal of Information Science*, 15(3): 179–89.

Lowndes, V., Pratchett, L. P., and Stoker, G. (2001), 'Trends in Public Participation: Part 2 – Citizen Perspectives', *Public Administration*, 79: 452–3.

Lowndes, V., Pratchett, L., and Stoker, G. (2006), 'Diagnosing and Remedying the Failings of Official Participation Schemes: The CLEAR Framework', *Social Policy and Society*, 5: 281–91.

Ludwig, T., Buchholz, C., and Clarke, S. (2005), 'Using Social Marketing to Increase the Use of Helmets Among Bicyclists', *Journal of American College Health*, 54: 51–8.

Lunch, C. and Lunch, N. (2006), *Insights into Participatory Video: A Handbook for the Field*, Oxford: InsightShare, http://insightshare.org/resources/pv-handbook [accessed 16 May 2011].

Lupia, A. and Sin, G. (2003), 'Which Public Goods are Endangered? How Evolving Communication Technologies Affect the Logic of Collective Action', *Public Choice*, 117: 315–31.

Lupia, A., McCubbins, M., and Popkin, S. (2000), *Elements of Reason Cognition, Choice, and the Bounds of Rationality*, Cambridge: Cambridge University Press.

Luskin, R. C., Fishkin, J. S., and Iyengar, S. (2006), 'Considered Opinions on US Foreign Policy: Face-to-Face versus Online Deliberative Polling', paper available from the Center for Deliberative Democracy, Stanford, CA: Stanford University, http://cdd.stanford.edu/research/index.html [accessed 5 January 2019].

Lyas, J.K., Shaw, P. J., and Van Vugt, M. (2004), 'Provision of Feedback to Promote Householders' Use of a Kerbside Recycling Scheme – A Social Dilemma Perspective', *Journal of Solid Waste Technology*, 30: 7–18.

Macedo, S. (1999), *Deliberative Politics: Essays on Democracy and Disagreement*, Oxford: Oxford University Press.

McGann, M., Blomkamp, E., and Lewis, J. M. (2018), 'The Rise of Public Sector Innovation Labs: Experiments in Design Thinking for Policy', *Policy Sciences*, 51: 249–67.

McKenzie, C. R., Liersch, M. J., and Finkelstein, S. R. (2006), 'Recommendations Implicit in Policy Defaults', *Psychological Science*, 17(5): 414–20, doi: 10.1111/j.1467-9280.2006.01721.x.

McKenzie-Mohr, D. (2000), 'Promoting Sustainable Behaviour: An Introduction to Community-based Social Marketing', *Journal of Social Issues*, 56: 543–54.

McKenzie-Mohr, D. and Smith, W. (1999), *Fostering Sustainable Behavior: An Introduction to Community-Based Social Marketing*, Gabriola Island, Canada: New Society Publishers.

Mangan, C., Needham, C., Bottom K., and Parker, S. (2016), *The 21st Century Councillor*, Birmingham: University of Birmingham.

References

Manosevitch, E., Steinfeld, N., and Lev-On, A. (2014), 'Promoting Online Deliberation Quality: Cognitive Cues Matter', *Information, Communication & Society*, 17(10): 1177–95.

Mansbridge, J., Hartz-Karp, J., Amengual, M., and Gastil, J. (2006), 'Norms of Deliberation: An Inductive Study', *Journal of Public Deliberation*, 2(1), article 7, www.publicdeliberation.net/jpd/vol2/iss1/art7 [accessed 5 January 2019].

March, J. and Olsen, J. (1989), *Rediscovering Institutions*, New York, NY: Free Press.

Margetts, H., John, P., Escher, T., and Reissfelder, S. (2011), 'Social Information and Political Participation on the Internet: An Experiment', *European Political Science Review*, 3: 321–44.

Margetts, H., John, P., Hale, S., and Yasseri, T. (2015a), *Political Turbulence: How Social Media Shape Collective Action*, Princeton, NJ: Princeton University Press.

Margetts, H., John, P., Hale, S. A., and Reissfelder, S. (2015b), Leadership without Leaders? Starters and Followers in Online Collective Action, *Political Studies*, 63: 278–99.

Marteau, T. M., Ogilvie, D., Roland, M., Suhrcke, M., and Kelly, M. P. (2011), 'Judging Nudging: Can Nudging Improve Population Health?', *British Medical Journal*, 342: 263–5.

Mason, D. P. (2016), 'Recognition and Cross-cultural Communications as Motivators for Charitable Giving: A Field Experiment', *Nonprofit and Voluntary Sector Quarterly*, 45(1): 192–204.

Meyer, C. and Tripodi, E. (2018), 'Image Concerns in Pledges to Give Blood: Evidence from a Field Experiment', SSRN: https://ssrn.com/abstract=3132289.

Micheletti, M. (2010), *Political Virtue and Shopping: Individuals, Consumerism, and Collective Action*, New York, NY: Palgrave Macmillan.

Miller, D. (1992), 'Deliberative Democracy and Social Choice', *Political Studies (Special Issue: Prospects for Democracy)*, 40: 54–67.

Mohan, J. (2011), 'Is there a British "Civic Core"? Evidence from the Citizenship Survey on Patterns of Volunteering, Donations to Charity, and Civic Participation', Third Sector Research Centre Working Paper No. 73, www.birmingham.ac.uk/generic/tsrc/documents/tsrc/working-papers/working-paper-73.pdf [accessed 5 January 2019].

Morales, L. (2009), *Joining Political Organisations: Institutions, Mobilisation and Participation in Western Democracies*, Colchester: ECPR Press.

Moseley, A. and Stoker, G. (2013), 'Nudging Citizens? Prospects and Pitfalls

References

Confronting a New Heuristic', *Resources, Conservation and Recycling*, 79: 4–10.

Moseley, A. and Stoker, G. (2015), 'Putting Public Policy Defaults to the Test: The Case of Organ Donor Registration', *International Public Management Journal*, 18(2): 246–64.

Moseley, A., James, O., John, P., Richardson, L., Ryan, M., and Stoker, G. (2018), 'The Effects of Social Information on Volunteering: A Field Experiment', *Nonprofit and Voluntary Sector Quarterly*, 47(3): 583–603.

Munnell, A. (1987), *Lessons from the Income Maintenance Experiments*, Boston: Federal Reserve Bank of Boston.

National Council for Voluntary Organisations (2017), *UK Civil Society Almanac 2017*, London: NCVO, https://data.ncvo.org.uk/a/almanac17/volunteering-overview/ [accessed 17 February 2019].

National Council for Voluntary Organisations (2018), *UK Civil Society Almanac 2018*, London: NCVO, https://data.ncvo.org.uk/category/alma nac/voluntary-sector/volunteers-workforce/ [accessed 17 February 2019].

Neblo, M., Esterling, K., Kennedy, R., Lazer, D., and Sokhey, A. (2010), 'Who Wants to Deliberate – and Why?', *American Political Science Review*, 104: 566–83.

Neblo, M. A., Esterling, K., and. Lazer, D. (2018), *Politics with the People Building a Directly Representative Democracy*, Cambridge: Cambridge University Press.

Nelson Dias (Org.) (2018), *Hope for Democracy: 30 Years of Participatory Budgeting Worldwide*, Cimpress TM, supported by Ministry of Finance of the Russian Federation/World Bank, https://thelivinglib.org/hope-for-democracy-30-years-of-participatory-budgeting-worldwide/ [accessed 17 February 2019].

New, W., Solomon, M., Dingwall, R., and McHale, J. (1994), *A Question of Give and Take: Improving the Supply of Donor Organs for Transplantation*, London: King's Fund.

Newton, R., Pierce, A., Richardson, L., and Williams, M. (2010), *Citizens and Local Decision-making: What Drives Feelings of Influence?*, London: Urban Forum.

NHS Blood and Transplant (2018), *Organ Donation and Transplantation – Activity Figures for the UK as at 6th April 2018*, https://nhsbtdbe.blob. core.windows.net/umbraco-assets/1343/annual_stats.pdf [accessed 3 January 2019].

Nickerson, D. (2006), 'Volunteer Phone Calls Can Increase Turnout:

Evidence from Eight Field Experiments', *American Politics Research*, 34: 271–92.

Nomura, H., Cotterill, S., and John, P. (2011), 'The Use of Feedback to Enhance Environmental Outcomes: A Randomised Controlled Trial of a Food Waste Scheme', *Local Environment*, 16(7): 637–53.

Norris, P. (2001), *Digital Divide: Civic Engagement, Information Poverty, and the Internet Worldwide*, Cambridge: Cambridge University Press.

O'Donoghue, T. and Rabin, M. (1999), 'Doing It Now or Later', *American Economic Review*, 89: 103–24.

Office for National Statistics (2017), *Billion Pound Loss in Volunteering Effort*, 16 March 2017, London: Office for National Statistics, www.ons. gov.uk/employmentandlabourmarket/peopleinwork/earningsand-workinghours/articles/billionpoundlossinvolunteeringeffort/2017-03-16 [accessed 17 February 2019].

Olken, B. A., Onishi, J., and Wong. S. (2014), 'Should Aid Reward Performance? Evidence from a Field Experiment on Health and Education in Indonesia', *American Economic Journal: Applied Economics*, 6: 1–34.

Oliver, A. (2013), 'From Nudging to Budging: Using Behavioural Economics to Inform Public Sector Policy', *Journal of Social Policy*, 42(4): 685–700.

Oliver, A. (2017), *The Origins of Behavioural Public Policy*, Cambridge: Cambridge University Press.

Oliver, P. (1980), 'Rewards and Punishments as Selective Incentives for Collective Action: Theoretical Investigations', *American Journal of Sociology*, 85: 1356–75.

Ontario Ministry of Health and Long Term Care (2016), *Behavioural Insights Project – Organ Donor Registration*, Ontario Ministry of Health and Long Term Care, Trillium Gift of Life Network, the Ministry of Government and Consumer Services and Treasury Board Secretariat's Behavioural Insights Unit/ Behavioural Economics in Action at Rotman Centre, www.ontario.ca/page/behavioural-insights-pilot-project-organ-donor-registration [accessed 3 January 2019].

Oostveen, A.-M. and van den Besselaar, P. (2004), 'Security as Belief: User's Perceptions on the Security of Electronic Voting Systems', in A. Prosser and R. Krimmer (eds), *Electronic Voting in Europe: Technology, Law, Politics and Society*, Bonn: Gesellschaft für Informatik.

Oostveen, A.-M. and van den Besselaar, P. (2006), 'Non-Technical Risks of Remote Electronic Voting', in A.-V. Anttiroiko and M. Malkia (eds), *The Encyclopedia of Digital Government*, Hershey, PA: Idea Group Inc.

Organisation for Economic Co-operation and Development (2017),

References

Behavioural Insights and Public Policy: Lessons from Around the World, Paris: OECD.

Osborne, D. and Gaebler, T. (1993), *Reinventing Government: How the Entrepreneurial Spirit is Transforming the Public Sector*, New York, NY: Penguin.

Panagopoulos, C. (2010), 'Affect, Social Pressure and Prosocial Motivation: Field Experimental Evidence of the Mobilizing Effects of Pride, Shame and Publicizing Voting Behavior', *Political Behavior*, 32: 369–86.

Pattie, C. and Seyd, P. (2003), 'Citizenship and Civic Engagement: Attitudes and Behaviour in Britain', *Political Studies*, 51: 443–68.

Pattie, C., Seyd, P., and Whiteley, P. (2005), *Citizenship in Britain: Values, Participation and Democracy*, Cambridge: Cambridge University Press.

Pawson, R. and Tilly, N. (1997), *Realistic Evaluation*, London: Sage.

Pestoff, V. (2019), *Co-production and Public Service Management: Citizenship, Governance and Public Service Management*, New York, NY: Routledge.

Peters, B.G. (1998), *Comparative Politics: Theory and Methods*, London: Macmillan.

Petrosino, A., Turpin-Petrosino, C., and Buehler, J. (2003), 'Scared Straight and Other Juvenile Awareness Programs for Preventing Juvenile Delinquency: A Systematic Review of the Randomised Experimental Evidence', *Annals of the American Academy of Political and Social Science*, 589: 41–62.

Petrosino, A., Turpin-Petrosino, C., Hollis-Peel, M. E., and Lavenberg, J. G. (2013), 'Scared Straight and Other Juvenile Awareness Programs for Preventing Juvenile Delinquency', *Cochrane Database of Systematic Reviews*, 4. No.: CD002796. doi: 10.1002/14651858.CD002796.pub2.

Pichert, D. and Katsikopoulos, K. V. (2008), 'Green Defaults: Information Presentation and Pro-environmental Behaviour', *Journal of Environmental Psychology*, 28(1): 63–73.

Phillips, A. (1991), *Engendering Democracy*, Cambridge: Polity.

Phillips, A. (1995), *The Politics of Presence*, Oxford: Oxford University Press.

Pisani, E., Franceschetti, G., Secco, L., and Christoforou, A. (2017), *Social Capital and Local Development: From Theory to Empirics*, Basingtoke: Palgrave.

Prabhakar, R. (2010), 'Nudge, Nudge, Say No More', *Guardian*, 9 March, www.theguardian.com/public-leaders-network/engagement?page=9 [accessed 24 February 2019].

References

Price, V. (2006), 'Citizens Deliberating Online: Theory and Some Evidence', in T. Davies (ed.), *Online Deliberation: Design, Research, and Practice*, Chicago, IL: University of Chicago Press.

Przeworski, A. and Teune, H. (1970), *The Logic of Comparative Social Inquiry*, New York, NY: Wiley-Interscience.

Putnam, R. (1993), *Making Democracy Work*, Princeton, NJ: Princeton University Press.

Putnam, R. (2000), *Bowling Alone: The Collapse and Revival of American Community*, New York, NY: Simon and Schuster.

Putnam, R. and Pharr, S. (2000), *Disaffected Democracies: What's Troubling the Trilateral Countries?*, Princeton, NJ: Princeton University Press.

Puustinen, S., Mäntysalo, R., Hytönen, J., and Jarenko, K. (2017), 'The Deliberative Bureaucrat: Deliberative Democracy and Institutional Trust in the Jurisdiction of the Finnish Planner', *Planning Theory & Practice*, 18(1): 71–88.

Quinn, M. T., Alexander, G. C., Hollingsworth, D., O'Connor, K. G., and Meltzer, D. (2006), 'Design and Evaluation of a Workplace Intervention to Promote Organ Donation', *Progress in Transplantation*, 16: 253–9.

Read, A. D. (1999), 'A Weekly Doorstep Recycling Collection, I Had No Idea We Could! Overcoming the Local Barriers to Participation', *Resources, Conservation and Recycling*, 26: 217–49.

Reams, M. A. and Ray, B. (1993), 'The Effects of Three Prompting Methods on Recycling Participation Rates – A Field-study', *Journal of Environmental Systems*, 22: 371–9.

Rebonato, R. (2012), *Taking Liberties: A Critical Examination of Libertarian Paternalism*, London: Palgrave.

Reisch, L. and Sunstein, C. R. (2016), 'Do Europeans Like Nudges?', *Judgment and Decision Making*, 11(4): 310–25.

Reno, R. R., Cialdini, R. B., and Kallgren, C. A. (1993), 'The Transsituational Influence of Social Norms', *Journal of Personality and Social Psychology*, 64: 104–12.

Renwick, A., Allan, S., Jennings, W., Mckee, R., Russell, M., and Smith, G. (2018), 'What Kind of Brexit do Voters Want? Lessons from the Citizens' Assembly on Brexit', *The Political Quarterly*, 89: 649–58.

Reubsaet, A., Brug, J., Nijkamp, M. D., Candel, M. J. J. M., Hooff, J. P., and Borne, H. W. (2005), 'The Impact of an Organ Donation Registration', *Social Science and Medicine*, 60: 1479–86.

References

Richardson, L. (2008), *DIY Community Action: Neighbourhood Problems and Community Self-help*, Bristol: Policy Press.

Richardson, L. (2013), '"We Need to Decide!" A Mixed Method Approach to Responsiveness and Equal Treatment', in P. Esaiasson and H. Narud (eds), *Between-election Democracy: The Representative Relationship Out of the Shadow of Elections*, Colchester: ECPR Press.

Richardson, L. and John, P. (2012), 'Who Listens to the Grassroots? A Field Experiment on Informational Lobbying in the UK', *British Journal of Politics and International Relations*, 14: 595–612.

Richardson, L., Durose, C., and Dean, R. J. (2018), 'Why Decentralize Decision-making? English Local Actors' Viewpoints', *Governance*, 32: 159–76.

Rithalia, A., McDaid, C., Suekarran, S., Norman, G., Myers, L., and Sowden, A. (2009), 'A Systematic Review of Presumed Consent Systems for Deceased Organ Donation', *Health Technology Assessment*, 1326, doi: 10.3310/hta1326.

Rogers, B. (2004), *Lonely Citizens, Report of the Working Party on Active Citizenship*, London: IPPR.

Roth, A. E. (1995), 'Introduction to Experimental Economics', in J. H. Kagel and A. E. Roth (eds), *The Handbook of Experimental Economics*, Princeton, NJ: Princeton University Press.

Rowe, I. (2015), 'Civility 2.0: A Comparative Analysis of Incivility in Online Political Discussion', *Information, Communication & Society*, 18(2): 121–38.

Ryan, M., Stoker, G., John, P., Moseley, A., James, O., Richardson, L., and Vannoni, M. (2018), 'How Best to Open Up Local Democracy? A Randomised Experiment to Encourage Contested Elections and Greater Representativeness in English Parish Councils', *Local Government Studies*, 44(6): 766–87.

Sack, W. (2005), 'Discourse Architecture and Very Large-scale Conversation', in R. Latham and S. Sassen (eds), *Digital Formations: IT and New Architectures in the Global Realm*, Princeton, NJ: Princeton University Press.

Salamon, L. M. (ed.) (1989), *Beyond Privatisation: The Tools of Government Action*, Washington, DC: Urban Institute.

Samuelson, W. and Zeckhauser, R. (1988), 'Status Quo Bias in Decision Making', *Journal of Risk and Uncertainty*, 1: 7–59.

Sanders, M., Snijders, V., and Hallsworth, M. (2018), 'Behavioural Science and Policy: Where Are We Now and Where Are We Going?', *Behavioural Public Policy*, 2(2): 144–67.

References

Santana, A. D. (2014), 'Virtuous or Vitriolic: The Effect of Anonymity on Civility in Online Newspaper Reader Comment Boards', *Journalism Practice*, 8(1): 18–33.

Sartori, G. (1987), *The Theory of Democracy Revisited*, Chatham, NJ: Chatham House.

Savani, M. M. (2018), 'The Effects of a Commitment Device on Health Outcomes: Reputational Commitment and Weight Loss in an Online Experiment', *International Journal of Applied Behavioral Economics*, 7(4): 1–20.

Saward, M. (2001), 'Making Democratic Connections: Political Equality, Deliberation and Direct Democracy', *Acta Politica*, 36: 361–79.

Saxton, J., Madden, M., Greenwood, C., and Garvey, B. (2007), *The 21st Century Donor*, London: nfpsynergy.

Schultz, P. W. (1998), 'Changing Behaviour with Normative Feedback Interventions: A Field Experiment on Kerbside Recycling', *Basic and Applied Psychology*, 21: 25–36.

Schultz, P. W., Nolan, J. M., Cialdini, R. B., Goldstein, N. J., and Griskevicius, V. (2007), 'The Constructive, Destructive and Reconstructive Power of Social Norms', *Psychological Science*, 18: 429–34.

Schwartz, D., Chang, J., and Lee, M. (2008), 'Instrumentation and Innovation in Design Experiments: Taking the Turn towards Efficiency', in A. E. Kelly, R. A. Lesh, and J. Baek (eds), *Handbook of Design Research Methods in Education*, London: Routledge.

Scottish Government (2018), *Human Tissue (Authorisation) (Scotland) Bill*, www.parliament.scot/parliamentarybusiness/Bills/108681.aspx [accessed 3 January 2019].

Setälä, M. and Smith, G. (2018), 'Mini-publics and Deliberative Democracy', in A. Bächtiger, J. Dryzek, J. Mansbridge, and M. E. Warren (eds), *The Oxford Handbook of Deliberative Democracy*, Oxford: Oxford University Press.

Setälä, M., Grönlund, K., and Herne, K. (2007), 'Comparing Voting and Common Statement Treatments: A Citizen Deliberation Experiment', paper prepared for the American Political Science Association's Annual Meeting, Chicago.

Shadish, W. R., Cook, T. D., and Campbell, D. T. (2002), *Experimental and Quasi-experimental Designs for Generalised Causal Inference*, Boston, MA: Houghton Mifflin.

Shapiro, I. (2005), *The Flight from Reality in the Human Sciences*, Princeton, NJ: Princeton University Press.

References

Shapiro, I. R., Smith, M., and Masoud, T. (2004), *Problems and Methods in the Study of Politics*, Cambridge: Cambridge University Press.

Shaw, P. J. (2008), 'Nearest Neighbour Effects in Kerbside Household Waste Recycling Resources', *Conservation and Recycling*, 52: 775–84.

Shaw, P. J. and Maynard, S. J. (2008), 'The Potential of Financial Incentives to Enhance Householders' Kerbside Recycling Behaviour', *Waste Management*, 28: 1732–41.

Shaw, P. J., Lyas, J. K., Maynard, S. J., and Van Vugt, M. (2007), 'On the Relationship Between Set-out Rates and Participation Ratios as a Tool for Enhancement of Curbside Household Waste Recycling', *Journal of Environmental Management*, 83: 34–43.

Silva, C. N. (2013), *Citizen E-Participation in Urban Governance: Crowdsourcing and Collaborative Governance*, Hershey, Pennsylvania: IGI Global.

Simon, H. (1945/1997), *Administrative Behavior*, New York, NY: Free Press.

Simon, H. (1996), *The Sciences of the Artificial*, Cambridge, MA: MIT Press.

Sirianni, C. (2009), *Investing in Democracy: Engaging Citizens in Collaborative Governance*, Washington, DC: Brookings.

Smith, G. (2005), *Beyond the Ballot: 57 Democratic Innovations from Around the World*, London: Power Inquiry.

Smith, G. (2009), *Democratic Innovations: Designing Institutions for Citizen Participation*, Cambridge: Cambridge University Press.

Smith, G. (2018), 'The Institutionalization of Deliberative Democracy: Democratic Innovations and the Deliberative System', *Journal of Zhejiang University (Humanities and Social Sciences)*, 4(2): 5–18.

Smith, J., Gerber, A., and Orlich, A. (2003), 'Self-Prophecy Effects and Voter Turnout', *Political Psychology*, 24: 593–604.

Smith, G., Sturgis, P., and Smith, G. (2013), 'Taking Political Engagement Online: An Experimental Analysis of Asynchronous Discussion Forums', *Political Studies*, 61: 709–30.

Spital, A. (1995), 'Mandated Choice: A Plan to Increase Public Commitment to Organ Donation', *Journal of the American Medical Association*, 273: 504–6.

Spital, A. (1996), 'Mandated Choice for Organ Donation: Time to Give It a Try', *Annals of Internal Medicine*, 125: 66–9.

Spotswood, F. (2016), *Beyond Behaviour Change*, Bristol: Policy Press.

Stoker, G. (2006), *Why Politics Matters*, Basingstoke: Palgrave Macmillan.

Stoker, G. and Greasley, S. (2008), 'Mayors and Urban Governance:

References

Developing a Facilitative Leadership Style?', *Public Administration Review*, 68: 720–8.

Stoker, G. and Hay, C. (2017), 'Understanding and Challenging Populist Negativity towards Politics: The Perspectives of British Citizens', *Political Studies*, 65(1): 4–23.

Stoker, G. and John, P. (2009), 'Design Experiments: Engaging Policy Makers in the Search for Evidence About What Works', *Political Studies*, 57: 337–73.

Stutzer, A., Goette, L., and Zehnder, M. (2006), 'Active Decisions and Pro-Social Behaviour: A Field Experiment in Blood Donation', Working Paper No. 279, Institute for Empirical Research in Economics, Zurich: University of Zurich.

Sugden, R. (2018), *The Community of Advantage: A Behavioural Economist's Defence of the Market*, Oxford: Oxford University Press.

Sunstein, C. R. (2001), *Republic.com*, Princeton, NJ: Princeton University Press.

Sunstein, C. R. (2006), *Infotopia: How Many Minds Produce Knowledge*, New York, NY: Oxford University Press.

Sunstein, C. R. (2014), *Simpler: The Future of Government*, New York, NY: Simon and Schuster.

Sunstein, C. R. (2016a), *The Ethics of Influence: Government in the Age of Behavioural Science*, Cambridge: Cambridge University Press.

Sunstein, C. R. (2016b), 'Do People like Nudges?' *Administrative Law Review*, 68(2): 177–232.

Sunstein, C. R. (2017a), 'Nudges That Fail', *Behavioral Public Policy*, 1: 4–25.

Sunstein, C. R. (2017b), *Human Agency and Behavioral Economics: Nudging Fast and Slow*, Cham: Palgrave Macmillan/Springer.

Sunstein, C. R. (2019a), *How Change Happens*. Cambridge, MA: MIT Press.

Sunstein, C. R. (2019b), *On Freedom*, Princeton, NJ: Princeton University Press.

Sunstein, C. R. and Reisch, L. (2016), *The Economics of Nudge* (four volumes), Abingdon, Oxon: Routledge.

Sunstein, C. R., Reisch, L. A., and Kaiser, M. (2018), 'Trusting Nudges? Lessons from an International Survey', *Journal of European Public Policy*, forthcoming.

Sweeting, D. and Copus, C. (2013), 'Councillors, Participation, and Local Democracy', in B. Egner, D. Sweeting, and P. J. Klok (eds), *Local Councillors in Europe*, Urban and Regional Research International Volume 14, Germany: Springer: 121–37.

References

Tajfel, H. and Turner, J. C. (1986), 'The Social Identity Theory of Inter-group Behavior', in S. Worchel and L. W. Austin (eds), *Psychology of Intergroup Relations*, Chicago, IL: Nelson-Hall.

Tajfel, H., Billig, M., Bundy, R. P., and Flament, C. (1971), 'Social Categorization and Intergroup Behaviour', *European Journal of Social Psychology*, 1: 149–78.

Tang, A. (2016), 'Uber Responds to vTaiwan's Coherent Blended Volition', https://blog.pol.is/uber-responds-to-vtaiwans-coherent-blended-voli tion-3e9b75102b9b#.drbt5s7u9 [accessed 17 February 2019].

Teele, D. L. (2014), 'Reflections on the Ethics of Field Experiments', in D. Teele (ed.), *Field Experiments and Their Critics: Essays on the Uses and Abuses of Experimentation in the Social Sciences*, New Haven, CT: Yale University Press, 115–40.

Thaler, R. H. (1980), 'Toward a Positive Theory of Consumer Choice', *Journal of Economic Behavior and Organization*, 1: 39–60.

Thaler, R. H. (2015), *Misbehaving: The Making of Behavioral Economics*, New York, NY: Norton.

Thaler, R. (2016), 'Behavioral Economics: Past, Present, and Future', *American Economic Review*, 106(7): 1577–600.

Thaler, R. H. (2017), 'Much Ado about Nudging', Behavioral Public Policy blog, https://bppblog.com/2017/06/02/much-ado-about-nudging [accessed 17 February 2019].

Thaler, R. H. and Bernartzi, S. (2004), 'Save More Tomorrow: Using Behavioural Economics to Increase Employee Saving', *Journal of Political Economy*, 112: 164–87.

Thaler, R. H. and Sunstein, C. R. (2008), *Nudge: Improving Decisions about Health, Wealth and Happiness*, New Haven, CT and London: Yale University Press.

Thomann, E. (2018), 'Donate Your Organs, Donate Life! Explicitness in Policy Instruments', *Policy Sciences*, 51(4): 433–56.

Thomas, C. (2006), *Recycle for Hampshire – Campaign Evaluation Report*.

Timlett, R. E. and Williams, I. D. (2008), 'Public Participation and Recycling Performance in England: A Comparison of Tools for Behavior Change', *Resources Conservation and Recycling*, 52: 622–34.

Tjoa, P. (2018), *Rebalancing the Power: Five Principles for a Successful Relationship Between Councils and Communities*, London: Local Trust.

Torgerson, D. and Torgerson, C. (2008), *Designing Randomised Trials*, Basingstoke: Palgrave.

Tremblay, C., Jayme, B., Openjuru, G., and Jaitli, N. (2015), 'Community

Knowledge Co-creation Through Participatory Video', *Action Research*, 13(3): 298–314.

Tucker, P. (1999), 'Normative Influences in Household Waste Recycling', *Journal of Environmental Planning and Management*, 42: 63–82.

UK Transplant (2008), *UK Transplant Activity Report 2007–2008*, London: NHS Blood and Transplant.

US Department of Health and Human Services (2017), *Organ Donation Statistics*. US Government Information on Organ Donation and Transplantation, www.organdonor.gov/statistics-stories/statistics.html [accessed 3 January 2019.]

Vabo, S. I. (University of Oslo), Winsvold, M. (University of Oslo), and Sørensen, E. (Roskilde University), 'Designing Institutions for Interactive Political Leadership in Local Governments – Possibilities and Contingencies'. Paper prepared for ECPR, Hamburg, August 2018.

van Diepen, M., Donkers, B., and Franses, P. H. (2009), 'Does Irritation Induced by Charitable Direct Mailings Reduce Donations?', *International Journal of Research in Marketing*, 26(3): 180–8.

Varotto, A and Spagnolli, A. (2017), 'Psychological Strategies to Promote Household Recycling: A Systematic Review with Meta-analysis of Validated Field Interventions', *Journal of Environmental Psychology*, 51: 168–88.

Verba, S., Nie, N., and Kim, J. (1978), *Participation and Political Equality*, Cambridge: Cambridge University Press.

Verba, S., Schlozman, K. L., and Brady, H. (1995), *Voice and Equality: Civic Voluntarism in American Politics*, Cambridge, MA: Harvard University Press.

Vesterland, L. (2016), 'Using Experimental Methods to Understand Why and How We Give to Charity', in J. H. Kagel and A. E. Roth (eds), *The Handbook of Experimental Economics*, Volume 2, Princeton, NJ: Princeton University Press.

Vinokur, A. D., Merion, R. M., Couper, M. P., Jones, E. G., and Dong, Y. (2006), 'Educational Web-based Intervention for High School Students to Increase Knowledge and Promote Positive Attitudes Toward Organ Donation', *Health Education Behaviour*, 33: 773.

Waldron, J. (2014), 'It's All for Your Own Good', *New York Review of Books*, 9 October 2014, www.nybooks.com/articles/archives/2014/oct/09/cass-sunstein-its-all-your-own-good [accessed 17 February 2019].

Walker, R., Hoggart, L., Hamilton, G., with Blank, S. (2006), *Making Random Assignment Happen: Evidence from the UK Employment Retention and*

Advancement (ERA) Demonstration. DWP Research Report No 330. London: Department of Work and Pensions.

Walker, T. and Lawson, S. (2018), *From Transactions to Changemaking: Rethinking Partnerships Between the Public and Private Sectors*, London: New Local Government Network.

Warman, M. (2018), *Who Governs Britain? Democracy and Local Government in the Digital Age*, London: Centre for Policy Studies.

Warren, M. and Pearse, H. (eds) (2008), *Designing Deliberative Democracy: The British Columbia Citizens' Assembly*, Cambridge: Cambridge University Press.

Waste and Resources Action Programme (2006), *Step by Step Guide to Door-to-Door Canvassing*, www.wrap.org.uk [accessed 5 January 2019].

Waste and Resources Action Programme (2010), *Improving the Performance of Waste Diversion Schemes: A Good Practice Guide to Monitoring and Evaluation*, www.wrap.org.uk [accessed 17 December 2018].

White, M. and Lakey, J. (1992), *The Restart Effect: Evaluation of a Labour Market Programme for Unemployed People*, London: Policy Studies Institute, London.

Whitefield, S. D. and Rovny, J. (2018), 'Issue Dimensionality and Party Politics in Turbulent Times', *Party Politics*, 25 (1): 4–11.

Whitehead, M., Jones, R., Lilley, R., Pykett, J., and Howell, R. (2017), *Neuroliberalism: Behavioural Government in the Twenty-first Century*, New York, NY: Routledge.

Wiepking, P. and Maas, I. (2009), 'Resources That Make You Generous: Effects of Social and Human Resources on Charitable Giving', *Social Forces*, 87(4): 1973–95.

Williams, J. W. (2007), 'The Power of Local Political Debates to Influence Prospective Voters: An Experiment at the Congressional Level', American Political Science Association – Panel on Congressional Campaigns and the Media, Chicago, IL.

Wilson, C. D. H. and Williams, I. D. (2007), '"Kerbside Collection": A Case Study From the North-west of England', *Resources Conservation and Recycling*, 52: 381–94.

Woodward, R., Bench, M., and Harder, M. K. (2005), 'The Development of a UK Kerbside Scheme Using Known Practice', *Journal of Environmental Management*, 75: 115–27.

World Bank (2015), *World Development Report 2015: Mind, Society, and Behavior*, Washington, DC: World Bank.

References

Wright, S. and Street, J. (2007), 'Democracy, Deliberation and Design: The Case of Online Discussion Forums', *New Media and Society*, 9: 849–69.

Xenos, M. and Kyoung, K. (2008), 'Rocking the Vote and More: An Experimental Study of the Impact of Youth Political Portals', *Journal of Information Technology and Politics*, 5: 175–89.

Young, V., McHugh, S., Glendinning, R., and Carr-Hill, R. (2017), *Evaluation of the Human Transplantation (Wales) Act: Impact Evaluation Report*, Welsh Government, Statistical Research No. 71/2017. https://gov.wales/docs/caecd/research/2017/171130-evaluation-human-transplantation-wal es-act-impact-en.pdf [accessed 3 January 2019].

Index

Note: page numbers followed by 't' refer to tables, page numbers in italic refer to figures.

Abadie, A. 160
active decision choices 24
activists 183, 187, 210
Alexander, G. C. 160
altruism 124, 128
AmeriCorps 79
Amnesty International 125
anti-social behaviour, online debate
        170–3, *171*
Ariely, D. 128
Aronow, P. M. 107
associative democracy 207–8

behaviour
    anti-social 170–3, *171*
    pro-social 64
behaviour change
    citizens' 1–6
    influences on 24–5
    organ donation experiment 147–9,
        158–9
behavioural economics 15, 34, 158–9,
        245

beliefs, moral 124
Best, S. J. 110
Beveridge, William 77
Beyond the Ballot (Smith) 188
bias 42–3, 49, 246
Bielaczyc, K. 56
Bimber, B. 121
blogs 120, 216
book donation experiment 128–36,
        210, 216, 242t
bounded rationality 18–21, 34
boycotting 78
Brady, H. 82
Braintree District Council 69
Brannan, T. 208
Brown, A. 57
budgeting, participatory 26, 161, 177,
        209
Building Links project 198

Cameron, David 79
Campbell, D. T. 50
canvassing 76, 106, 207, 210

approach for 70–2, 101, 102t
and recycling experiment 62, 64, 65–70, 213, 217, 242t
and voter turnout 64, 99, 101, *103*, 106, 216, 242t
carrier bag petition 113
celebrity endorsement 154
Center for Deliberative Democracy 175
chat-rooms 164
Chicago Community Policing 178
China and Tibet petition 115, *118*
choice architecture 19–20, 22–3, 33–4, 35
    and defaults 23
    and organ donation 144–5, 150–1, 158–9, 242t
    and recycling experiment 74–6
Chorley Smile 125
Cialdini, R. B. 133
citizens
    activists 183, 187, 210
    behaviour change 1–6
    and bounded rationality 18–21
    consent 31–2
    defining good 11–12
    influencing decision-making 195–7
    mini-publics 26–7, 164, 171–3, 177, 209–10
Citizens' Assembly, Ireland 26
civic behaviour theory 17
CLEAR model 83, 84t, 93, 94–5, 197–8
climate change petition 115, 117, *118*
cluster bomb petition 115, *118*, 119
Cobb, P. 56
coding framework, in linking experiment 201
cognitive consistency 23–4
Coleman, S. 164
Collins, A. 56

commitment 22–3, 24
    pledging 117–19, 119–20, 125–7, 132–4
community cohesion 9, 163, 165, 169–70, 172–3
Community HEART 129
Community Organisers programme 79
comparison, in testing 43–4
compromised experiments 52–3
conjecture driven tests 56
consent, of citizens 31–2
consistency, cognitive 23–4
control groups, defined 245
controversy 212
Cook, T. D. 50
co-production *see* volunteering
Corporation for National and Community Service 79
cost 108, 159, 211
    giving 124–5
    of voting intervention 106
councillors *see* local government
counterfactuals 42–3, 43–4, 245
cues, social 3, 98, 106, 173

Darfur petition 115, *118*, 119
debating 9, 161–75, *171*, 207, 242t
decentralization 10, 176, 179, 186, 207–8, 217
decision-making 18–21
defaults 89, 211
    and choice architecture 23
    and organ donation experiment 150–1
deliberation 20–1
    and behaviour change 146, 159
    and inclusion 176–88, 216
    and the internet 161–2, 172–3
    mini-publics 26–7, 164–5
    polls 170
    and think 17–18, 26–7, 29

Index

deliberative democracy 17–18
Deliberative Democracy Consortium 175
democracy
  associative 207–8
  deliberative 17–18
democratic theory 16, 187
design experiments 6, 54–9, 59, 207, 209, 214
  and inclusion 179–88
design partnerships *see* design experiments
differential selection 52
discounting 22–3
discussion streams 120
Dolan, P. 15–16
donation (organ) 9, 138–60, 211
  petition for 113
  and registration systems 138–50
Druckman, J. 48

education/schools 57–8
EMERGE, recycling experiment 65
endowment effect 21
equality/inequality 177
  and the internet 163
ethical buying 78
ethics
  of behaviour change 30–5, 158
  and experimental research 54
ethnic minorities 88
European Convention on Human Rights 144
Everyday Democracy 188
expectations 75
experimental method 50–9
experiments 5–6, 38–60
  defined 245
  experimental method 50–9
external validity 245
extrinsic motivation 124

face-to-face forums 174–5, 180, 216
false positives 43
Fearon, J. 20
feedback 109, 207, 215
  internet and 108–9
  recycling experiment 62, 63, 64–5, 70–3, *72*, 242t
  and volunteering 91–2, 94
  and voter turnout 64–5
Festinger, L. 23–4
field experiments 48–9, 54
Fishkin, J. 165, 170, 175
flaming 163, 167, 172–3, 173
food waste recycling 70–3
'foot in the door' techniques 126
forums, face-to-face 174–5, 180
Fung, A. 178, 208

Gaebler, T. 4
Gay, S. 160
Gerber, A. S. 48, 99, 104–5, 105
Gerber, E. R. 192–3
Get Out the Vote campaign 8, 99, 100, 106, 128, 213
  as example of randomization 46–7
giving 8–9
  charitable 123–38, 216, 242t
  costs 124–5
Goldberg, Denis 129
Green, D. P. 48, 99, 105, 107
Greenberg, D. H. 53
Gutmann, Amy 175

habit 12, 19–20, 23, 34, 76
  and recycling 62, 68, 76
  and voting 105, 213
Hale S. 111
Hallsworth, M. 15–16
Halpern, D. 15–16, 208
Harder, M. K. 62
Hawthorne effect 43, 43t, 245
Hirst, P. 207

Index

Hollingsworth, D. 160
hyperbolic discounting 22

identification/identity 19
  and commitment 126–7
  group 25, 64, 76
identity cards, petition 113
image motivation 124, 128
Improvement and Development
    Agency (IDeA) 191
incentives 35
  for online debating 166, 167
  for participating in petitions 113,
    115
  for recycling 63
including 9, 176–88, 181t, 242t
inequality/equality 177
  and the internet 163
inference, defined 246
influences, and behaviour 24–5, 63,
    74, 118
information, and nudging 13
informational lobbying 203
informed consent 140–1, 143, 147–8,
    149t
Institute for Political and Economic
    Governance 101
Institute of Government for the UK
    Cabinet Office 15–16
intent to treat effect 103, 105–6
inter-group bias 25
internal validity 41–2, 41t, 51, 246
International Volunteer Day 79
internet 209
  and debating 161–75, 171, 215,
    242t
  online surveys 148, 149
  and petitioning 108–22, 215–16
interrupted time series 44, 246
interventions
  cognitive-driven 21–4
  defined 246

interviews
  for inclusion video 180–1
  intrinsic motivation 124
  for voting canvass 101
Ipsos MORI 148, 166

Janssen, D. 164
John, P. 54–5, 208
Joseph, D. 56
Journal of Public Deliberation 175

Kickstarter 111
Kies, R. 164
King, D. 15–16
Krueger, B. 110

Ladewig, J. 110
laws 4
  on organ donation systems 144
linking 9–10, 189–205, 218–19, 242t
Linkz, D. 53
lobbying experiment 198–205, 219
local government 217
  and inclusion 179–82, 185–6
  and linking 189–205, 242t
  and volunteering 84–5
loss, prevention of 21–2
Lowndes, V. 83
loyalties, group 25, 76
Lupia, A. 108
lurkers 169
Luton Borough Council 69

McDaid, C. 159
Macedo, S. 175
McGrath, M. C. 107
McKenzie-Mohr, D. 133
mandated choice system 139, 145,
    148, 149t, 150, 159
Mandell, M. 53
manipulation 33, 217–18
Margetts, H. 111

Index

media technology, used in inclusion 9, 176
Meltzer, D. 160
method, experimental 50–9
Mill, J.S. 44
Miller, D. 17
mini-publics 26–7, 164, 172, 177, 209–10
mobilization
 and charitable giving 135
 and petitioning 111, 120
 and volunteering 82–4, 89–90, 93
 and voting 98–9, 105–6
motivation, and charitable giving 124, 127–8
Myers, L. 159

National Coalition for Dialogue and Deliberation 175
National Conference for Citizenship 79
National Day of Remembrance petition 113
National Organ Donor Register (UK) 148
Newton, R. 192
Nickerson, D. 104–5
Norman, G. 159
nudge 3, 13–15, 20
 and charitable giving 123–38, 216, 242t
 and cognitive-driven interventions 21–4
 criticism of 217–18
 limitations of 210–15
 and petitioning 8, 108–22, 242t
 and recycling 1–2, 7–8, 61–76, 68–9, 72–3, 210, 212, 213, 242t
 and responsiveness of local government 189–205
 and social influences 24–5

and think 27–30, 28t, 35, 36–7, 151–9, 153, 156t
and volunteering 8, 77–95, 189–91, 210, 213–14, 218, 242t
Nudge: Improving Decisions about Health, Wealth and Happiness (Thaler and Sunstein) 14–15

Obama, Barack 120–1
observational data 43, 44, 48–9, 62, 148–9, 208, 209, 246
O'Connor, K.G. 160
Oldham (Greater Manchester) 70
online deliberative polling (ODP) 165–75, 215–16
Oostveen, A.-M. 110–11
opt-in system see informed consent
opt-out system see presumed consent system
organ donation 9, 211
 and behavioural change experiment 147–9, 242t
 and nudge and think experiment 151–9, 153, 156–7t, 216, 242t
 petition 113
 and registration systems 138–50
Osborne, D. 4
ownership 21–2
OxLab 112, 114

participation 18, 106, 208–11
 linking 9–10, 189–205, 218, 242t
 mini-publics 26–7, 164, 177
 petitioning 8, 108–22, 109, 242t
paternalism 13, 28, 33, 36, 158
petitioning 8, 108–22, 242t
Phillips, J.H. 192–3
pledging 120, 125–7, 128–36, 207, 242t
 and organ donation 138
policy-makers
 and ethics of behaviour change 30–1

as experts 30
and nudging 15–16
polls *see* questionnaires
Porto Alegre (Brazil) 177–8
  participatory budgeting 26
Prabhakar, R. 34
pragmatic trials 54
Pratchett, L. 83
pre-moderation 167–8
prescriptions petition 113–14
presumed consent 138, 140–5, 148–9, 149t, 150, 159
proof, standards of 40–3
pro-social behaviour 64
prospect theory 21, 154
psychological discounting 23
public authorities *see* local
  government

questionnaires, in the debating
  intervention 166–8
Quinn, M. T. 160

randomization 45–50, 51, 53, 59–60
randomized controlled trials 5–6, 38–40, 45–50, *45*, 54–60, 207, 209, 246
  and charitable giving 8–9, 123–38, 216, 242t
  on linking 198–203
  and recycling 61–2, 64–76
recognition, of giving 127–8, 135
recommendation systems 109, 119–20
recycling 1–2, 7–8, 61–76, 69, *72*, 210, 212, 242t
registration systems, and organ
  donation 138–50
regression analysis 202–3
regulations 4
reputation systems 109, 120
researchers 54, 57
responsiveness 217

of local government 191–205
results, local 51
Richardson, L. 209
Rithalia, A. 159
Rockefeller Fund 191
Roth, A. E. 50

Saward, M. 159
Scared Straight 39
Schlozman, K. L. 83
schools/education 57–8
Schultz, P. W. 65
selection bias 246
Shadish, W. R. 50
significant, defined 246
Simon, Herbert 19
Sin, G. 108
Sirianni, C. 208
smiley/frown faces 62, 65
Smith, G. 209
Smith, W. 133
social capital 208
social cues 3, 14, 98, 106
social influences 152–4
  and nudging 24–5
South Africa, book experiment 129
Sowden, A. 159
Spital, A. 160
standards of proof 40–3
status quo 23, 141
Stoker, G. 54–5, 83, 208
sub-goal identification 19–20
Suekarran, S. 159
Sunstein, Cass 4, 14–15, 33, 211
surveys 38–43, 45–7, 63, 216
  organ donation 143, 146, 148–9, 149t, 159
  response to 42–3
  voting 102

telephone canvassing 216
  for voter turnout 99, 100–4, 242t

Index

Thaler, Richard 4, 14–15, 33, 211
think 214, 217
  and bounded rationality 20–1, 34
  defined 4, 14–16
  and deliberation 17–18, 26–7
  and linking 9–10, 197–8
  and nudging 28t, 29–30, 36–7,
    151–9, *153*, 156–7t
Thompson, Dennis 175
Tibet and China petition 115, *118*
Timebanking 94
Torgerson, C. 39, 54
Torgerson, D. 39, 54
trade rules petition 115–16, 117–18,
  118
Trafford Metropolitan Borough
  Council (Manchester) 65
transparency 33, 35
treatment groups 45, 47, 52, 246
  charitable giving *132*
  organ donation 148–9, 155, 156–7,
    156t
  petitioning 114, 116
  recycling 66, 71–2
  voting 100–1, 103–5
trust 208
  in government 191, 194–5
turnout, voter 100–6, *104*, 127, 242t
Twitter 120, 154

United Kingdom (UK)
  including 179–82
  organ donation 138, 143, 145, 146
  responsiveness of local government
    191–7
  volunteerism 79, 80, 81

United Nations 79
United States (US)
  internet and participation 121–2
  and organ donation 138, 145, 146
  volunteerism 79, 80–1
  and voter turnout experiments 99,
    104–5, 127
University of Manchester 85–6
user feedback applications 109,
  120

validity 41–3, 41t, 246
van den Besselaar, P. 110–11
Verba, S. 83
video, used in inclusion 180–8, 181t,
  187, 242t
video-sharing sites 120
Vision TwentyOne 102
Volunteer Bureaux 84
volunteering 8, 77–95, 189–91, 210,
  213–14, 218, 242t
voting 8, 32, 64
  Get Out the Vote campaign 8, 46–7,
    99, 100, 106, 128
  importance of 96–8
  mobilization 98–9
  turnout experiment 96–137, *104*,
    242t

Wall of Life 154
whaling petition 113, 115, *118*
Wiltshire Council 218
  inclusion experiment 179–82
women, and online debating 169

youth volunteering 79

.